509

Eddie Connolly

A COP'S COP

by Superintendent Edward F. Connolly
and Christopher Harding

Quinlan Press
Boston

Copyright © 1985 by
Quinlan Press, Inc.
All rights reserved,
including the right of reproduction
in whole or in part in any form.
Published by Quinlan Press, Inc.
131 Beverly Street
Boston, MA 02114
(617) 227-4870
1-800-551-2500

Library of Congress Catalog Card Number
85-60300
ISBN 0-933341-03-2

First printing August 1985

To my wife Irene of so many years, I dedicate this book filled with cases and investigations of which she was kept unaware. Like every good policeman's wife, she waited and prayed for her husband during his long nights of duty, never knowing where he was, what he was doing or the dangers that he was facing.

Being married to a policeman, she learned early in life not to cry or show her feelings . . . even when she had to hurry to the hospital where her husband lay injured.

Thank you, Irene, for all that you have given me despite the little I could give you in return . . .

Attorney Thomas C. Troy of Reading
Friend, Counselor, and Advisor

Table of Contents

Introduction

The year 1919 was a momentous one in the history of the city of Boston. It was the year of the Great Molasses Flood, a unique catastrophe in which a huge holding tank exploded and deluged the North End with two million gallons of sticky syrup. It was the year of the Boston Police Strike, a "work action" that left the city without police protection; all strikers were fired and replaced. 1919 was also the year Edward F. Connolly was born.

Superintendent Connolly epitomizes a breed of policeman, who apparently is no longer in favor — at least not in the Boston Police Department today. After 38 years of service, he is fighting just to continue doing the job he loves most — being a street cop.

I first met the Super in the fall of 1984, when we decided to collaborate on a book on some of the highlights of his career. At that time my idea of what police work was like had been determined by the portrayal of cops' lives on TV and in the movies. Quickly I learned how far these film versions deviate from reality.

Hill Street Blues may have won more than two dozen Emmy Awards, but its scriptwriters misrepresent policework almost as badly as those writing *Charlie's Angels*.

"The closest television ever came to capturing the feel of real police work was in that *Kojak* series. The station wasn't that clean. Kojak depended on his informants a lot. The idiosyncrasies of the characters in the show are typical of cops everywhere," Connolly once remarked, "I'd watch Telly Savalas reruns 100 times before I'd watch these young studs in *Miami Vice* and these other supposedly realistic shows."

The routine of real-life cops is at once more humdrum and more exciting than most of their glamour-boy video counterparts. On the tube you'll see two partners hitting a pusher's pad by themselves. That may be the way it's done in Hollywood, but in Boston the men in the Drug Unit get as many guys as they can together and approach very cautiously because you never know what you'll find on the other side of a door.

Superintendent Connolly has dedicated most of his life to the Boston Police Department. He has not gotten rich in the process. He still rents his modest home in a nice suburban neighborhood. Not only has he refused hundreds of thousands of dollars in bribes, even in a time when slipping the local cops a few bucks was routine, but he also turned down a legitimate offer of a 100% pension when he was wounded in 1979. He'd rather prowl than loaf.

He thrives on the unpredictability and danger of night work, and he recalls his years as the first head of the Boston Drug Control Unit as the most memorable of his career. The respect and affection with which the former members of that unit still speak of him attest to the superb leadership he showed.

But even though he loves the action, he is scrupulous about serving the public in any way he can. He approaches anyone who looks lost and gives concise directions to faraway places. His familiarity with every sidestreet in Boston (and which direction the one-way streets go) is astounding.

Often when he notices that traffic at an intersection is getting fouled up, he trots out into the midst of the cars and starts directing, a skill most thought had gone the way of making real stained glass.

For those unfamiliar with the geography and various neighborhoods of Boston, the diagram on the opposite page should help. A distinctive architectural feature of the residential sections of the city is the high percentage of "triple-deckers," the three-story, three-family wood-frame houses that were built side by side to accommodate the great influx of immigrants during the latter part of the nineteenth century. Boston is truly one of this nation's greatest cities, and its police department, for all its past and present flaws, has not received a fraction of the recognition its dedicated staff deserves.

The Boston Police Department lays claim to the title of being the oldest in the nation, tracing its roots back to the night watchmen who checked the locks on doors back in 1630 when Boston was incorporated as a town.

The BPD was the first in the country to use automobiles in its work. In July, 1903 a Stanley Steam automobile was purchased but, according to Commissioner O'Meara, "it has never, except in cases of necessity, gone over six miles an hour." By 1906, four one-man vehicles were out chasing after speeding roadsters. A sedan was reserved for the use of the superintendent.

A Cop's Cop is one attempt to preserve some fairly accurate information about some scattered moments in the recent history of the Department and of the city. The fact that Superintendent Connolly is not the main actor in several of these chapters demonstrates once again that he is a leader who knows how to share the responsibility and the credit, a man more interested in the truth than in personal glory.

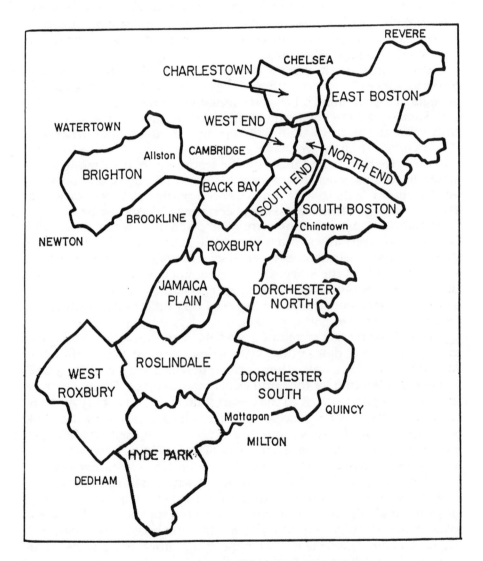

BOSTON'S NEIGHBORHOODS

Though the material in *A Cop's Cop* is autobiographical, the book is not a conventional autobiography. Besides being written in the third person, it contains very little information about the Super's personal life. Furthermore, it didn't seem desirable or even practical to chronicle every transfer, promotion or award of a medal during his nearly four decades of service.

Instead, this work ranges over a variety of episodes in the Superintendent's career, chosen because they reflect different aspects of a policeman's life and Connolly's character.

In sketching a few incidents of the Super's career, we aim to tell a little more of the truth than has appeared in newspaper articles or TV reports. Though we have reviewed print and video records carefully, we have relied more on the testimony of the men who actually lived these episodes of local history. In doing so we have unearthed many facts that have never been published before or which flatly contradict official versions of certain incidents. So be it.

By nature, most policemen are suspicious of — if not downright hostile to — journalists, often for excellent reasons. Reporters can deride, distort, insinuate, even accuse, and police officers rarely get to air their side of the story. Only the confidence that Boston police officers have in Connolly made them open up to me with their versions of the incidents that were depicted very differently by the press and even in written police reports.

The stories you will be reading are true. Most chapters contain the actual names and dates of the crimes described. In a few instances, identities, locations and other surface details have been disguised out of consideration for the families of those involved. Often when we are a little vague, such as in the description of Jeff's robbery attempt in Chapter 25, it is because some of the felons depicted in the book are back out on the street and might take it into their heads to get revenge on those who betrayed them. (The Epilogue, however, is fiction — a short story in which the Superintendent synthesizes events that have happened at different police funerals over the years.)

We have steeled ourselves against those who will tell us, "You guys got it all wrong. That's not the way it happened . . ." or complain "How come you didn't put me in your book?" We realize *A Cop's Cop* isn't perfect, but we believe it's much truer to life than practically anything else that's out there.

However, we do want to express our sincere appreciation for those who helped us to verify facts and ferret out information by sharing their recollections and private records:

Dep. Comm. Bill Murphy　　Capt. Arthur Cadegan
Sgt. Maurice Wall　　　　　Det. John Shepard, retired
Det. Tom Moran, retired　　Det. Arthur Linsky

Det. Jack Parlon	Det. Walter Robinson
Super. Earl Hamilton	Lt.-Det. Walter Tower
John Best	Det. Joe Smith
Ptl. Kevin Foley	Michael Donato
Peg Leahy	Vera Mahoney
Ptl. Al LaFontaine	David Hurley

Our thanks as well to the following people and all the staff at Quinlan Press:

Carolyn Moran	Peter Pearsall
Sandra Dailey	Sandra Bielawa
Kevin Kelly	Deborah Mulcahy

For the photographs that illustrate this book, we are grateful to Bill Brett and the *Boston Globe* Photo Department as well as to the *Boston Herald* Photo Department and to many of the men listed above, who provided pictures from their private collections.

Special thanks to Bill Noonan, Boston Fire Department Photographer, for the present-day portrait of Superintendent Connolly on the cover.

In particular, we want to thank Irene Landry for compiling news clippings about her father and binding them into a memorial volume that saved us hundreds of hours of research.

Chris Harding
June 1985

1

Another Rainy Funeral

Every time Superintendent Edward Connolly attended a policeman's funeral, he couldn't help thinking back to all the other services for deceased officers that he had been to in the same church. Since it was not unusual for him to go to three funerals a week, he had quite a backlog of memories from his 38 years on the Boston Police Department.

On this raw, drizzly morning in March of 1985, the 65-year-old man stood at attention outside St. Anthony's in the Brighton section of Boston, waiting for the cortege to arrive. Ignoring the stray drop here and there that plunked on his face, his mind wandered back to the funerals of the two Schroeder brothers, both of which had been held here in their home parish of St. Anthony's.

On September 23, 1973, Patrolman Walter Schroeder had responded to a call that a robbery was in progress at the State Street Bank and Trust on Western Avenue in Brighton. As Schroeder was getting out of his cruiser, William "Lefty" Gilday, the lookout for the gang hitting the bank, sprayed the parking lot with bullets from a .45 caliber semiautomatic rifle. Walter slammed face first onto the asphalt, and soon died.

Late that night, Eddie Connolly was still at Headquarters. He got word from the New Hampshire police that Gilday had been seen in a restaurant in his home town of Hampton Beach, flashing a wad of $5000 and a gun, with which, he bragged, he had just "dusted a Boston cop."

Every one of the detectives in the Drug Control Unit, which Eddie headed, volunteered to go up to New Hampshire, but Connolly had room for only 11. They piled into two unmarked cars and roared across the state line.

Outside the coastal summer resort town of Hampton, they found that the New Hampshire police had set up roadblocks. With the cooperation of the local law enforcement officials, a small army of Boston and New Hampshire cops crept across the wide field around the Gildays' beachfront home.

Just as dawn was breaking over the ocean, Connolly led the men up to the house, cautioning them to keep quiet. But with so many inexperienced men with guns there, the inevitable happened: someone accidentally fired his weapon.

Connolly and a couple of his men knew there was no stopping now, so they just barrelled through the front door and up to the second floor, where they found only Gilday's terrified wife and children.

For the next two days, the Boston Police Department combed the area with choppers, set packs of canines loose, and broke into boarded-up summer cottages, but found no trace of Gilday. Later Lefty was nabbed by Massachusetts State Police at a tollbooth on the Mass. Turnpike.

Walter Schroeder's funeral brought officers from police departments and law enforcement agencies as far away as Alabama. Between 800 and 900 men assembled in a Brighton shopping mall and set off for St. Anthony's, disrupting traffic for about an hour as they marched the mile and a half to the church.

That day was a rainy one, too. St. Anthony's was packed, and several hundred officers stood outside in the downpour while the ceremony they couldn't even hear was conducted inside. The massive effort expended in the manhunt and the extraordinary turnout for the funeral demonstrated what no words could completely describe — the fierce solidarity among cops.

A few years later, Walter's brother Jack was checking out a character reference at Lenox Loan Co., a pawnshop on Washington Street. Out of nowhere, some holdup men appeared, and in the confrontation that followed, a second Schroeder boy lost his life while on duty.

The Boston Police Department honored these two by naming its highest medal of valor after them. Eddie himself wore the Schroeder medal, given to him after he was gravely wounded when trying to get a psychotic to release the family he was holding hostage.

But Eddie was not one to be very impressed by any man, not even himself. It was not what anyone did in the past that mattered, but how dependable he would be in any upcoming crisis.

"The Schroeders were two of the few that deserved all the glory they got," he thought, shrugging the rainwater from his shoulders. "I've seen many a heel in the department turn into a hero, and many a hero end up a heel."

The hearse had arrived; the coffin and honor guard moved into the church, and the mourners, eager to get out of the wet, hurried in as well. Since the deceased had been retired for several years, the pews were nowhere near as crowded as they had been for the Schroeders' ceremonies. But it was a respectable turnout. Eddie's blue eyes, still sharp at 65, flickered over familiar faces or noted the names of the towns on the arm patches of those people he didn't recognize.

St. Anthony's filled up pretty quickly, but Eddie managed to squeeze into a space in one of the rear pews. No sooner had Connolly got settled than a man in the middle of Eddie's pew began to make his way back out into the aisle. Seeing this poor fellow stepping on people's toes, banging into their knees and whispering apologies reminded Eddie of an incident when he too had had to make an awkward exit in the middle of another rainy-day funeral.

A black officer had shot his wife and then committed suicide. Everyone felt a little awkward at the double-coffin service. Eddie settled into a relaxed posture, doing his bit to add a touch of dignity to the proceedings. He tried to concentrate on what the minister was saying.

Out of the corner of his eye, he noticed an usher waving at him, trying to capture his attention.

"Call home," the usher called. "It's urgent."

Cursing under his breath, Eddie bumbled over the seated deputy superintendents and lieutenants, sprinkling them with water from the overcoat he held over his arm.

He finally made his way out of the clapboard church and onto the street. What with the rain and his lack of change, it took him quite some time to locate a phone and call his wife, Irene.

"It's me. What is it?"

"The dog is dead," the voice sobbed on the other end. "He had a heart attack on the kitchen floor."

"What do you want me to do about it?"

"Come home right away!"

"I'm right in the middle of a funeral. I'll be home as soon as —"

"You get over here now," Irene cried and hung up.

The funeral was about to break soon anyhow, so Eddie found his car and drove the short distance from the Grove Hall neighborhood of Boston to the town of Milton.

When he walked dripping into the kitchen, there was Sergeant, a magnificent white German shepherd, stiff and lifeless.

Irene's eyes were red from crying, and she dabbed at them with the tissues she had in her hand.

"Poor Sergeant," she sniffled. "He died right there. I just can't get anything done with him lying there."

Eddie considered for a moment and then said, "Okay, I'll take him up to the dump and dump him."

Irene was horror-struck at the suggestion.

"The dump? How can you even think about doing such a thing?" she remonstrated. "Sergeant's got to be buried."

"Alright," Eddie conceded. "When the rain stops, I'll dig a hole out back."

"Sergeant's going to be buried on the front lawn, and you're not going to wait. I can't stand to see him a moment longer."

Eddie knew better than to argue. He pulled on his boots, found a spade, went out and started chopping up the grass. The front lawn sloped down to busy Randolph Avenue. The drivers whizzing by, sending up sheets of gray water, wondered what the hell the old man was doing, digging up his front lawn in a rainstorm.

Every time Connolly hoisted a shovelful out of the hole, the rain would wash more mud right back in. Whenever he looked up, he saw his red-headed wife at the window, making sure that he kept at it.

Finally, he wrestled the 100-pound corpse outside and into the shallow pit and slopped the mud over the white-haired creature.

Filthy and exhausted, he reappeared at the kitchen door and announced, "No more dogs in this house!"

A peal of organ music roused Superintendent Connolly from his reverie. He continued his survey of the congregation at St. Anthony's. He saw the widow and, by her side, two sons, both in uniform.

Eddie naturally compared these two to his own children. His son Billy had served two years with the Washington Metropolitan Police before joining the BPD where he had been employed for the past 18 years. Billy had been out for a while with a bad hand injury, but was now back working with the Harbor Police.

Daughter Irene was a traffic enforcement officer, a meter maid. She loved working outdoors and would ticket up to 200 cars a day.

Of course, being a meter maid was not all that exciting.

"But then again," Eddie reflected morosely, "It's a hell of a lot more than I'm doing these days."

Connolly had been forced to retire shortly after his 65th birthday last November. He had gotten a 120-day extension from former Police Commissioner Joseph Jordan, but that time was fast trickling away. Jordan's successor had taken away Eddie's responsibilities as Chief of the Bureau of Administrative Services and put him off when-

ever he asked for a new assignment. Sitting in an office with nothing
to do was torture by stagnation. Eddie didn't need a little birdie to tell
him the new regime wanted him out A.S.A.P.

Eddie had only one chance, and it was a long shot. He was trying
something that had never been done by a high-ranking police officer
before. He was hoping to get a bill passed through the state
legislature that would permit him to keep on working for the Department until he reached 70.

But the bill had been blocked in 1984, and there really wasn't
much hope that he could get it passed in the few weeks left of his
reprieve.

Connolly looked at the coffin. "Will I be dragging my ass like this
guy did for ten years . . . nothing to do but watch the soap operas?"

He thought with a touch of envy of the Schroeders. They went out
the way policemen should go out.

"Still I can't complain," he told himself, "Thirty-eight years on the
force . . . narcotics, robberies, murders, forgeries, riots. There
wasn't much I didn't get to do . . . and wouldn't do today, if only
these bastards would let me . . . ."

2

Joining the Force

In 1947 when 27-year-old Edward Francis Connolly landed back in his hometown of Boston, he discovered that his eight years in the service had left him with a few thousand dollars in the bank, an unshakeable sense of duty and an insatiable appetite for adventure.

He had enlisted before World War II began, and his second hitch carried him beyond the end of that conflict. As a member of the Coast Guard, he had traveled to many far-off ports and seen plenty of action. He had escorted convoys from New York to Londonderry, Ireland. He had sailed around the Caribbean and through the Panama Canal. He had landed troops in Osaka during the invasion of Japan. In Alaska he spent months on weather patrol. From Greenland to the Philippines, from Cuba to Casablanca, Eddie had "seen the world," but now it was time to come home.

In his final months as a chief gunner's mate stationed in Boston, Eddie decided that as a civilian he would like to continue to wear a uniform and work for an organization dedicated to the public good. Hence, he took a variety of qualifying examinations for Civil Service departments: Post Office, Metropolitan District Police, Capitol Police, Fire Department, Boston Police. Prior to this time, when stationed in San Francisco, he had taken a test for a federal job with the Border Patrol.

When he was discharged from the Coast Guard in August of 1947, he decided to put off getting his high school diploma and entering college. After all his travels, he needed time to readjust to civilian life and to consider if school was what he really wanted. Like so many other veterans, he did odd jobs for a while, trying to sort out exactly what he wanted to do with his life.

Then in one week he received job offers from three of the organizations for which he had taken tests: the Boston Police, the Metropolitan District Police and the Border Patrol. After talking over the Border Patrol possibility with friends, he decided that, as much as he would have enjoyed working on the Canadian-US border, it was more likely that he would be sent to swelter in the heat of New Mexico or Texas — an unappealing alternative to a man used to the bracing New England winters.

He toyed with the idea of joining the Metropolitan Police, but eventually came to the conclusion he would probably be packed off to the Quabbin Reservoir in the western part of Massachusetts where there would be nothing to do but shoo away poachers. That left the Boston Police Department, where he hoped at least to see some of the action that had made his tour of duty in the Coast Guard bearable.

So on October 3, the blue-eyed, fair-haired young man reported to the Police Academy, located in the upper stories of the Milk Street Station. Edward W. Fallon, the sole superintendent on the force, and Police Commissioner Thomas Sullivan swore Connolly in and gave him a badge. Even though the Property Clerk's Office was located in the Milk Street building, no uniforms were issued on that day.

Connolly was told to return the following morning to begin classes and to report that afternoon for on-the-job training at Station 11, located in the Fields Corner section of Dorchester, the largest residential part of the city of Boston. Since Station 11 was only a ten-minute walk from his house on Vaughan Avenue, Eddie was not displeased at the assignment, although he would rather have been sent to the South End, where he had been born and raised and where he had worked with his father and brothers prior to entering the service.

So that afternoon, Connolly along with six or seven other fledgling officers gathered in front of the sergeant's desk inside Station 11.

"What do you want?" the sergeant growled, eyeing the bunch scornfully.

"We're the new police officers," someone finally stammered.

"Well, go in and see the captain and leave me alone!"

Connolly, who had expected to be welcomed by his brother officers with open arms, immediately began to have misgivings about having joined the Boston Police force. Despite the chilly reception, the men crowded into the office of Captain Justin McCarthy. Behind the desk sat a chunky, white-haired man. When Connolly studied the rosy, chubby cheeks and the light blue eyes of the captain, he didn't realize that he was looking at the very image of the man he himself would turn into once his blond crewcut gave way to a balding head.

Instead of giving the men the lecture they expected on crime and the adventurous life that lay before them, McCarthy talked about things that surprised Connolly. The captain emphasized the need for the strictest integrity. He warned them that the bookmakers had already corrupted much of the police force through bribery.

"Take only the money you receive as your pay. Take no other money."

The concept of dishonesty in the department was one that had never even occurred to Connolly, but in the years to come he found that the captain's concern was well-founded.

The men were immediately impressed by the captain's words. Besides hammering home the point that they were to take nothing from anyone, McCarthy encouraged them to do their job to the best of their ability and not to get upset if they slipped up. Members of the Department would understand that everyone makes an error once in a while. Connolly soon found that this particular bit of advice was wrong; very few people in the Department did understand and back a man up if he made a mistake, even an honest one.

Connolly's Academy Class Picture

The new recruits quickly learned that the high-minded captain was not as important in the day-to-day operations as the sergeant. Sarge was the disciplinarian, the ultimate arbiter. Men were not supposed to go running into the captain with their complaints or problems. The sergeant might respond to an officer's question or he might shrug it off, but he would not allow the issue to go beyond his desk. The guiding principle was "Keep your mouth shut. Either quit or do what you're told."

On the whole, the police department was not turning out to be what Connolly had expected it to be like. The next morning he and the other 127 members assembled at the Academy. All the men were veterans from various branches of the service. Of the 128 men who started in 1947, only 11 were still members of the department in 1985.

From nine to noon each day they would study traffic control, the law, rules and regulations. They would go out to the firing range in a quarry in West Roxbury to perfect their marksmanship, but when they headed to their afternoon assignments at the various stations around the city, they had to leave the bullets behind. The range was a makeshift affair, far inferior to the more sophisticated set-ups the men were used to from the military.

Only one of the classroom teachers had a college degree, yet the lessons went on well enough, with mock trials to familiarize the officers on the proper way to behave and testify in court. At least at the Academy, the officers were interested in helping the new men along.

Quite the reverse was true at the stations. When Connolly reported to Station 11 on the second afternoon, he came up to the sergeant and said, "Sergeant, I'm a new man reporting for duty."

"Yeah, well, go into the guardroom and sit down. There'll be someone along to pick you up."

As he sat waiting for someone to come to talk with him or at least tell him what to do, Connolly became aware of how old the building at 195 Adams Street was. The cells, located in the basement, resembled a dank dungeon. The cell walls were made of granite blocks. The lighting was very dim, and of course there was no air conditioning. The bunks were simply planks of hard wood. The flushing mechanism for all the toilets was operated by the guards, who only attended to this task every few hours.

After waiting for hours alone in the guardroom, Connolly was relieved when an older officer finally ambled in. Without greeting Eddie or introducing himself, the man said, "Come on. You're going to be with me."

Connolly was expected to tag along behind the more experienced policeman as he walked his beat. Eddie was made to feel like a Japanese woman required to trail a certain number of paces behind her husband.

Eventually, his uncommunicative companion said, "We'll go hit a box."

The pair walked to Park Street where one of the police boxes was located. The boxes contained telephones with direct lines to the station. "Hitting a box" meant calling in your location.

At the station, a Signal Service man who received the call that Officer Jones had hit the 24 box would record the time on a page in his journal. The call was also recorded on a tape, transcribed and turned into a log which was sent the following day to Headquarters so that the higher-ups could double-check that the neighborhood was being patroled sufficiently.

Before the days when there were radios in every car and walkie-talkies on the belts of every foot patrolman, the boxes were crucial to the communication system. Some boxes were attached to the wall of a building, but most were mounted on their own stanchions, usually located on street corners.

The boxes themselves were silver with a blue base, but above the box was a round red light that would flash when the station wanted the officer to call in. When an officer happened to notice a light blinking, even if it were not on his beat, he was supposed to run to the box, open it and use the telephone to find out what the emergency was all about.

Hanging from the bottom of the locked box was a hook, known as "the citizen's alarm." Anyone who wanted to summon a policeman had only to pull the hook. The call would be recorded on a tape at the station, and an officer would be dispatched to meet the person at the box to see what the trouble was.

There was a police emergency phone number, DEvonshire 8-1212, but unlike today's 911, it would cost a person a nickel to use the phone. Besides, in 1947 there were many people who didn't have a phone, nor were payphones as ubiquitous as they are today. So it was much simpler to pull the hook and wait for help to arrive.

Naturally, the hook presented a temptation to youngsters, and many a time a policeman would rush to a box only to hear giggles fading in the distance and see pranksters scampering away.

To unlock the box a policeman needed a large brass skeleton key. Most officers kept their key attached to a leather fob or a metal chain that hung from one of the buttons of their tunics. At roll call, when the men fell in for inspection, each officer would hold up his box key for the sergeant to see. In New York it was a tradition for each policeman to present his nightstick before going out, but in Boston it was the brass key.

One of the major things a rookie had to learn about a new beat was where the boxes were located. He had to know the direction in which to run when he needed to summon help. When a cop was alone and wanted reinforcements to subdue a criminal or needed a wagon to cart off a drunk, he would somehow have to drag the man to the nearest box and with his free hand call for assistance.

So on his first day tagging along, Connolly learned how to hit the 24 box and then walked about three-quarters of a mile to the next box and hit it, too. Out in Dorchester, the boxes were spaced pretty far apart; downtown, they were much closer together.

At Station 11, an officer might be given two or three routes because Dorchester covered so much territory — one-quarter of the

entire city, as a matter of fact. Since the boxes were located generally
on main streets, such as Dorchester Avenue, a man might not patrol
the side streets unless there was a box down there to hit because it
took him so long just to get from one box to the next in a direct route.

When assigned to a particular beat, a man was supposed to go to
each one of the boxes on his route in succession. From then on he had
to hit a box every 40-minutes. Although he couldn't ring the same one
twice in a row, he could return to a box if he had gone to another one in
between. However, if he kept hitting the same couple of boxes, he
would usually get a reminder that he'd better start calling in from some
different locations because the log of exactly which boxes he'd rung
was being sent to Headquarters first thing in the morning.

The 40-minute check-ins also gave the Signal Desk man frequent
opportunities to send a man off on errands, some of which seemed
very unimportant. A patrolman might get word to tell a certain man
to shovel the snow off his section of a sidewalk or disperse a gang of
boys from a street corner. By the time the officer had walked a mile
or two out of his way, the snow might have melted or the kids gone
home to supper.

Besides demonstrating the duties of an officer, Connolly's close-
lipped mentor introduced him to the unofficial aspects of a
policeman's routine. For example, Eddie found himself being led to
the backroom of a storefront embalming establishment. Though he
got no information from his companion, Eddie gathered the room
had been set up as a place for policemen to warm up or rest their feet
when they weren't pounding their beat.

There was nothing in the room but a few chairs, so they sat down.
The other man lit up his pipe, had a leisurely smoke, and finally announced, "I'll be right back."

He wandered out to hit a box while Connolly sat alone — again.
Soon the fellow returned, and they sat in silence until it was time to
call in once more.

The sickening smell of embalming fluid hung heavy in the air, and
the strange sounds of the undertaking process could be heard from
the adjoining room. In fact, every once in a while, the undertaker or
his assistant would request the policemen's aid in carrying in the big
wicker baskets that were used in those days to hold bodies.

It was getting late in the afternoon, and the quiet was broken as the
old-timer heaved himself into a standing position and mumbled,
"Let's head in."

As he was about to put his hat on, the man caught sight of a piece
of paper he'd put in the inner band earlier in the day. "Almost forgot
I have that summons to serve."

The pair walked two or three miles through the streets of Dorchester without exchanging as much as a word. When they got to the

right address, they climbed the stairs to the top floor of a three-decker. Not bothering to knock or to attempt to serve the summons personally, the veteran cop just slipped the folded paper under the door and started to trudge down the stairs.

By the time they had completed the long walk back to the station, Connolly figured they had covered at least ten miles. Like most of the other men on the day shift at Station 11, this fellow was a 30-year veteran and a great walker. He seemed to be perfectly content to spend the rest of his days walking, walking, walking.

The veterans were big strapping fellows, many of whom seemed to have joined in 1919 as replacements during the great Boston Police Strike. Others came aboard during the war as provisionals to fill in for the young men who had gone off to fight, but they managed to pass the test and become permanent. They had no ambition to be promoted or transferred. They didn't like anything to upset their tranquil routine — especially not thrill-hungry rookies.

Though the hours were long by modern standards, the pace was leisurely. The day shift went from 7:45 to 5:45 with an hour and a quarter break for lunch. Most men just went out to buy a sandwich and spent their free time in the guardroom playing dominoes and having a quiet smoke.

Finally, Connolly and the other recruits were ordered to report to the Property Clerk to get a uniform. Unlike today where the Department gives each officer $440 a year to buy and maintain uniforms, in those days the Clerk reissued old pairs of pants or jackets that had been worn by men who had left the service or died. The summer uniform consisted of a gray shirt, black tie, single-breasted jacket, pants and a hat. At that time, an officer was never supposed to be without his hat — unless he were in church or court. A policeman would be put down on charges if he appeared in public without the official headgear.

The Clerk also issued a nightstick, a gun, and six bullets, but no handcuffs.

For the first week, each day was the same, following a veteran around. Occasionally, someone might share a tidbit of information about what the neighborhood was like, but basically the recruits were expected to pick up the procedures by observation and deduction during the long, conversationless patrols.

Connolly enjoyed stretching his legs as much as the next man, but wandering the streets was not his idea of police work. Neither did he relish the thought of a life where the highlight of the day was matching black wooden tiles with little spots or staring into space in the backroom of an undertaking parlor.

3

"Nothing Ever Happens on the First Floor"

After the first week, Connolly was assigned to the night shift, when, so he had heard, all the real action took place. The men on the night squad were slightly younger, and Connolly was expecting big things.

Full of anticipation, Connolly reported promptly at midnight and was assigned to the rear end of the wagon. Each wagon or van had a driver and a man in back to ride with the prisoners and see that they behaved themselves. The old "Black Maria" had brass bars to hold onto when climbing the step into the back of the van; inside were two benches.

When Connolly arrived at the wagonhouse, he discovered the old-timer who was supposed to be driving the vehicle lying on a cot in a tangle of blankets. The white-haired character moaned that he was deathly ill, but the smell of alcohol told another story. In any case, he was clearly unfit to drive.

Connolly waited alone by the telephone, wondering if a call from the station would come and if it did, what he would do. Around 2 am, the phone jangled, and he found out.

"You're needed down at 25 Port Norfolk Street."

"Okay, then."

Connolly went into the darkened back room to rouse the driver.

"We got a call to go to Port Norfolk Street."

"I can't go. I'm too sick."

Connolly called the station back. "The driver's sick. We can't go."

"Then take the wagon down there yourself."

"I don't know how to drive the wagon."

"Well, you'd better learn. Now just get down there."

"I don't even know where Port Norfolk Street is," Connolly said, still hoping to wiggle out of the assignment.

"When you leave the wagonhouse, take a left, then another left and then just keep going straight ahead. You'll come to a big square. There's a fire station there. Ask one of the firemen how to get to Port Norfolk Street."

"Alright," Connolly said reluctantly. He went out to the garage and found the keys in the ignition. The GMC wagon had four on the floor and a clutch that stuck a little.

Since he was not accustomed to handling a wagon, Eddie drove cautiously and followed the streetcar tracks down Neponset Avenue. The firemen and strangers on the street that he asked for directions thought it rather odd the officer driving the police wagon didn't know where to go in his own neighborhood, but their amused expressions didn't deter Eddie from getting to his destination.

On Norfolk Street he sighted the police car that had summoned the wagon. A woman on the third floor of a triple decker was in labor. At that time, the police wagons were the only ambulance service available.

The policemen carried the moaning mother-to-be down the stairs on a chair. Connolly pulled out the stretcher and blanket that were kept in the back of the wagon, and they made her as comfortable as possible, trying to keep her warm on this chilly night.

Connolly said, "I got no one to help me."

"One of us will have to go along," the responding officer replied. One of the patrolmen climbed in back to steady the stretcher and keep it from sliding around when the wagon went up a hill.

Without any further ado, Connolly found his way back to Massachusetts Avenue and headed for Boston City Hospital. As the orderlies helped the woman off the stretcher, Eddie saw how stained and unsanitary the stretcher was. On one ride the stretcher might be holding a corpse or bloody accident victim, the next a lice-ridden bum, and then a delicate woman like this. The only time the stretcher got cleaned was when someone got around to laundering the blankets and washing off the stretcher the best way he could think of.

The next night, there was a new driver, and the two had barely introduced themselves when there was a call to do some more ambulance work.

When they arrived at the address on Dorchester Avenue, they learned that the sick woman was on the top floor. As the officers hustled up flight after flight, Connolly remarked, "You know, the lady I took in last night, she was on the third floor, too."

His new partner laughed, "You mark my words, Eddie. It's always on the second or third story. Nothing ever happens on the first floor."

This woman, in her late 50's, was unusually large and complained dramatically that "The devil's own cramps are tormenting my belly!"

"We'll need the sturdiest chair in the house," the driver said under his breath, "Let's look in the kitchen."

When they had settled on a strong, straight back chair, the driver asked, "Got any rope or belts around to strap her to the chair?"

"Belts wouldn't get around this one," Connolly whispered and then in a normal voice requested some sheets.

With the assistance of a man from the patrolcar, they secured the woman to the chair, binding her arms to stop them from flailing. They started down the winding staircase with Connolly in front and the other two men supporting the chair from the back.

No sooner had they started down than the woman began to make gagging sounds. Connolly was about to pray that the woman wouldn't vomit all over him, but he was too late.

Smoky hot, yellowish-pink slime erupted from the fat woman's face and shot through the opening of Connolly's right cuff. As the woman emptied her stomach down his sleeve, the vomit coursed down the space between his shirt and skin, into his undershirt and leaked down to his chest and stomach, leaving a sticky, warm trail along the right arm and right side of his body. Because he was supporting her tremendous weight on a rather steep staircase, he couldn't let go to protect himself or even let his body shudder the way it wanted to.

Connolly was bullshit.

"What a fuckin' job this is," he fumed internally and didn't refrain from saying aloud, "Lady, we shoulda had you in the artillery. You would have got 100% for marksmanship. That's what I call deadly aim."

But the woman was too busy coughing, crying and trying to wipe her chin off on the sheets to understand what he was saying. With every step down, the vomit sloshed around, smearing his stomach and seeping down to his shorts.

Once outside, they unknotted the vomit-drenched sheets and struggled to get the poor woman onto the stretcher and into the back of the wagon. In the cold of the night air, the regurgitated food began to congeal and become clammy. Connolly stayed in back with the woman as the driver sped to City Hospital, but he was careful to stay out of the line of fire.

When the woman was in safe hands, Connolly stopped a nurse and asked, "Where can I change?"

"What happened to you?"

"A lady we just brought in puked all over me."

She showed him to a washroom and gave him a stack of towels. He stripped to the waist and wiped his torso clean and rinsed out his shirt and undershirt. Then it was time to put on the damp clothes again and head back.

At the wagonhouse, Connolly began to get undressed again, intending to dry his shirts off by draping them over the radiator, but before he had even gotten his gray shirt unbuttoned, the driver had picked up the ringing phone.

"Fighting drunk down on Freeport Street," the driver laughed, adding mischievously, "Third floor."

Back into the uniform, out to the wagon, through the streets and up, up the stairs to the top floor of the house on Freeport Street they went.

As they climbed, they could hear the argument raging above. When the drunk became aware that the police had arrived, he bellowed, "Come on, you fucking assholes. You think you can take me? I'll kick the living shit out of you. I'll rip your lungs out."

These threats, delivered in the thickest of brogues, were intermingled with the cries of his wife who pleaded, "Help me, someone. He says he's going to murder me!"

As Connolly and the driver neared the top landing, the scarlet-faced man shouted, "You two keep your distance or I'll drown the both of you in piss."

Undaunted Eddie started up the last few steps, but the man was as good as his word. He ripped open his fly and produced a pint-size penis that miraculously showered quarts of urine.

Eddie shielded his eyes as he advanced, but the spray liberally doused his hat, shirt, jacket and pants.

As the two subdued the drunk, Connolly said, "He's been at some kind of rotgut bourbon and Pickwick ale. You can smell it coming out of his dick."

Both cops grabbed the drunkard and dragged him downstairs and threw him into the wagon. Now the drunk turned weepy and sentimental.

"Come on, fellas. I didn't mean it," he sniffed with tears welling up in his eyes, "There's no reason to pick on me."

They dumped him off at District 11 and headed back to the wagonhouse.

"We shoulda killed that prick when we had the chance," the driver growled.

"Too bad," Connolly agreed, "We'll get him next time."

When Eddie got home the next morning, his mother was taken aback at his disheveled appearance and peculiar odor.

"For heavens' sakes, what happened to you?"

"Can't you smell it?"

"What is that?"

"Beer . . . booze of the cheapest vintage . . . vomit in every color of the rainbow."

"Here," she said, "get out of those clothes and get into the bath. Your father will have your uniform cleaned."

Eddie scrubbed himself as he had never scrubbed before, then tumbled into bed. While he slept his mother washed his shirt and underclothes; his father was good friends with a local cleaner and was able to get the jacket, pants and hat spic and span by the time Eddie was ready to dress for work.

While night duty on the wagon undoubtedly had its drawbacks — wear and tear on the uniform, not to mention the nostrils — it certainly had a little more excitement to it than strolling down the street.

Most of the men walked beats; cops of the old school didn't get fat sitting behind a desk. Even the sergeant patroled the streets. He was out there checking to see that the men were where they were scheduled to be. Each officer was given a little notebook in which he was supposed to write whatever he saw of significance on his route. If nothing important happened, he still had to write about the weather or the traffic or something. These books would be carefully inspected and compared to see that they did not contain works of fiction.

"Connolly," the sergeant said one night at roll call, "From now on, you're on routes 6, 8 and 10."

"Where are these routes? I don't even know them."

The sergeant shook his head and beckoned to a veteran.

"Doran, show Connolly where his beat is."

On a big map pinned to the stationhouse wall, Doran traced the routes that Connolly had been ordered to cover.

"Jeez, that's a lotta walking," Eddie said when Doran had finished.

"Come on, we'll take care of you," Doran said. Like most of the younger men on the evening shift, he was willing to help a rookie out, unlike the old-timers on the day shift who would just as soon see him bumble around forever.

Doran and his partner were assigned to a patrolcar that night.

"We won't get a call for a while," Cimino explained, "We'll give you a ride around the outskirts of your route. I know it's kind of hard to picture where you're going just from looking at a map."

In addition to driving Eddie along the perimeter of his new route and showing him where the local landmarks were, the two fellow officers pointed out the trouble spots. Soon, however, they got a call and had to let Eddie out. He thanked them sincerely, but as they drove off, he couldn't help envying their being assigned to a car.

Eddie's route ran from Fields Corner to Lower Mills, an area of some four square miles which he was supposed to cover on foot. His main task was to try the shop doors, both front and rear, to make sure that they were secured. More a night watchman than anything else, he would rattle and tug on doorknobs.

If he did discover an open door, he would try to phone the owner. In the event that the proprietor couldn't be contacted, Eddie would Dutch-lock the door. To do so he would have to scare up a hammer, nails and a scrap of wood. After nailing the wood to the floor near the door, Connolly would then wedge another piece of wood between the block on the floor and the knob as he slid out the door. If the careless owner had a key to the back door, there would be no problem removing the makeshift barricade in the morning. But to get into a Dutch-locked store that had only one entrance, that was the proprietor's headache.

Basically, everyone seemed to be obeying the law, which was nice from one point of view, but made for somewhat boring patrols.

After all the bars closed at 1:00 am, the streets became positively desolate. Sometimes walking along, Connolly would hear the cry of a baby. Then a window would light up somewhere as the mother got up to give the child a bottle or her breast. After a few minutes, the lights would go down behind those curtains, and all would be dark and quiet once again.

Toward morning, more and more people would appear, and the city would come to life. Horses drawing milk-wagons would go clip-clopping down the streets as the milkman clinked the bottles of milk and cream onto people's porches or stoops.

The breadman would deliver freshly baked loaves and rolls and deposit them in special breadboxes that many families kept by their doors. At that time no one would dream of pinching a neighbor's quart of milk or loaf of rye.

Around 3, Eddie became lonely and would stop anyone he saw just to have a little human contact. One night he struck up a conversation with a man in the Lower Mills area.

"What are you doing here?"

"I'm a baker. On my way to work."

"Oh . . ."

"Why don't you come along? I'll give you a cup of coffee."

The baker took Connolly into the back of his shop where his brother was already hard at work cutting doughnuts.

"Anytime you're in this area, drop in for coffee and a doughnut."

The coffee was good. The doughnuts were good. So for the short time that he did the night patrol Connolly made a habit of dropping in on the two brothers. Since there was no place open to buy coffee, the warm bakery was a godsend.

There was a modicum of suspense in reconnoitering dark alleys. With one hand pointing his flashlight and the other on the grip of his pistol, Connolly was never quite sure what he would find as he ventured into the darkness. A rat would scurry underfoot, or he would step on an alley cat which would hiss and swipe at him, but no public enemies were ever found lurking in any ashcans.

The only kind of disturbances that broke the silence and the tedium of those nights were the antics of the drunks — harmless, most of them. One night walking down Dorchester Avenue from Peabody Square toward Gallivan Boulevard, Eddie spotted a man with his arms wrapped around a tree. When Connolly got closer, he saw the man was nuzzling and kissing the trunk.

"What do you think you're doing, mister?"

"I'm in love with this tree. Isn't it the most beautiful thing you've ever seen?"

The man's breath indicated that he was intoxicated with more than just love. Connolly pried the man away from his bark and pulled him toward the callbox which was about 40 yards away. The man kept struggling to get free and return to his darling elm. The two of them stumbled and spattered themselves in mud, the man all the while disturbing the neighbors by singing the praises of his tree. As Connolly finally wrestled the man, who had a good four inches on him, to the box, he felt the ridiculousness of his situation. "Here I am in the middle of the night fighting with a drunk who's in love with a tree."

On Christmas Eve, Connolly was inclined to be a little more lenient toward those who had drunk a bit too much. One snowy December 24, he spotted a man staggering down the street near Ashmont Station. Eddie was more concerned with getting the man home to his family than jailing him.

"Where do you live?" Connolly demanded.

The man was so far gone that he had a hard time stammering out the words "A-avon . . . Avondale. . . ."

"Don't worry now. I'll get you there."

Connolly hailed a bus that was leaving the station and headed for Brockton and the South Shore.

"Do you go through Avon?" Connolly asked the driver.

"Yeah . . ."

"Well, this guy lives in Avon or Avondale . . . somewheres around there. He's done a little too much celebrating."

"Put him on," the driver said agreeably. "What the hell. It's Christmas."

Connolly boosted the protesting, disoriented man aboard and thanked the driver. "Just leave him off in Avon. The local police will see he gets home."

Hours later, Connolly was again walking by Ashmont Station and noticed the same driver on his return trip. Connolly waved. The driver stopped and signaled him to approach.

"Hey, I just got stopped by the Avon police. They just arrested that guy."

"What for?"

"Kickin' up a tremendous ruckus."

"Why?"

"He don't live in Avon. He didn't want to be there."

Connolly shook his head. "I stopped him and asked him. He said he lived in Avon."

The bus driver laughed. "He lives on Avondale Street. That's right around the corner from here. He was sure pissed off that you sent him way off to the South Shore."

"I guess he won't be home for Christmas, will he?" Connolly said sheepishly and thought to himself, "This is what happens when you try to do a guy a favor."

4

"Dead Bodies Can't Breathe in Your Face"

Being assigned to a night tour of duty put Connolly into contact with a whole new set of brother officers. There weren't many older men assigned to the night shift, but those that were didn't see any point in socializing with the rookies. The old-timers would stick together and play dominoes or smoke their pipes off in some corner.

The younger officers, however, were eager to impress the rookies with tips on how to deal with a tough street gang or where to go (or not go) for a cup of java.

There was one old-timer who was as pleasant and helpful as the younger men. Wally was 60 or 64, but he looked as if he were 70 or 74. His face was thin and usually in need of a shave. His weather-beaten uniform hat was developing patches of non-regulation colors. His "Bennie," or heavy winter overcoat, hung on his gaunt frame looking at least two sizes too large. His baggy-kneed trousers were in desperate need of a cleaning and press. Anyone within six feet of him couldn't help noticing the odor of Jim Jameson on his breath.

Yet the superior officers, lieutenants and sergeants overlooked Wally's shabby appearance and seemed to regard him with a lot of respect. The citizens of Dorchester seemed to feel the same way.

Wally was nothing more than a route officer, a walking cop, in one of the poorer sections of Dorchester, but almost everyone on his beat from the toddlers to the old folks knew "Wally the Cop."

Seldom was there any trouble on the route he plodded along so faithfully each day. Toughs would move along when Wally gave the word. Not that he was big or imposing; quite the opposite he was skinny, pale and old, but he was the law, and he called all the locals by their first name and knew their families as well.

Connolly found out just how deep the respect for Wally was one cold December night.

Connolly had just come down an alley after having inspected both doors to Sol Levine's Deli. No sound broke the stillness of the night, except the intermittent clashes between some scruffy alley cats, and one or two rats rustling around inside a garbage can.

As he reached the sidewalk, the 11-wagon pulled up right in front of him.

"Eddie, have you hit a box lately?" Charlie Sweeney called from the observer's side of the wagon.

Connolly nodded.

"By the way, the sergeant is looking for Wally. They haven't heard from him since he hit his first box at 12:35 at Orchardfield and Dot Ave. Have you seen him?"

"Nope."

Just then the radio blared out a call: "11-wagon, see a woman at 560 Sumner Street, relative to a sick man on the second floor. Possible heart attack. 11-wagon, make that in a hurry."

"OK," Sweeney told the dispatcher, "11-wagon has got the message."

The driver Ed Tate took compassion on the bored young patrolman and said casually, "Hop in the back, Eddie, and we'll all go for a ride."

"Oh, boy," Connolly thought as he swung himself up onto the hard bench in back, "Something else to do besides shaking hands with door handles."

Since Dorchester Avenue was completely deserted, the wagon whizzed down to Savin Hill Avenue, to Pleasant Street, to Stoughton and then turned off at Sumner Street, pulling up in front of 560. The wagon had been there many times before on a variety of calls. The wide, battleship-gray Victorian had been converted into a roominghouse, and at one time or another most of the lodgers had required the services of the men in blue.

While Sweeney and Connolly scrambled up the porch, Tate reached into the compartment under the rear seat and withdrew the stretcher and a blanket. He lugged the equipment up the stairs where his two fellow officers had paused, taking in a not altogether pleasant sight.

Framed in the doorway was an enormous 55-year-old woman, blubbering and gesticulating wildly. Her hair, dyed an unlikely flaming golden-red, flared out around her tear-streaked face.

The bright hallway lamp revealed more than her silhouette. The merciless rays cut through her flimsy, green negligee, outlining every lump and bump, highlighting every discolored splotch and birthmark on the layers of fat that drooped over her hips. The outline of the shaggy thicket between her legs made it all too clear that she had not had time to climb back into her undies when misfortune had driven her out on the porch.

"Come quick, please," she panted on the verge of hyperventilating. "It's Wally. He collapsed. I think he's . . . dead!"

"Where is he?" Sweeney demanded.

"Second floor right," she screeched. "I'll show you."

Huffing and puffing, the blowsy behemoth hobbled up the stairs in her bare feet which ended in chipped, dark red toenails. The rear prospect of her churning masses of flesh was equally unappetizing. The unusual exertion of lumbering up the stairs caused the emission of noxious gases from what had to be the largest posterior in the world.

Anxious as Sweeney was to rush to the side of his fallen friend Wally, the string of wet farts forced him to keep several paces behind the weeping woman and to hold his breath.

At the second floor landing, she slumped against the wall and pointed a bloated finger towards the dimly lit interior.

"Wally, Wally," she gasped and at the same time fumbled to force her mottled left breast, which had flopped out during her heroic struggle up the steps, back underneath the sheer green wrapper.

Sweeney led the way into the 10 by 12 room, which contained a bed, a table, two chairs and a sink. On the sagging mattress and box springs was a form covered with a gray blanket with the words "US NAVY" printed in black and the name "A. K. Cortez" stenciled in fading white paint in one corner.

Connolly turned to Tate, who was still out in the hallway with the folded stretcher under one arm and his blanket trailing along on the floor. "We better call the fire department and get some oxygen for him."

"It's no use," Sweeney said sadly as he uncovered old Wally's face. "He's stone dead. Looks like he's been dead for some time."

He let the Navy blanket droop down again for a moment while he regarded the sniffling woman.

"Hey, baby, how long has Wally been laying here like this?"

"Since one o'clock. He . . . uh . . . came by for . . . uh . . . a cup of tea and he said that he had a headache . . . and . . . asked me if he could lie down for a while."

Her enormous bosoms jostled one another as she erupted in a convulsion of tears and coughing.

No one believed her story for a second. Sweeney snapped the blanket off the corpse. There lay Wally in his grimy long johns, his shriveled penis dangling out as dead and pasty as the rest of him.

Sweeney, Connolly and Tate just looked at one another for a moment. They couldn't help wondering if Wally had had the life squeezed out of him by his lard-assed lady-friend.

Finally, Charlie said, "OK, baby, quit sniveling. Keep your mouth shut, and we'll take care of everything."

"Now," he asked, peering around in the darkness, "where're his clothes?"

"Under the bed," she sobbed, "and on that chair over there."

"Eddie Tate, you watch the door. Eddie Connolly, you get over here and help me dress him."

Connolly and Tate had a very uneasy feeling, but they shuffled to their designated locations. After all, Sweeney was an experienced street cop, who presumably knew exactly what to do in emergencies like this.

"Get his uniform from under the bed," Charlie ordered. Connolly got down on his knees and groped around, retrieving various garments and passing them to Charlie who had collected the rest of the clothes from the straight-backed chair.

"Help me pull the bed away from the wall. I'm going to have to hold him while you dress him."

"It won't be easy in this light," Connolly ventured.

"Just move that bed."

When the creaky bed was repositioned, Sweeney climbed up onto the pillows and hoisted Wally's stiffened body into a sitting position.

Connolly felt like an embalmer as he wrestled to pull the smelly shirt and then the sweater over the pitifully scrawny frame of old Wally. When Wally's upper half was covered, Charlie moved to the other end of the bed and held up the dead cop's heels. Connolly was perspiring and cursing under his breath as he tried to yank the pants over the rigid, clammy legs and to fit the socks and shoes around the bony, cheesy feet.

Tate meanwhile had a much easier job; he leaned in the doorway, keeping watch and shooing away nosy roomers who wanted to know why their neighbor was whimpering.

Finally, the task was completed; Connolly and Sweeney extricated themselves and the corpse from the welter of sheets and brushed the sweat from their brows.

"Tate, open that stretcher. Eddie and I will tie him to it; you can cover him with your blanket."

As they gently carried their companion from the bed and placed him on the stretcher out in the hall, Connolly inquired, "What are we going to use to tie Wally on with?"

"Anything you can find. Rip up the sheets or the blanket on the bed."

Connolly dutifully tore the Navy blanket in half and proceeded to make long strips.

"My blanket!" the redheaded beauty cried in protest.

Charlie had just about had it.

"By the way, honey, what is your name?"

"Mabel James."

"Nice name, Mabel. Anyway, look, I'm sorry that we're leaving you with only half a blanket. The next guy that you invite up here will just have to bring his own blanket."

She slammed the door on them.

"Goodnight, Mabel."

A series of strange noises continued to issue from behind the door as the men finished strapping the body to the stretcher and shrouding it with the blanket from the wagon.

"Eddie Connolly and myself will take the bottom. Tate, you take the top — it's lighter."

"OK," Tate replied, "Let's go."

All three men grunted a bit as they lifted the body. Very gingerly the officers maneuvered down the winding, ill-lit stairs, unable to fend off roomers who now were no longer content to observe the proceedings from barely open doors, but emerged to supervise the removal of the body.

The corpse shifted from side to side during the descent. At one point the blanket slipped off the head, and Wally's grizzled chin came to rest against Tate's cheek.

"Can't somebody help me up here?" he squawked. "Wally's breathing in my face, and his breath stinks."

"Dead bodies can't breathe in your face," Connolly said in exasperation.

"Bullshit! You just come up here and switch ends with me."

"Just a few more steps," Sweeney tried to coax his two assistants into remaining calm.

Somehow they managed to bundle the body into the back of the wagon.

"Get in back and pull down the shade," Sweeney told Connolly.

Straddling the body of his fellow cop, Connolly did as he was told, but couldn't suppress a shudder. "I can't wait till we get Wally to the morgue."

"Not so fast, Eddie," Charlie said. "This is where we think about Wally's wife and family."

"What the hell do you mean by that?" Connolly asked.

Sweeney smiled sadly and shook his head. "You still have got a lot to learn, rookie."

Charlie drove the wagon along and after a few minutes called back to Eddie, who was miserably sitting guard in the rear.

"What route do you have?"

"4-6-14."

"What route did Wally have?"

"The opposite side of the street . . . 16-18-26."

"I thought so," Charlie commented tersely, but didn't say anymore until he coasted to a halt.

Sweeney came to open the back door for him. Connolly was glad to leave his vigil over Wally's body and step out into the night air.

"Tate," Charlie whispered, "Put out the lights."

A moment later the beams were fading, but not before Eddie was able to get his bearings and recognize that they had stopped behind Pitnoff's Stove and Furniture Store.

"No flashlights," Charlie warned.

Then addressing Connolly, Sweeney said, "Help me with the stretcher."

When the stretcher had been gently lowered to the ground, Sweeney ordered him to remove the blanket and untie the strips that bound the body to the stretcher.

"Hold my hat," Charlie said, handing his cap to the mystified rookie. Then Sweeney leaned over, hoisted the body over his shoulder and stumbled through the pitch dark alley. Then he carefully leaned Wally against the rear door to Pitnoff's.

"Give me my hat back first," Sweeney called in low tones, "then fetch Wally's hat — I put it on the rear seat."

Tate brought the cap to his superior. Charlie reverently arranged the hat on Wally's head. Sweeney blessed himself, bowed his head for a moment and then breathed the words of praise, "He was a great cop."

The moment of sentiment was over, and the authority returned to his voice. "Connolly, get in the back. Tate, let's get the hell out of here, but don't make a sound."

Tate slowly rolled the wagon out of the alley down onto Duncan Street.

Connolly's eyes were demanding an explanation. When they had gotten far enough away from Pitnoff's, Sweeney gave him one.

"Wally was one of us, a cop. In his day, he was a detective, one of the best. He saved my life one day when I was a rookie, just like you. He disarmed a guy with a .45, who would sure as hell have killed me."

"Look, Eddie," he continued in a softer tone, "we're not doing anything wrong. All men are weak in some way. The newspapers in one edition would knock Wally's balls off, and his family would be disgraced. Let them think of him as they knew him, as a husband, a father and a grandfather . . . a good guy . . . a cop."

They drove on for a few minutes in silence. Sweeney cleared his throat.

"Connolly, you will now call the station from box 13 on the Avenue. You will tell them that you found Wally collapsed behind Pitnoff's. Got that? Say nothing else."

"What if they ask me what I was doing on his side of the Avenue?"

"Tell them that you thought you had both sides of the street. After all, you're just a green rookie. They think all rookies are stupid. Show us how smart you really are and do this thing for Wally right."

Connolly sighed his assent.

"Most likely the call will be put over the air as soon as you call in," Sweeney explained. "Tate and myself will make sure that we're the first ones there."

It only took two minutes for Connolly to run to box 13 and call in. As Sweeney had predicted, the wagon was the first to respond, but the 11-A and 11-T cars arrived soon after with blue lights flashing and sirens blasting.

Sergeant Tom Mundy pulled up in the 11-T car. Connolly was nervous confronting him.

"Down here, Sergeant. I found Wally out behind Pitnoff's Furniture Store," Connolly blurted out, "I think he's dead."

"You think he's dead," Mundy retorted sharply. "What are you . . . a doctor?"

"Sure," Sweeney laughed. "Didn't you know Eddie was a neurosurgeon before he joined the force?"

"I don't like wise guys, Charlie," the sergeant snapped.

Mundy viewed the body and ordered Sweeney and Tate to take Wally to Boston City Hospital for pronouncement and then on to the morgue.

"Get his gun and badge, Sweeney," the grim-faced sergeant reminded him as they carted Wally's remains back to the wagon.

When they left, Mundy turned to Connolly who was still breathing uneasily. "OK, kid. Go to the station and make out your report about finding Wally. You did a good job, but just remember you're not a doctor."

Connolly returned on foot to Station 11 on Adams Street. At the front desk sat Lieutenant Bowes, the man in charge. Connolly nodded to him as he headed for the guardroom.

"If you have any trouble with that report, one of the clerks will help you out."

"Thank you, sir."

Connolly was struggling with his report and his conscience when the doors to the guardroom opened. Charlie Deary, the night clerk, summoned him, "Eddie, some guy at the morgue wants to talk to you."

Connolly's guts were thrashing around inside him as he picked up the phone.

"Are you Edward Connolly?"

"Yes, sir. This is Officer Connolly."

"Were you the one that found the body of the officer that was just brought in?"

"Yes, sir. I did."

"Did you notice anything unusual about the body?"

"Not that I can recall, sir."

"How long ago did you find him?"

"About an hour."

"The man is as stiff as a board. Rigor mortis set in a long time ago."

"Well, I'm not a doctor," Connolly stammered, "but it was pretty cold out there in that alley."

"I see. Perhaps you could explain something else to me?"

"I-I'll try, sir. . . ."

"How come Wally had his pants on backwards and two socks on one foot?"

"I don't know, sir. I'm just a rookie — you know how stupid us rookies are. Do you want me to ask the lieutenant why policeman put their pants on backwards?"

"Kid, I know exactly how stupid you are by your answer. Don't ask the lieutenant a thing. Keep your mouth shut, and nobody will know how stupid you are."

The morgue attendant slammed down the receiver.

Minutes later Sweeney and Tate came through the front door, chuckling and congratulating themselves. They called Connolly over into a corner.

"Well, Eddie. You're a smart boy. You did everything right. Old Wally would have been proud of you."

"Thanks, Sweeney, but I would rather be a rookie and stupid. Nobody asks you questions that way."

5

Blood and Guts

High-speed chases through the streets of Boston, thrilling gun-fights, bushels of stolen jewels triumphantly recovered . . . young Eddie Connolly had dreamed that police life was actually the way it was portrayed in pulp novels and comic books. After a year or so on the force, he had finally come to the realization that most police work was much more mundane than hack novelists would have their readers believe.

The only gangs he got to chase were gangs of kids playing ball in the street. He would be more likely sent out to quiet a barking dog than to silence Public Enemy No. 1.

Sure, once in a while, Eddie would get his name in the papers, but not for saving a flimsily clad beauty from white slave traders. No, Eddie got a couple of column inches for rescuing a kitten.

One Sunday morning, the plaintive cries of a cat were heard issuing from the sewer at the corner of Blakeville and Bowdoin Streets. Patrolmen Paul Zaniewski and Ed Connolly answered the call from concerned neighbors. While a crowd of parishioners coming home from Mass looked on, the officers pried the grating loose, but still could not reach the meowing animal.

The two men stripped off their coats, and Zaniewski held Eddie by the legs as he lowered himself into the foul-smelling catch basin. After a few swipes, Connolly managed to grasp the scruff of the cat's neck. The bedraggled creature was too busy trying to keep afloat to offer much resistance.

On Eddie's signal, Paul hauled him and the now limp kitten back up into the daylight. The churchgoers burst into applause, and the cat bounded away as soon as Eddie set it on the ground.

Eddie did feel some measure of satisfaction when he would deliver a baby that arrived enroute to the hospital as he was tending the mother in the back of the wagon. But these opportunities to pinch-hit for an obstetrician were not enough to make up for all the monotonous days when he seemed to be frittering his life away.

Connolly started thinking about finding another way to make a living — perhaps one that paid more than the low weekly wages of a cop. After all, he had met a beautiful redhead named Irene, who worked in a dry cleaning shop on his beat. Before he knew it, he had a wife and son to provide for.

So one day, Eddie found himself standing, hat in hand, before Captain McCarthy.

"I think I'll go back into the service. This is not at all what I thought a police job would be like. No action, nothing ever happens."

"Oh, come on," McCarthy said in his most soothing tone, "There's a lot of excitement . . ."

"Not out here. A few drunks, a few family fights. It's taking care of sick people mostly, busting up ballgames on the street because some old battle-ax don't want the boys to have any fun . . ."

"Tell you what, Eddie. I'll put you in a car."

"I dunno . . ."

"The least you can do is try it."

Station 11 had three patrol vehicles — the A-car, the O-car, and the T-car — one for each of the sectors into which Dorchester was divided.

Eddie reluctantly agreed to give this new assignment a whirl. Things picked up a little; once in a while there was a bank robbery or a stolen car chase to make life a little more lively. Captain McCarthy began grooming Connolly for a career with the Vice Squad by sending him out to bring in bookmakers who were operating out of local bars and shops. But basically in the late 40's and early 50's crime was at a low ebb in Dorchester. The top three kinds of calls the police got were housebreaks, vehicle accidents and injured children.

Sooner or later, however, the day had to come — the day that Connolly would get his baptism of blood, the day he learned that, though most of a policeman's hours are filled with necessary, but humdrum work, there are also minutes so full of horror that years of routine work can never erase them from his memory.

One spring afternoon Connolly and Patrolman Bill McDonald were out cruising in the O-car.

McDonald was Connolly's first partner, a gentle family man from South Boston, who was always ready with some fatherly advice to steer his young companion in the right direction.

They had just left Fields Corner and were headed south on Dorchester Avenue towards the Ashmont section. The quiet of the afternoon was broken by the dispatcher's voice.

"Eleven-O car, woman under train at Shawmut Station. Fire Rescue on the way."

Since the Shawmut rapid transit station lay in between Fields Corner and Ashmont, the men in the Eleven-O car knew it was up to them to respond.

"It's right around the corner," Eddie said excitedly, hoping that at last he was going to be involved in a memorable incident.

"Take it easy, Eddie," McDonald reminded him, "This is a job for the fire department. They're the experts at this type of work. We're just going there to take the report."

By the time the Eleven-O car reached the Shawmut stop, the ladder truck and rescue company were just pulling up.

A distressed-looking train starter directed the policemen to the outbound side of the tracks, and they hurried down the steps to the dank, underground station.

Firefighters were everywhere, hauling hydraulic jacks down the stairs, across the platform and down on to the track bed. Other men were erecting portable floodlights that illuminated the subterranean scene with a harsh, unnatural glare.

The train had stopped a few feet into the station, and the firemen had already begun to hoist the first car off the tracks with the jacks. There were too many men in heavy coats milling around for the policemen to get a clear view, but the voice of the fire chief, calm, controlled, and just a little sad, rung in everyone's ears.

"She's under the right front wheels, and she's dead."

The fire chief continued to direct the operations with serenity and confidence.

"Our wagon just got here," whispered McDonald, tapping Connolly on the shoulder. Connolly joined the policemen carrying a stretcher and a blanket as they walked to the edge of the platform and made ready to jump down onto the tracks.

"We don't need the stretcher down here," the fire chief said with a little shake of his head. "We can use our bag. We'll put the bag on the stretcher once we get it up on the platform."

Connolly felt a twinge of disappointment at the thought that the firefighters were going to get to do everything themselves, but then the fire chief added a moment later: ". . . but I do need a couple of you young policemen down here to help to pull the body out."

Connolly was not the tallest or the strongest officer around, but he was certainly the youngest, so he hopped down onto the rails, eager to be in the thick of things. He scrambled breathlessly under the train which a team of firefighters were jacking higher and higher.

"Oh, Jesus, my God," he gasped.

The front wheels had sliced the shoulder, the arm and the entire left side off the body. Blood was still flowing. The arm lay alongside the train, mangled in the greasy gravel of the track bed.

Two firemen were holding the rubberized canvas body bag, and Connolly and some other men tried to edge the remains into the bag.

"Easy does it, boys," the fire chief said. "Ease her out and let her fall into the bag."

A fireman at Connolly's side suggested, "Watch out for the blood."

But the warning came too late. Connolly's gray shirt and pants were covered with the corpse's blood and internal jellies. He felt the warm liquids soaking through and sticking his skin to his clothes.

As the rookie cop and the veteran firemen struggled to heave the poor woman's remains free from the track, all sorts of organs began sliding out of her side . . . heart, liver, kidneys and miles of intestines plopped onto their pants legs and shoes.

"My God, what a mess!" Connolly thought, cursing himself for being so anxious to get involved in this sickening spectacle.

As they juggled the corpse into the canvas container, Connolly wondered about the person who only minutes before had resided in the body. All he could tell from looking at her was that she was about 35 and had auburn hair. Too much of the face was gone to tell whether she had been pretty or not. Was it an accident or suicide? This wasn't the moment to try to resolve these speculations.

When she was completely inside, one fireman swiftly lashed the cover shut; the men lifted the bag up to another team of firemen who were kneeling and crouched on the platform to receive it. The police wagon crew had unfolded the stretcher ready to bring the body to the hospital for pronouncement and then on to the morgue.

A gray-haired priest from St. Mark's had arrived and was murmuring the last rites over the bag.

Bill Leyden, the wagon driver, got the fire chief's attention.

"Are you sure you got all of her in there?"

"No," said the fire chief. "We didn't know you wanted the arm and all these other pieces . . ."

"We want it all," Leyden replied grimly. They passed the arm up to him; he unlashed the bag and tossed it in.

Bill then went over to a rubbish barrel, rummaged around until he found a discarded issue of the *Record*. With the newspaper under his arm, he hopped down onto the track and began to collect the various internal organs that lay scattered on the sooty rocks along the track. Liver, kidneys, whatever, he flopped into the newspaper like a butcher at the delicatessen.

Connolly had his eyes closed, trying to keep his stomach from erupting and disgracing him.

Bill McDonald nudged him and remarked, "Bill Leyden knows what he's doing. The Medical Examiner gets mad if you don't get everything. He'll send you back if there's even one little piece missing."

Patches of blood-soaked cloth on Connolly's shirt and pants had begun to stiffen. No going home to change in those days; you stayed in the uniform you wore till the end of your tour of duty.

When Leyden had scraped together all he could, the grisly bundle was added to the bag, and the wagon crew put the canvas bag on the stretcher and took her away, the elderly priest trailing behind.

"Well, Eddie, that was a messy one," McDonald sighed, "but before you get through with your career, you will see hundreds, maybe thousands of bodies . . . smashed up, chopped up, ripped up, blown up, burnt."

Bill McDonald's rueful prophecy came true . . . over the next four decades, Connolly saw thousands of corpses, many disfigured by freak accidents or fiendish humans. From infants to the helpless elderly, the body count was staggering.

6

"How Do You Tell the Parents?"

A policeman learns to deal with people of all types, sizes, colors, and personalities. Meeting a wide cross-section of mankind comes along with the badge, and it's impossible to like everyone. A responsible officer does not allow his personal prejudices to interfere with the performance of his duty.

There are two groups, however, that every man in blue can't help liking: the very old and the very young. Senior citizens inspire respect, and their unsteady, trembling walk often evokes pity. The innocent, wide-eyed stare of a baby, the carefree giggle of a toddler, and the open-faced earnestness of a child manage to penetrate the armor of even the most jaded cop.

There's also one thing that an officer, no matter how experienced he is, never really gets used to — the neglect and cruelty with which some unfortunate youngsters are treated by some of the adult population.

When a policeman has to pick up a dead or dying child, mangled in an accident, he can't refrain from thinking about his own child or in later years his grandchildren. Still there's no percentage in trying to figure out why a particular little boy or girl was singled out to suffer some gruesome death due to the carelessness of adults who should have been watching over him or her.

With siren blasting in the bitterly cold December air, Patrolmen Joe Gambino and Eddie Connolly headed for the intersection of Columbia Road and Dorchester Avenue. It had snowed heavily in the last weeks. The city plows had pushed the white stuff into high heaps on either side of Columbia Road. The surface snow had melted and then refrozen, making the mountains crusty with a thin glaze of ice.

There were two elementary schools on that stretch of Columbia Road — a public one, the William Russell School, and a parochial one, St. Margaret's. Before school, during recess, and after classes, fledgling mountaineers would scale the heights of these roadside Everests, but it now looked as though the fun had ended in tragedy.

Within forty seconds from the time they had received the dispatcher's call, Gambino and Connolly arrived at the snarl of traffic on Columbia Road. The officers rushed toward the group of storekeepers and neighbors who had gathered beside a large truck.

"He's under there," a man in a white apron told them, pointing at the huge wheels, "I think he's dead."

Joe and Eddie hit the street on their knees at the same instant. They could see that the sand- and ice-covered surface of the street was smeared with the black of oil and the bright red of fresh blood.

There lying in his school uniform, his little skull horribly crushed, was a six-year-old boy. Heedless of their own uniforms, the officers crawled on their stomachs over the ice, oil and blood towards the body of the second-grader.

"My God, the wheel went right over his head," Joe cried to Eddie in the confined space of the grimy underbelly of the truck, "I hope the poor kid didn't feel it."

The two policemen with the assistance of a pair of firefighters who had also wiggled underneath tugged the body slowly across the surface of the road and out into the sunlight. The wagon had arrived; the stretcher was ready. Joe tenderly placed the body on the white sheet. The wagon driver quickly covered the little fellow's body with a blanket.

The fire chief shouted to Eddie and the fireman who had remained under the truck, "Have we got everything?"

"No," said Eddie, as he pulled himself out from under, "I have his woolen hat and one green mitten."

He dropped the blood-and-mud soaked articles of clothing onto the blanket.

"Chief!" yelled the fireman who was still under the wheels.

"Yeah?" answered the chief.

"I found one of his eyeballs on the ground here."

"Bring it out. We'll send it to the morgue with the body."

Not many people had the stomach to watch as the young firefighter maneuvered himself into a standing position, cupping in his right hand the child's eyeball. This too was deposited inside the sheet.

The stretcher was lifted into the wagon for the trip to the hospital and finally to the morgue. The faces of the policemen and firemen, usually so impassive and tough, reflected the sadness and pain they shared. Many an eye was watery, and not just from the icy gusts of wind.

Gambino had been questioning a crowd of the boy's schoolmates. They told him how the boy had slipped while playing King of the Mountain and slid all of a sudden under the wheels of the truck. They gave Gambino the name and address of the young victim.

As a rookie, Connolly took the accident rather hard. Even more excruciating than the recovery of the body was the trip to the parents' home to notify them that their little Teddy had been crushed during recess.

Around 4:30 pm, the late school bus stopped at the corner of Baker and Vermont Streets in West Roxbury. The bus driver parked the vehicle on a slight grade and slipped out, leaving the door open. He darted into the corner drugstore to tell his girlfriend he was behind schedule.

The bus was still more than half full of kids. All of a sudden, it started to slide down the hill. The children began to shriek, and the panic swept through the yellow bus in a flash.

A ten-year-old girl named Jane who was near the door started to jump out only to become pinned between the bus and a streetpole. Her head and body were mashed instantly. Connolly brought her remains to the hospital.

Jane's mother had just come home from work when Connolly and the parish priest rang the bell. She still had her coat on when she answered the door.

Connolly and Father Mulkern broke the news as gently as possible, but the woman was devastated. When they inquired when her husband would be getting home from work, she turned to them with eyes brimming with reproach and despair and said, "He won't be coming home. He died two weeks ago in a car accident."

Neither the clergyman nor the policeman knew how to begin to console her in the face of this double tragedy.

"I have no family," she kept sobbing, "I . . . have . . . no . . . family."

It was the kind of day that all kids dream about: no school and perfect weather. The sun was warm and bright, just the day to bat a ball around, go for a bike ride or wander the neighborhood to see what the adult world was doing.

Six-year-old Tommy was glad he didn't have to be inside a schoolroom. Playing in his yard, he detected exciting mechanical buzzing sounds coming from the neighbor's yard. When he looked up, he saw strange men with ropes and power saws, climbing an old tree.

To get a closer look at the men's activities, Tommy climbed up on the fence that separated his yard from the Lambertis'. It was a perfect position from which to study the way the workers trimmed the branches and to watch the boughs fall with a rustling and then a thump to ground.

All too soon for Tommy's taste, the men moved out of the tree. With axes and loud power saws they attacked the trunk. The joking nurserymen didn't notice that forty yards away right in the path where the tree was to fall the little boy sat, drinking in their every move.

Before anyone knew what happened, the diseased elm snapped, then roared to the earth.

"Goddamn," one of the men said. "There's gonna be hell to pay."

"Yep," his partner agreed. "I wonder how much damages we'll have to fork out for that fence."

Patrolmen Joe Murphy and Ed Connolly took their time responding to a call about a "damaged fence."

"I don't know why people can't settle these things between themselves instead of dragging us into everything," Murphy groused as the officers stepped out of their car.

The two policemen drifted over to the fence and idly began breaking away branches to determine the extent of the damage to the fence. Only then did anyone notice the striped shirt, the blue jeans and the pulverized body.

"I think . . . there's a kid under here."

"What?"

"He's all twisted and dead," Connolly whispered.

The workmen, who had kept their distance, ran over. One offered to help the officers disentangle the body from the branches and fence posts.

"What the hell was he doing here?" another worker demanded, his show of anger masking his guilt and horror.

"What was he doing?" Connolly replied. "Just being a little boy, enjoying something different on a beautiful day . . . yeah, the beautiful day on which he died . . . God help him."

When Joe Murphy and Eddie Connolly got to the apartment in the Beachland Street Housing Projects in Roslindale, they found the fire crew had already arrived. A four-year-old boy had swallowed an unknown object and was slowly asphyxiating.

The mother and neighbors stood by, paralyzed with apprehension as the firemen placed an oxygen mask over the little face.

"For some reason, he's not responding to the oxygen," a firefighter confided to Connolly, "We've got to get him to a hospital."

"My baby! Oh, my God! My baby!" the mother cried as her son's skin began to show a bluish-green pallor.

Connolly and Murphy carried the child to the wagon while the fireman walked alongside keeping the mask over the boy's nose. They continued to administer oxygen as they raced to the Faulkner Hospital.

Then Connolly ushered the distraught mother and a neighbor who seemed to be a best friend into the police car to take them to the hospital. As the car was pulling away, the mother called to a man, "Charlie, get Jim. He's at work. Bring him to the Faulkner."

Once at the hospital, the officers escorted the woman into the emergency waiting room. Out of the corner of his eye, Connolly saw the firefighter coming out from behind a curtained alcove with a dejected expression. A nurse motioned to Connolly to come up to her.

"Officer, the doctor wants to speak with you."

A moment later, the physician introduced himself. "I'm Dr. Shea. It's too late. The boy was dead upon arrival. We did everything we could. How is the mother?"

"Not too good," Connolly admitted, "She's waiting for her husband. She sent a neighbor to fetch him at work. Maybe you better hold off with the news until he arrives."

Over the doctor's shoulder, Connolly could see the young boy stretched out on a gurney which was draped with a white sheet. A white towel covering the youngster's throat was spotted with blood.

"What was it, Doc?" Connolly asked softly, "A stone, a piece of candy?"

"No, Officer, this!" Dr. Shea replied, and held up a small red balloon. "He must have had it in his mouth . . . chewing on it or something, and it somehow got stuck in his windpipe. We tried a tracheotomy, but it was too late."

Connolly contemplated the little rubber sac and then ventured, "I hate to ask this, but did all that oxygen we were pumping into him do more harm than good? I mean was there any chance that the balloon was being blown up in his throat when we put that mask on him?"

"It's impossible to tell," Shea said sympathetically, "In any case, we all did what we thought was best. There's no sense . . ."

Murphy interrupted their conference with news that the father had arrived. Murphy's eyes too traveled to the little corpse on the table. Connolly knew he was thinking about his two sons who were roughly the same age as the dead boy.

The officers went out to the parents and confirmed what they had been dreading. Murphy and Connolly stood by as the husband and wife clutched each other, shaking and overwhelmed with grief.

Haunted by the memory of the choking, blue face of the boy and the pain of the bereaved parents, Connolly developed a habit of trying to stop children from playing with balloons. Whenever he would see little kids trying to inflate a brightly colored balloon, he would caution them against it and would warn the parents about how dangerous it was to let little ones chew on balloons.

Often he was rebuffed, insulted and told to mind his own business. Even his wife Irene was embarrassed at the way Eddie would interfere with strangers' children if he saw them playing with a balloon. She protested until he shared the story that still tugged at his heart. Then she understood: "You're just trying to stop a little angel from returning to heaven too soon."

7

In the Shithouse

As a young policeman, full of idealistic dreams of ridding the city of vice and corruption, both inside and outside the department, Eddie Connolly soon found that most of his superiors hated him for playing a different game from theirs.

Eddie's success in carrying out Captain Justin McCarthy's orders to clean up the bookmaking in District 11 was brought to an abrupt halt as soon as the Captain went on vacation.

Eddie was sitting in the guardroom, thumbing through the *Morning Post* when he heard himself summoned by the sergeant.

"Connolly, come in here."

"Yes, sir," Connolly responded, tossing the paper aside and hurrying out of the guardroom out to the front desk. "Here I am, Sergeant."

"You've been doing such an excellent job with the bookies, Connolly, I've decided you're ready for an even bigger problem. Do you think you can handle it?"

"Exactly what is it you want me to do?"

"Stop the sacrilegious larceny that's going on in the church, that's what!"

"I never heard anything about that, Sergeant," Connolly replied, furrowing his brow.

"Haven't heard about it! It goes on all day long. People are going in and out of St. Peter and Paul's stealing holy water in broad daylight, and I think you're the man to put a stop to it."

The other policeman in the office laughed at the thought of Connolly trying to stop people from wetting their fingers in the holy water font as they entered or left the church. Connolly joined in the chuckling when he realized that the sergeant was merely mocking him.

"Actually, I do have something special for you, something that's perfect for a brown-noser. I'd like you to meet these gentlemen, Inspector Jonas and Inspector Lee of the Boston Elevated Railway Police. You'll work with them for the next week on a vice assignment . . ." An unpleasant curl of the lips between a smile and a sneer played around the sergeant's mouth as he paused for emphasis: ". . . because you did such a great job cleaning up the bookies for Justin."

Before Connolly had time to analyze what the sergeant's ironic remark really meant, he found his right hand being crushed in the powerful handshake of a man with the build of a football professional who was saying, "I'm Burt Lee and this is Joe Jonas. Glad to meet you, Connolly."

Jonas was considerably shorter and fatter than Lee. He nodded. Lee explained that they had both been streetcar operators and motormen for the Boston Elevated Transit Authority. During the early 50's, they had been promoted to plainclothes Inspectors for the Police Unit of the Transit Authority.

"I'll get a car," Connolly said and moved to get the keys, but Lee stopped him by placing his big paw on Connolly's chest.

"We don't need a car where we're going. Remember you're with the Transit Authority now — buses and streetcars. Besides, we're only going as far as Fields Corner Station — that's just down the street from here."

Once the three men had left the station, Jonas remarked, "I don't think the good sergeant likes you, Eddie."

"What makes you say that?"

"All that talk about assigning you to a 'vice operation.' Why didn't he just come out and tell you that he was sending you to the men's room?"

"The what?"

"The men's shithouse."

"We've been getting a lot of complaints about the conditions there," Lee explained.

The naive young officer wasn't sure what the two were talking about.

"You'll soon see," Jonas chuckled.

A couple of blocks later, the trio reached the Fields Corner stop. A wave from Lee, and the coin collector released the turnstyle so the three men could walk through onto the platform.

The elevated trains stopped on this platform on the second story; on the ground level below people could make connections with the buses and streetcars.

"This way, Eddie," Lee said. With a small key in his ham of a fist, he unlocked a door painted with the six-inch high letters MEN.

One glance inside and one whiff told the whole story. The dimly lit interior contained three hoppers separated by partitions but without doors, two filthy urinals and a cracked marble sink with ancient fixtures. From the dust and cobwebs and the stains, it seemed inconceivable that the place had ever been cleaned since the place opened.

Lee and Connolly stepped inside to make a closer inspection; Jonas stayed out on the platform to smoke a cigarette. Connolly's nose wrinkled as he choked a bit on the oppressive, acrid stench of the place.

"Your eyes will soon get used to the light, but frankly I don't know anyone who ever really gets used to the stink."

Lee moved over to one of the walls.

"See these holes?" he said, pointing to quarter-inch openings that had been drilled in the wall at various heights.

"Yeah . . . what are they for?"

"Peepholes. We'll be on the other side of this wall, watching the action in here."

"Action?"

"Yeah, sometimes things get pretty hot and heavy in here."

"I've seen enough," Connolly said.

"You ain't seen nothing yet."

The two stepped back out into the daylight and fresh air briefly, then slipped through another door that led to the monitoring room. It was small, about 12 feet long and 4 feet wide affording space for a wooden bench, a chair and a stepladder, each positioned by peepholes at different levels.

"We'll take turns, Eddie," Jonas said. "As soon as you hear the door open, bend over so you can see through your peephole. Write down the time the subject entered and the time the second guy comes in. Make a note of the action, whatever they do."

Connolly didn't even want to think about what was in store for him during the ensuing days, but he was already mentally cussing out the superior officers who had rewarded his efforts to clean up the city with this degrading assignment.

"I'm going to take a little nap," Jonas whispered. "The men's room is unlocked so pretty soon you should get an education about some facts of life that your old man may never have told you about."

A few minutes after Jonas had departed, the door creaked open and Connolly hunched over to see who had entered. A well-dressed white male was wearing a trench coat, but no hat. His hair was carefully styled. He walked over to the urinal, zipped his fly open, relieved himself and jiggled the handle to flush the urinal.

"Well," Connolly thought, "he soon finished. No action here. Just a guy taking a leak."

But the gentleman lingered.

Connolly started to get angry. He wanted to say, "You did what you had to do, now get out, you bum."

But for the next ten minutes the man half-sat, half-leaned against the marble sink.

Then the door burst open, and in rushed a big black man about 45 years old. He was carrying a lunchbox and chomping on a cigar. He was at least 6'2" and could have weighed 300 pounds. From his overalls, red plaid workshirt and cap, Connolly could tell this guy was a hard-working man who had to go in a hurry.

Even before he got into the stall, he was slipping the straps of his overalls off his shoulders. He wrestled his pants and shorts down to the floor and positioned himself on the hopper, puffing on his stogie, the smell of which he hoped would counteract that of the toilet.

Suddenly Connolly realized that the well-groomed man in the trench coat had left his position by the sink and had slipped into the stall next to the workman's and was unbuttoning his coat.

"What the hell is going on?" Connolly whispered to Lee.

"Just keep your eye on him. He's up to something."

Though it was difficult to get a complete perspective from any one angle, a disbelieving expression on the black man's face indicated that something had happened.

He was glowering at the rigid head of a penis that was worming its way through a hole in the partition until 6 or 8 inches were quivering and straining to get closer to his face.

The black man kept sucking on his cigar until its tip glowed red. He calmly took the stogie from his lips, flicked off the ashes at the end and took careful aim at the slit in the head that was leaking beads of pearly lubricant.

He jabbed the burning cigar end down with triumphant spite in his eyes. There was a sizzle as slimy little helmet was first touched, then a scream that they could hear clear across the bay to Chelsea. The white guy wrenched his singed dick through the gloryhole and ran wailing to the sink. He fumbled with the handles and was bathing his injured apparatus as the black guy laughed merrily to himself and finished his business.

"Boy, he got it right on the old knob," Jonas whistled from behind the wall. "Grab both of them."

Scrambling over each other and the furniture in the tiny room, the three men tumbled into the men's room.

"Hold it. Police." Connolly called as they wedged themselves into the now-crowded room.

"What's goin' on?" the black man demanded, hoisting his overalls up.

"You're both under arrest." Jonas informed him.

"Officer," the man at the sink whined, "He burnt my thing."

"What thing?"

"This thing," he sniffed. Even under the rushing water, it was clear that his "thing" was seriously burnt.

"The doctor at the station will take care of you. Now, get a move on, both of you."

"What are you arresting me for?" the black man hollered. "I was minding my own business, taking a shit, when this faggot shoves his cock in my face. I was so surprised that the cigar fell out of my mouth."

"Good story. Tell it to the judge in the morning. Maybe he'll buy it," Connolly replied.

"This brute tried to burn me up," interrupted the man whose scorched penis had shrunk considerably by this time. "I intend to press charges against him."

"You've got a lot to answer for, buddy," Jonas snapped. "You started the whole thing."

"I did not! I had to make pee wee. I thought that hole was a urinal and all of a sudden this sadist scorches me with his cigar!"

"Another good one. You too can tell your story to the judge. Now let's get the hell out of this dump."

The arguing and counteraccusations continued, but finally the Transit Police and Connolly breathed a sigh of relief as they watched the wagon from District 11 pull away with the black man and the white guy he had scarred for life.

"Back in the hole!" Jonas reminded them. "We got a long day ahead of us!"

"You want more?" Connolly asked incredulously, "We already got a pinch. That's a good day's work."

"Eddie, you remember what your friendly sergeant said, 'This is a big vice operation,' " Jonas chuckled.

" 'Shithouse operation' is more like it," the young officer grumbled.

"No more stalling. Just think of the vice experience you'll get out of this."

As they trudged back toward the observation room, Connolly was thinking of ways to get back at the sergeant for giving him this assignment. "This is no joke. This is just plain depressing."

"I think I'll get us some lunch," Lee announced. "You two go ahead."

"What's the matter? Being a Peeping Tom ain't fun no more?" Connolly remarked.

"Just for that. I'm going to bring you back a roasted weenie for lunch," Lee laughed and left.

Jonas and Connolly squeezed back into the closet-like space and waited for the parade of perverts to continue. One fellow stopped into take a leak on his way to visit his wife in the hospital where she had just given birth to a bouncing baby boy. Daddy was propositioned by a middle-age insurance salesman for oral sex. But in the middle of a blow job, the policemen popped in on them, ordered them to zipper up, and marched them down to street level to wait for the wagon.

Lee was back from a local deli carrying three brown paper bags.

"Aw, gee," he said in mock disappointment. "I guess I missed the action. Joe and Eddie, can't you wait for me? You two want all the glory for this shit caper? Geez, some people just can't share."

Connolly was not amused.

"I'm eating my sandwich out here on the bench in the open air. You two can eat in the rathole if you want."

"Eddie, you may miss a pinch while you're enjoying your corned beef on rye," Lee teased.

"That's OK. I'll chance it."

They all ended up munching their sandwiches on the bench, but fifteen minutes later they were at their spyhole posts in "the Blue Room."

About an hour later a Transit bus driver and a young fag from the Back Bay were in there, fiddling around in each other's pants.

"Well, what do you know? I used to work with the driver," whispered Jonas, "Never knew he was queer."

"His job is gone," Lee said curtly, "Come on, let's pry the two lovebirds apart."

By evening, Connolly's head was reeling, whether from the stale air or the sickening scenes he had witnessed, he couldn't say.

"We only got six today," Lee said, "but we got a late start, what with breaking Connolly in. We'll do better tomorrow."

"Now, Eddie, don't forget, tomorrow before we spend another day gazing into the beautiful Blue Room, we'll have to arraign today's guys in court first."

"So I guess I'll meet you two at the station around 8 am," Connolly said and, dreading what the new day would bring, hopped a streetcar home.

All six men had been bailed out, and all showed up in Dorchester Court. All the complaints were made out in Connolly's name. Though the Transit Police inspectors had all the authority of a regular Boston cop on their own turf, Lee and Jones as a courtesy named Connolly as the complainant.

Clerk of the Court Tony McNulty approved the complaints, which were signed and sworn to.

Judge William Lynch, the presiding justice, was sitting in the first session that day. Lynch was well-liked by the police, whether he handed down a guilty or a not-guilty. A product of South Boston, he had been a city councilor, a state representative and Clerk of the South Boston Court, before being named Judge of the Dorchester District Court.

All the defendants were arraigned, and Connolly gave a synopsis of each arrest. Lynch continued the cases for a week and advised every man to get himself a lawyer.

As the policeman were gathering their notes, preparing to leave the courtroom, a court officer tipped them off to the fact that a pack of reporters were waiting in the corridor, expecting some sort of a statement.

Not relishing the prospect of seeing their names in all the papers in connection with the shenanigans in a public toilet, the three cesspool sleuths ducked out the back way and returned to the Blue Room of the Fields Corner Transit Station.

Even though the trio arrived comparatively late in the day, 11 am, by 1:30, they had arrested four men for lewd behavior and various kinds of sex. There was a lull during the afternoon, but between 4 and 5, another four were arrested, the second group including a juvenile.

So, on the third day, the Shithouse Squad was back in front of Judge Lynch to issue complaints against the eight alleged sex offenders. Seven of the defendants were arraigned, and the underage boy was held for juvenile court.

The deepening scowl on Lynch's face during the proceedings indicated that he was very angry that conditions at the transit stop men's room had been allowed to deteriorate to this point. Strangely enough, he continued all seven cases to the same date as the one set for the men who had been arrested the day before.

By now the news was spreading that the police were making arrests in Fields Corner Station. When Eddie went back to Station 11 to pick up his paycheck, he was greeted by the smirking sergeant.

"I hear you're a natural at this men's room job, Connolly. When Justin gets back from his vacation, I'm going to tell him what a grand job you've been doing!"

Connolly kept his mouth shut, dreaming of a chance to repay this smart aleck.

That afternoon, Lee, Jonas and Connolly were discussing when they could wrap up the surveillance at the Fields Corner men's room.

"I think you can tell your boss that we've got this mess pretty well cleaned up," Connolly said hopefully, "We can close this operation tomorrow."

"Yeah, the word has gotten around that we've got our eye on the shithouse," Jonas agreed. "The fags and degenerates will stay clear for a while."

"Besides, between you and me," Lee put in, "I think Lynch is bullshit about us bringing up so many queers into his courtroom."

"We'll give it one more day, and then we'll call it quits," Jonas decided, and then they all said goodnight and headed home.

The following morning the three men met at Station 11, had coffee and doughnuts at Charlie's Spa and steeled themselves for another day at the peepholes.

The day dragged on interminably. By one o'clock nothing suspicious had happened. The men's room was being used only for what it had been designed for. The Shithouse Squad was secretly glad that there would be no more arrests.

But their relief was premature. Around 2 pm, a slim, carefully dressed man about 33 entered, a man who apparently not heard the rumors about police monitoring the use of the restroom.

He positioned himself by the urinals and spoke to anyone who came in and who was his own age or younger. From behind the wall, the policemen couldn't make out what he was saying, but it was clear from the shrugs and glares of the other men that he was propositioning them.

Even after the fourth rejection, he continued to loiter, looking a little disappointed, but still determined.

"This guy is not giving up," Jonas whispered.

"He's going to get his today, whatever it is," Connolly returned.

"Boy, he must be roasting with that trench coat on in there," Lee added.

Then his patience paid off. The door to the outer platform opened for a moment, flooding the room with light, and in breezed a blond fellow about a year younger than the man in the trench coat. The blond went to the urinal, and the other moved closer. The blond start to piss, but when he noticed that he was being watched, he took a step back so that his admirer could get a clear view of what he had to offer.

The two exchanged words, but what was said was muffled by the walls.

"The blond guy said yes," Jonas announced. "I read his lips. Be ready to get in there when these two go at it."

From his trench coat pocket, the first man produced a small jar of Vaseline and handed it to his new-found friend. While the blond smeared the Vaseline over his penis, the patient waiter flung the tails of his coat up over his shoulders and yanked his trousers and shorts to the floor.

"Grease me," he cried, and his partner obliged by rubbing the petroleum jelly deep into the crevice of his ass. The first guy then bent over the marble sink and grabbed the faucets to stabilize himself.

The blond wasted no time with preliminaries and jabbed his dick into his willing victim's butt.

This loveplay elicited an unearthly moan from the man spread over the sink, "Mooooaaaah, MoooAAAHHH!"

The cries resembled those of a cow in agony, but they only prompted the guy in the saddle to redouble his efforts. He was pumping away harder and harder, and the man in the trench coat screamed louder with every hearty thrust.

Finally, the rectal roughhousing reached its ecstatic pitch. The man let out a climactic "MOOOOOOAAAAH"; his body was buckling and writhing in such a frenzy that he ripped the faucets right out of the marble.

Twin geysers shot up almost to the ceiling, and the accident just added to the men's frenzy. It was long past time to move in.

Connolly led the way in, shouting, "You're under arrest, both of you. This is the police."

Unfortunately, Eddie slipped in the puddle that had formed on the floor. Jonas and Lee were also thrown off balance, and before anyone could figure out what had happened — what with the uncontrolled gushing of the faucets and the tangle of bare buttocks — the two transit inspectors and the two sodomists had tumbled out onto the platform.

Reflexively, Lee grabbed the man in the trench coat, and Jonas latched onto the blond before realizing that both men had their pants and shorts around their ankles and were thus presenting the horrified passengers on the platform with a very clear view of their swollen penises.

Ladies waiting for the inbound train shrieked in disbelief.

"Pull up your pants!" Jonas screamed into his man's ear.

"Then let go of my arms . . . give me a chance will you?" the blond man said, struggling to get free. Jonas and Lee tried to screen the men from the view of the public as the two men adjusted their soaking underpants and trousers.

Lee hollered to Connolly who had just emerged from the Blue Room, "Call the wagon. Tell them we got two wet ones."

When the wagon rolled up in front of the Fields Corner Station, the two prisoners and their equally drenched captors piled into the back.

Back in the guardroom, the brother officers were absolutely merciless with their wisecracks. As Connolly and the two transit inspectors stood dripping in front of the desk, the sergeant nearly wet his own pants laughing at the ridiculous spectacle they presented.

That Monday complaints were made out for the pair that had destroyed the sink, and their case continued until the date to which Lynch had continued all the other cases.

When that day arrived, the judge meted out justice swiftly. In the case of the cigar burn, the black man was dismissed with a warning not to burn anyone no matter what the provocation. The other defendant was given a six-month sentence in the House of Correction on Deer Island.

The other cases were heard and received the same six-month sentence to Deer Island. All the defendants appealed; the juvenile was handed a suspended sentence and turned over to his parents.

When it was all over, Judge Lynch called the Transit Police and Connolly up to the bench and said, "I want you to put a padlock on that men's room and keep it locked. Let people find some other place to go."

"Thank you, Your Honor," Connolly said with sincere gratitude.

On the courthouse steps, he prepared to say goodbye to Jonas and Lee.

"It was great working with you both . . . even if it was a shithouse operation. Thanks for everything. I'm glad it's all over."

Connolly put out his hand to shake, but Jonas slapped a map of the transit system into Eddie's palm.

"I don't get it," Connolly said.

"We just wanted to show you where our next stop is . . . right here, the men's room at South Station. Then we'll be going on to Milk Street and so on," Jonas laughed. "See you bright and early tomorrow."

8

Learning the Vice Game

Eddie had Wednesday off that week. He and Irene hadn't quite decided what they were going to do with the day when the phone rang.

It was Justin McCarthy, recently appointed to the rank of Deputy Superintendent by Commissioner Thomas Sullivan. He wanted to know whether Eddie could meet him within the hour.

"Sure, Deputy, name the place."

"Where do you live?"

"On Brent Street just off Codman Square. I don't have a car so it would have to be somewhere in walking distance."

"How about the school at Washington Street and Welles Avenue?"

"The Pierre School? See you there in an hour."

Connolly stood on the sidewalk across from the school, considering why the Deputy Superintendent wanted to see him on a day off when McCarthy's black 1950 Pontiac pulled up.

"Hop in."

Connolly climbed into the front seat. McCarthy was not one to waste words.

"I'm going to make some changes in the Vice Squad. How would you like to come in town and be a part of it?"

He seemed as if he expected an immediate positive response. Thanks to the Dorchester High School Band, Connolly got a few minutes' reprieve to consider the offer.

The deafening blare of imperfectly played martial music assaulted the two men's ears. Then right down the middle of Washington Street from the direction of Dot High marched the young men of the Dorchester High School band. They were dressed in street clothes, practicing for the annual city-wide Schoolboy Parade that was coming up in a few weeks.

The din of the instrumentalists and the disruption of the traffic made it impossible for the two men to speak for several minutes. When the noisy contingent had gotten far enough away so that conversation was once again possible, McCarthy gave Eddie a look that demanded an answer.

"I don't know, Deputy," Connolly began. "I'm near home. I got a good partner. I get a detail every two weeks. I'm happy here in Eleven."

"There will be a detective rank in it for you in a couple of years," McCarthy countered.

As Connolly hesitated, the Deputy went on. "The main reason I want you is that I know you're a willing worker and you're honest. There's a lot of money floating around this squad. I want men that I know and can trust without question."

"Why don't you give the job a try?" he continued. "If you don't like it, I'll transfer you out whenever you say the word."

"Fair enough, Deputy. OK, I'll try it."

"See you at Headquarters next week," he said.

With the same crisp directness, he ended the conversation.

"Get out of here now. I want to be gone before that band comes back."

Connolly stepped out onto the street, wondering how this decision would change his life and his career as a police officer. The Dot High troops were marching back, and Eddie raced across Washington Street and Welles Avenue to break the news to Irene.

"Oh, shit," he thought. "I've only got one suit."

Taking a plainclothes job meant having a presentable wardrobe of business wear, but as a policeman he had always worn a uniform. The one outfit he did have was one he purchased from Raymond's Department Store right after he got out of the service. He hadn't worn it much — to his wedding and to a few funerals, including his father's.

"It'll have to do for a while," Irene pointed out sensibly. She took the announcement well. Whatever Eddie wanted was fine with her. "But maybe you can pick up some more paid details."

A few days later Captain Patrick O'Reilly, who had replaced Justin McCarthy as station commander when he was kicked upstairs, notified Connolly to report to the Vice Squad the following Wednesday at 7:45 am. O'Reilly was a two-fisted cop who had led reinforcements who came to Connolly's aid when the patrolman was fighting off a drunken crowd, and the captain had remembered Connolly's gutsiness.

"Vice is a touchy squad," O'Reilly told him over the phone. "You can make a lot of friends in the department or a lot of enemies. Use your head, Eddie. Good luck. You're gonna need it."

Early that Wednesday morning Irene surprised Eddie with a gray hat she had bought for the sum of $4.50 at the Adams Store in Codman Square. In his freshly pressed blue chalk-stripe suit, she thought, he looked like a real detective as he reported for his first day on the Vice Squad.

Eddie showed up at Berkeley Street Headquarters promptly at 7:45, but no one was there. Soon a handsome young man, who introduced himself as Jerry Sullivan from District 18 (Hyde Park), joined him and tried the handle to the office.

"Door's locked. Guess we'll just have to stand here and get acquainted till the regular crew shows up. The official starting time may be 7:45 but most of the characters who work here don't roll in till 9."

The two weren't waiting long before a burly fellow came limping down the hall. Lieutenant Bill Hogan knew Jerry and introduced himself to Eddie.

Hogan had lost a leg a few years earlier during assignment in the South End. While tracing telephone wires to a bookie office, he fell down an elevator shaft. Though he somehow survived the plunge, almost every bone in his big frame had been shattered. One leg had to be amputated, and he nearly lost the other.

Hogan was not one to quit on a disability. He stayed on the Vice Squad and handled the clerical end of things during the day. At night he ran a school for policemen studying for promotion exams. The basement of his home at 27 Knoll Street in Roslindale, where he held these classes, was affectionately known as "Club 27." Thanks to these cellar tutorials, hundreds of police officers, both in Boston and throughout the state, successfully prepared for qualifying examinations.

The rest of the Vice Squad began straggling in including the other new men in the unit: Sergeant John Byrne from District 11, Sergeant Frank O'Meara of District 19 (Mattapan), and Patrolman Tom Bevins, an old-timer from District 11.

When Deputy Superintendent McCarthy showed up, he introduced the veteran members of the Vice Squad, trustworthy men who had weathered the purge that McCarthy had ordered. Sergeant Joe Cunningham deserved his reputation of being a first-class cop who knew the city and everyone in it. Detective Jerry McCallum, born in Ireland but "dragged up in Southie," was reputed to be "as sharp as a whip and as straight as a dime."

In addressing his men, the Deputy spoke straight from the shoulder . . . no threats, no demands. Like any shake-up in the Vice Squad, this one had created headlines, but McCarthy did not feel that he had to justify his decision by demanding a massive vice and gaming clean-up.

"The city is yours," the Deputy began. "I don't expect any miracles. Don't feel that you have to be the broom that cleans up the city. All I expect of you is that you stay honest and do your level best."

That very day Sergeant O'Meara, Jerry Sullivan and Connolly made an arrest of a small-time bookmaker at the Reddy Hot Restaurant. This was the first of thousands of pinches made during the next five years by the new Vice Squad.

As he began working with the Racket Squad, Eddie was surprised at the sophistication of the bookmakers' equipment and their ingenuity in concealing their operations. Raids on the central offices, the places where the neighborhood bookies called their customers' bets in to, revealed rooms full of adding machines, banks of telephones, electrically controlled doors and cleverly constructed "stashes" or hiding places.

In Brighton, for example, the Squad found a trapdoor in the floor of a closet of a bookie raid. The trapdoor led to a space five feet high, two feet wide and two feet deep. Inside were a pair of telephones that automatically disconnected when the trapdoor was closed.

Even the men out in the street showed great imagination when it came to storing betting slips, as Eddie discovered during an investigation he made in late November of 1952.

The Racket Squad received a tip that Benjamin Ginns was running an illegal betting operation in Bartlett Square in Mattapan. Byrne, O'Meara, Sullivan and Connolly halted Ginns' canteen truck as it pulled up in front of a manufacturing plant, but a thorough search of the vehicle and his person revealed nothing.

The detectives were about to give up when the factory whistle sounded, and the employees congregated around Ginns' truck buying soft drinks kept cool in a battered metal washtub. When the luncheon crowd returned to work, the officers removed the remaining bottles from the basin and dumped out the ice and water.

The tub had a false bottom; a small door gave access to a compartment that contained 36 slips with 155 numbered pool plays and 30 other slips with horse racing bets — more than enough evidence to put Ginns out of the curbside, lunchtime betting business — for a while at least.

Connolly soon learned just how widespread bookmaking was in the city of Boston and how extensive the payoffs to the high-ranking police officers and judges were.

The protection system amounted to an elaborate game. On the one hand, the division would rack up their quota of collars by arresting nickel-and-dime streetcorner bookies. But any foolhardy officer who attempted to flush out the bosses was likely to find himself transferred to Siberia.

In any case, being arrested for bookmaking was a trifle. Bookies almost always got off with a fine or probation; rarely did one hear of a bookmaker being sent to jail.

Still both the bookie and his boss wanted to minimize arrests because they interrupted business. An arrest meant that the betting slips, the only memoranda of the transactions, were seized, and unscrupulous clients would come back after the bookie set himself up in business again claiming they had winning numbers that they wanted to be paid for. Buying protection from the courts and the police command staff was cheaper than losing customers and paying off phony claims.

Actually, a patrolman had more to fear from higher-ups in the department than from a bookie. It was unheard of that a bookie would use any sort of violence to resist arrest. Why should he? He knew that his boss would provide bail money and a lawyer.

An overly ambitious cop, on the other hand, just might collar someone who had paid insurance; that officer would find himself

Detective Edward F. Connolly of the Racket Squad examines a metal tub seized by police. The false bottom, shown by Connolly, was used to conceal betting slips.

transferred in a hurry to some very undesirable beat. Most patrolmen then just left the bookies to the plainclothesmen on the Vice Squad. They just couldn't afford to antagonize a superior officer.

There was a way around this ticklish position for the honest cop who wanted to see a bookie out of his beat, but who was afraid of possible career repercussions if he intervened directly. All the officer had to do was send an anonymous tip to the Vice Squad. The language in the note or phone call was usually a dead giveaway as to who was a law enforcement officer and who was, say, a rival bookie who was supplying information to the Racket boys to get rid of some competition.

Connolly and the others on the Squad felt lucky to have the complete support of the Deputy Superintendent. They could go after anyone in the gaming racket without fear of being moved to a new job the next morning. McCarthy stood firm, protecting his men from interference by other superior officers in the department.

The more big bosses the men in the Vice Squad arrested, the more they saw just how pervasive the corruption was throughout the justice system.

They began to perceive patterns. If a defendant had a certain lawyer and his case was continued several times until a particular judge was sitting, the verdict was inevitably not guilty. Of course, the fees involved were extraordinarily high, but that was part of the game.

The head bookmakers made no bones about attempting to bribe an officer and get him on the payroll, as Connolly soon found out for himself.

One morning around 7 am, Irene was preparing breakfast while Eddie was getting dressed. She answered the door and was greeted most courteously by a dapper gentleman who asked to see her husband.

"Eddie, there's a man at the front door. He says his name is Johnny and he would like to speak with you. He's very polite and good-looking."

"I'll be out in a minute."

While Irene had gone to fetch Eddie, Johnny had stepped over the threshold into the Woodrow Avenue apartment without being asked in. Eddie was a little taken back by his boldness.

"Nervy son-of-a-bitch," he muttered and then raising his voice asked, "What can I do for you?"

"I just want two minutes of your time."

"Go ahead. Two minutes."

Johnny, who looked very elegant in a midnight-blue three-piece suit, put on a doleful expression.

"Eddie, you're putting me out of business. You raided my office and took my pickup car. I've got a family to take care of. Come on, gimme a break."

"No way."

"Now, Eddie, why are you picking on me? Is it something personal?"

"I'm not picking on you. I'm just doing my job."

"What will it take? I'll give you five hundred a month if you want."

"Thanks, but no thanks."

"Think it over, Eddie."

"Johnny, your two minutes are up. Now leave. I don't want you to come to my home ever again. If you want to see me, you know where my office is."

Without another word, Johnny turned and let himself out.

Connolly returned to the kitchen and accepted a slice of freshly buttered toast from Irene.

"What did that nice man want?" she asked.

"He was working his way through college."

"That's strange. He looked kind of old to be going to college."

"Not really," said Eddie, crunching into his toast. "He's planning on going to an old college."

Other bookies were even more generous in their offers. When one boss learned that Connolly did not have a car and had to take the bus and subway to work, he tried to give Eddie a new car. Over the years Connolly had to say "no" to hundreds of thousands of dollars.

The other men in the Vice Squad were equally scrupulous about not taking bribes, no matter how big or how imaginatively presented. One afternoon Jerry Sullivan and Connolly raided a bookie joint in Charlestown. While waiting for the phone company to come to remove the phones, they decided to stop at a luncheonette for something hot to drink.

Sitting in a booth, they each ordered a coffee, but when the waitress returned, she had two cups and a sandwich on a plate, which she placed in front of Jerry.

"Did you order this sandwich, Eddie?" he asked, nudging the plate across the formica tabletop.

"Nope. What kind is it?"

Jerry lifted the top slice of bread, uncovering bills totaling $250.

"Would you look at this," he whistled.

Then Jerry summoned the waitress.

"Would you like anything else?" she cooed.

"Take this sandwich back, and tell the person who made it that I don't like lettuce on my sandwiches."

9

Quitting the Force

There were so many bookmakers in Boston in the 40's and 50's, practically one on every corner, that a member of the Vice Squad could make as many arrests as he had energy for. Connolly was always out in old street clothes dropping into bars, taverns, and variety stores where bets were being placed. He would follow known street bookies and trail the pickup cars that went from one small bookie joint to another gathering the slips for the central office.

When he was working with a partner, Eddie would duck into some establishment that doubled as a bookmaking operation and place a bet on the numbers or the ponies; then his partner would present himself, and together they would make the collar.

Occasionally when he was by himself and on foot, he would make an arrest and call a taxi. He got a kick out of making the hapless bookie pay the fare for transportation to headquarters.

Eddie was bothered by some underlying contradictions in the whole routine. For one thing, the newspapers would decry all the gambling and bookmaking that was going on in the city on page one, but in the sports section, there were detailed reports on all the horse races at the track at Suffolk Downs. While on-track betting was legal, the racketeers used the pari-mutuel payoff figures to determine the daily four-digit number for their illegal betting operation.

So, in effect, the papers were criticizing the bookmakers out of one side of their mouth, while performing a crucial service for the bookmakers with the other.

Even more disturbing to Connolly was the fact that Vice Squad members were assigned to work only in certain sections of the city. Little bookies who worked for certain big crime bosses were able to ply their trade freely.

It wasn't hard to figure out why. Someone, probably many people in the police hierarchy, were getting paid off. Though Connolly had definite suspicions as to who these bribe-takers were, he had no hard evidence. Betting was relatively harmless when you came right down to it, but the fact that Boston police officers could be so routinely bought off was very unsettling.

Connolly felt uneasy about the situation, but as long as no one offered him a bribe or no one directly forbade him to arrest certain people, he continued to haul bookies in each day.

There came a time when he could no longer close his eyes to the corruption that was all around him. One afternoon in the Vice and Gaming Office at Headquarters, Connolly's partner, who also happened to be his sergeant, announced that he was going out to get a shoeshine at a stand at the corner of Washington and Dover Streets. The sergeant always kept his wingtips spit-shined. His shoes didn't look as though they needed any attention, but it was really none of Connolly's business.

"Connolly, you stay here and take down any phone messages while I'm gone. Shouldn't be too long."

Eddie thumbed through an old paper and studied his own scuffed-up footwear. About a half hour later, the phone rang. It was a Massachusetts State corporal with some urgent information for the sergeant on some stolen whiskey.

"He's not here, Corporal. I expect him back soon though. Is there anything I can do?"

"Yeah, this can't wait," the corporal said, "They may move the load. I'll give you the information. Maybe you could go and find him and give it to him."

"Okay, what is it?" Connolly replied, reaching for a pencil and something to scribble on.

"A truckload of whiskey was hijacked yesterday in Worcester. We got a tip that it's in a garage at 56 Terrance Street in Roxbury. But they may move it at any time. So have the sergeant get someone over there to check this out immediately."

"I'll get on this right away. Good-bye," Connolly said. As soon as he dropped the phone back onto the cradle, he was stuffing the address into his inside jacket pocket. He grabbed his hat and ran out of the Vice Office. Soon he was in an unmarked car, heading for the shoeshine parlor at Dover and Washington Streets.

Connolly turned from Waltham Street onto Washington under the elevated, and when he got near Dover Street, he saw there was no place to park. He was considering double-parking when he spotted the sergeant walking out of Myer Murray's poolroom. The sergeant was chatting in a very friendly manner with a man whom Connolly recognized as one of the most infamous bookies in Boston, a fellow Connolly had known ever since he was a little boy in the South End.

As they walked down the sidewalk, the racketman passed an envelope to the sergeant who put it in his pocket. Without saying goodbye, the racketman turned sharply and started walking in the opposite direction toward Connolly. Eddie slid down under the steering wheel as the boss passed. When he popped back up, he saw that the sergeant was walking briskly up Dover Street toward Head-quarters.

Connolly knew that he had to beat the sergeant back to the Vice Office, so he put the car into gear and sped back on a parallel street. Fortunately, he was able to park the car in the same spot it had been in when the sergeant left for his shoeshine.

Eddie charged up the stairs, tossed his jacket and hat onto the coat rack, and was trying to catch his breath when the sergeant strolled in and asked nonchalantly, "Anything doing, Eddie?"

"Hi, Sergeant," Connolly answered, "There was one call. A State Police corporal called about a truckload of whiskey in a garage on Terrance Street. He said it was important. I was just heading over to Washington Street to get you."

"You should have. That's a big score. But then again, I guess it's lucky you didn't leave yet. I didn't go to the parlor on Washington Street. I went to the one on Tremont Street; it's closer."

"You fucking liar," Connolly thought. Now Eddie knew for sure that his partner and immediate superior was on the take and couldn't be trusted. But what could he do about it? Nothing.

Shortly after the Brinks robbery had rocked the city, the FBI had agents all over town. Naturally, the FBI men became acquainted with the officers of the Vice Squad and other units of the Boston Police Department in the course of their investigation or just by sharing a table at a restaurant.

There were many sources of information that the FBI had that the BPD had no access to. So there sprang up a system of reciprocation. The agents would pass on valuable information to the Vice Squad, but would expect something in return . . . often a list of phone numbers and names that were taken in raids.

Two of the top agents gave the Vice Squad information about a bookie office on Burbank Street in the Back Bay. They had every little detail from the precise apartment number to the full names of everyone involved.

The FBI had reason to believe that the Burbank Street bookie operation was being run by John Carlson. Carlson was known to be a close friend of "Specs" O'Keefe, one of the gang that pulled off the Brinks job, a man the FBI desperately wanted.

A bargain was struck between the federal agents and the Boston police. The local cops would keep the bookie operation under surveillance for a couple of weeks. At the right moment, the FBI would raid the place. Any incriminating evidence relating to bookmaking operations would belong to the BPD, but the little black book that Johnny carried would go to the Feds. They were hoping that somewhere among the phone numbers in Carlson's book would be one that would lead them to "Specs" O'Keefe.

The Burbank apartment house was put under strict surveillance. The detectives from the Vice Squad took turns observing the location.

Very quickly the Vice Squad learned who the inside man was, the person who received and kept track of all the bookie slips. It was Maxie Forsberg, a figure well known to members of the Squad.

Maxie had lost both his legs as a boy in some sort of railway accident. For a long time the Squad had been aware that he was involved in bookmaking, but everybody seemed to like Maxie Forsberg and shared the feeling, "With so many bookies around, why pick on a guy with no legs?" So whenever possible, the Vice Squad looked the other way when poor Maxie was involved.

Connolly would rotate with others watching the Burbank Street building from 10 am to 5 pm. As usual, around 11 am, a taxi pulled up, and Maxie struggled out of the cab and up the stairs on his crutches, clutching his racing forms in his hands.

There wasn't much to do but to keep an eye open for Johnny Carlson and company to show up, which they usually did around 5 pm. However, Eddie did notice that at about 3 pm a brown Oldsmobile would pull up and park on Burbank. The man inside would sit there, counting and sorting slips and envelopes. Eddie recognized the driver as Louis Blumberg, a pickup man for his brother Sam, one of the big-league bookmaking bosses in the area. Evidently, Louie had no connection with the office that Maxie was running for Carlson. He just happened to pick Burbank Street as a regular place to sort slips.

Connolly noted the number on the Oldsmobile's license plate. When he checked it that evening, he found that the car was registered to Mrs. Blumberg with an address in the neighboring town of Brookline.

Eddie cross-checked the names and addresses with the Brookline voters' directory. In the Identification Unit, he refreshed his memory about Louie's rap sheet; apparently he and his brother Sam were still wanted in connection with some gambling charges in the local Jewish community.

"Should I take this guy off?" Connolly wondered. "The FBI could be pissed if it jeopardizes the Carlson-Specky O'Keefe case, but I don't give a shit at this point. If Louie parks far enough down Burbank, Maxie wouldn't be able to see what's happening, even if he does decide to look out the window at the wrong moment."

Connolly volunteered for a second consecutive day of surveillance; he had no problem making the switch since no one else really liked to do that kind of tedious work. He was determined to arrest Louie, but he was sure as hell not about to inform the sergeant of his intentions, though regulations required that he do so.

The next morning, everyone was on schedule. Maxie thumped his way up the stairs shortly after 9 am. At 3 pm the brown Oldsmobile pulled into a parking spot on Burbank, a few cars ahead of Connolly's vehicle. Louie put on his reading glasses and began to arrange the papers on the empty passenger seat to his right.

"I'm okay as long as I stay to his left," Connolly told himself. Eddie had to walk in the street to get close to the Olds without being observed. He noted that the plunger on the driver's window was up, meaning the door was unlocked.

Praying that Maxie would not choose this moment to admire the scenery, Eddie burst into action. He yanked the car door open.

"Police, move over."

He flashed his badge in Louie's face and forced his way into the driver's seat, shoving Louie over to the passenger's side and scattering the slips and envelopes all over the mats on the floor.

"OK, OK. What's going on? Who are you?"

"Police. Detective Connolly. You're under arrest."

"Arrest? For what?"

Connolly swept up a handful of slips and thrust them under the bookie's nose, "What's this? Your homework?"

Eddie turned the key in the ignition. The bespectacled man was shaking with fear and indignation.

"What are you doing? This is my car."

"Nobody said it wasn't, but I'm using it to take you in."

"Where . . . to 16?"

"Headquarters."

Connolly pulled the car out into the traffic. Once they were on their way, Louie sunk back against the seat. "OK, kid, you win."

"Never mind the 'kid' shit. It's Detective Connolly to you."

Eddie found a spot right in front of Headquarters to leave the Olds. He gathered all the envelopes in one hand and held onto Louie's arm with the other. Together they went through the heavy brass-handled doors and walked up one flight to the Vice Office.

The instant the two came through the door, the sergeant's face reddened with anger. "What the fuck . . . What the hell do you think you're doing? Who told you to pinch this guy? You left your post!"

Connolly savored the sergeant's rage.

"I got this guy, and he was loaded. Thirty-five full envelopes . . . a couple thousand slips," Connolly said calmly and then added, "When have you made a pinch as good as this?"

"You do what you're told!" the sergeant insisted, even more infuriated at being taunted. "The Deputy's gonna hear about this!"

"Thanks for putting in a good word for me," Connolly smiled, then pulled the bookie back towards the door. "Let's go, Louie."

After Eddie booked Louie and left the slips at District 4, he got a lift back to his car on Burbank Street, just in time to see Johnny and a companion get out of a cab and hurry upstairs.

That evening Deputy Superintendent Justin McCarthy summoned Connolly to his office.

"What happened today, Eddie? The sergeant told me that you left your post to make an arrest."

"That's right, Deputy. We've been on that stakeout nearly three weeks. The same thing happens every day. I keep seeing this guy counting his play, so today I decided to arrest him."

"You got a good load; you do good work, but next time tell the sergeant," McCarthy said.

"OK, Deputy," Connolly said. He controlled the impulse to tell his old friend Justin that the sergeant's anger was proof that he was being paid to protect Louie and his co-workers from being arrested. But these circumstances were not severe enough for him to rat on a fellow officer, so he let the matter slide.

The case came up in court for arraignment and was continued for a month at the request of Louie's lawyer. In the meantime, Connolly was approached by several officers who suggested that Eddie give the man a break. They reminded Eddie that Louie was a disabled veteran and testified to the fact that he was basically a good guy who was just trying to support his family.

Connolly was amazed to find out how well connected Louie and his brother Sam were. Even one of Connolly's own uncles applied pressure, stating that he had known Louie and Sam as boys in the South End. Stunned by this infiltration into his family, all Eddie could reply to his uncle's overtures was a curt "No go."

It seemed everywhere he turned someone was coaxing him to change his story about the two brothers. Eddie wondered why he was getting so much heat about a misdemeanor, a lousy little bookie case. Once he asked around, Connolly found out the reason: "Louie is on probation, and the IRS is breathing down his neck. He's got the local people in his pocket, but no one can't screw around with Uncle Sam."

As the court date approached, Connolly's partner and nemesis, the sergeant, tipped his hand. He tried to jolly Connolly into charging Louie with a lesser offense: transporting lottery slips.

"He would plead to that," the Sergeant counseled. "Otherwise, we're in for a long case . . ."

"What do you mean 'we'?" Eddie snapped. "This is my pinch. Besides, both of us know this is a second lottery offense for this guy."

The sergeant insisted on signing the complaints and did everything in his power to take over the case. Justin McCarthy had died a few weeks earlier of natural causes. Since then, the Department had been changing; expediency, not integrity, was now the watchword with the Squad.

Connolly knew he was going to lose the case, but that certainty didn't prevent him from speaking the truth in court. However, when he walked into the courtroom and saw the "right" judge presiding and the "right" defense attorney, he knew there was nothing left to do but act out his part in this travesty of justice.

The brothers entered a plea of nolo contendere, essentially pleading not guilty, but accepting a finding of guilty and throwing themselves on the mercy of the court. After all, if the judge happened to hand down a decision they didn't like, they could always appeal.

As the proceedings opened, the sergeant brushed past Connolly on his way to the bench, mumbling, "I'll give them a brief outline of the case."

"How can you?" Connolly bellowed in open court, "You weren't there."

Eddie's little outburst did not seem to fluster any of the other performers in this legal farce. Within five minutes, the case was over. Louie was found not guilty of the lottery charge. He was fined $50 for transporting lottery slips.

It was a classic situation where a case was "bagged and bagged by a professional."

Connolly followed the sergeant out into the courthouse corridor. Eddie was angry, but not surprised at the outcome. He had been warned by fellow officers, and he had seen plenty of evidence of the sergeant's venality firsthand, such as in the shoeshine episode. Even if he hadn't seen the sergeant accepting bribes, it would not have been hard to figure out where he got the money for a new car every year, a fancy home, and frequent trips to Bermuda.

"You did a good job for Louie," Connolly muttered as he fell into stride with the sergeant.

"What do you mean?" the sergeant said darkly.

"You know exactly what I mean," Eddie replied and quickened his pace and strode out the door.

In the following months, this particular defeat rankled Connolly so much that he just couldn't forget the matter. Every time a bookie got off with a slap on the wrist, Connolly couldn't help wondering who was getting paid off and how much. He wondered how low the sergeant would stoop, and soon Eddie found out.

One morning Connolly was walking from the Dover Street elevated stop along the half-mile stretch to Headquarters. He passed by the second-hand clothing stores and the knots of diehard drinkers waiting restlessly for the honky-tonk bars to open so they could get their first slurp of alcohol of the day. Some others, even farther gone, were still crumpled in doorways or over heating grates, sleeping off yesterday's hangover.

Suddenly at the corner of Dover Street and Shawmut Avenue, Connolly spotted the familiar figure of Louie, getting into the same Olds that he used on Burbank Street. Eddie was elated, feeling higher than any of the alkies he had passed on his way to work.

Here was Louie in the jurisdiction of another court, the Boston Municipal Court, not the Roxbury one. That meant a different judge. Though he had not had the opportunity to do any sort of surveillance, Eddie went with the gut feeling that Louie was still picking up numbers.

On an impulse, he rushed the car and reenacted the same scene as before. Louie was absorbed in sorting slips on the passenger's side of the front seat. Eddie yanked the door open, simultaneously forcing Louie over and grabbing a fistful of slip-filled envelopes.

"Hi, Louie. It's me again." Connolly smiled, examining the contents of the envelopes. "Looks like I got you good."

"Eddie, please don't pinch me. I thought everything was alright between us."

"What do you mean by that?"

"The last time . . . after the court case . . . the sergeant told me he talked to you and he said you were OK. I gave him $800 bucks for you. He told me all about your wife being in the hospital and how you needed the dough."

"You fucking liar . . ."

"No, I swear. My brother Sam was there."

"Your brother Sam was there the day that Judas got his 30 pieces of silver."

"No, I wouldn't lie to you," Louie said, looking really frightened. "Take me over to Headquarters. I'll tell you in front of the sergeant."

"You would."

Connolly tried to control his feeling of rage at the sergeant so that he could think clearly. So the sergeant had been using the oldest, phoniest excuse in the book to ask for bribe and was doing it in Eddie's name!

Finally, Connolly came to a decision.

"OK, Louie, screw. I'm holding on to these slips. I still may get a complaint against you later. I have to think this whole thing over."

"Thanks, Eddie. Do what you want."

"But for your information, I never got your money or any other money from that bastard."

"Do you want me to talk to my brother? Sam can get that money back from the sergeant so you can pay your wife's hospital bills."

"My wife was never in the hospital. And I never want a red cent from you or your fucking brother," Connolly growled and got out of the car, leaving the door wide open, and stalked away.

He knew that Louie had been telling the truth. The closer Eddie got to Headquarters, the madder he got.

"I gotta get a transfer off this unit. Fuck, the whole job sucks. I'm quitting. Nobody's on the level. Maybe a few, hell, maybe a lot, I don't know, but that's just the point. If you don't know who the hell you can trust, how can you arrest citizens for doing what everyone in the Department is doing?"

As soon as he got to the Vice Office, Eddie went directly to the filing cabinet, yanked out a pink printed resignation form, and scrawled his signature and the date in the appropriate blanks. He asked Jerry Sullivan to hand it to Captain John Cunniffe, the acting commander of Vice since McCarthy's death. It was Holy Thursday, April 7, 1955.

Irene was startled to see Eddie back so soon.

"What are you doing here so early?" she asked. "Did you forget something?"

"I'm all through."

Irene glanced at the kitchen clock.

"How can you be through for the day? It's not even lunchtime."

"I'm through for good. I resigned the job."

"Why, Eddie, why?"

"I had it up to here."

Irene put down the bottle of bleach that she had in her hand and sat down at the kitchen table.

"Eddie, the job will never change. People will never change. By resigning now you're not going to hurt anybody but your family and yourself. Nobody cares but us. It will go on as before. They're probably glad you left."

Her tone softened.

"Still you're like a lot of other good cops, trying to do the impossible. You do your best, but nobody cares."

"Nobody cares," Eddie repeated and went into the bedroom to lie down.

Things were pretty rough for the next couple of months. Money was so tight it seemed like Lent came after Easter that year. If he had known how hard it was going to be on his family, Eddie might have stuck it out a little longer.

But it was too late for regrets. Throughout the summer, former Detective Edward F. Connolly was reduced to taking whatever menial labor was available. Initially, he thought he could find work as a private detective or a security guard. But everytime he wrote under Last Place of Employment "Boston Police Department, Detective, Vice Squad," he always got the same reply. "No opening. Come back next week." None of the agencies could swallow his explanation that he resigned because he felt the rest of the Department was behaving unethically. It seemed inconceivable that Eddie could really have left a secure job with the BPD for a less desirable one with a security company.

Even when he applied for other kinds of work, no employer would touch him. After all, who wants an ex-undercover cop prowling around the premises?

10

Jews vs. Christians

As disillusioning as Connolly's experience with bribery had been, he now found a previously unappreciated side to certain officers in the Department. Captain Patrick O'Reilly and Patrolman George Haskell dropped by to see the Connollys one evening. Though Eddie had never been particularly friendly with O'Reilly, there were five tens tucked under the sugar bowl on the kitchen table when the captain left that night.

Pat McDonough, a boyhood friend of Connolly's, got Eddie a job painting houses. It was sometimes brutally hot in the sun, lifting ladders, hoisting the rigging, and climbing over sticky shingled roofs. Other police acquaintances like Jerry Sullivan and Sergeants Matty King, Frank Joyce and Jerry McCallum stopped in whenever they had a lead on an odd job that Connolly could make some money on.

Both his former associates on the force and many personal friends kept trying to convince Eddie to join the Department again. After months of scrimping and being refused job after job, he realized that perhaps he had been too hasty in quitting. He agreed to petition the Department to be reinstated.

Bob Curtis, an aide to Mayor John B. Hynes, intervened to get Connolly reappointed to the force. Matty King and Frank Joyce used their connections at the State House, but Boston Police Commissioner Thomas Sullivan refused to reinstate Connolly because some of the brass in the Department didn't want him back in their ranks.

However, once the word spread that Eddie wanted back into the Department, friends rallied around his cause. Lieutenant Bill Taylor, who worked in the Clerk's Office, got Connolly put on the top of the Civil Service list as a disabled veteran. Captain O'Reilly and Sergeant King came through for him again by using their contacts at the Veterans' Administration to make sure that Eddie's service disability from a varicocele operation was promptly verified.

Finally on August 7, 1955, Bill Taylor swore him in again — as a patrolman. Frank Joyce, Matty King and Jerry McCallum were waiting outside the Clerk's Office for Connolly to come out. As soon as he appeared, they whisked him off in a police car to the Property Clerk's Office to get his uniform, then took him home with all his gear. As well as he could, Eddie tried to express his gratitude for all they had done for him.

Even their lobbying and good will had not been able to counteract all the resentment that certain other superior officers harbored against this "troublemaker." The brass who felt that Eddie had not been sufficiently punished for his "disloyalty" saw to it that his return was made as humiliating as possible. Not only did Connolly lose all his seniority and have to start over as a patrolman, but he was assigned to Division 17 in West Roxbury.

The old wooden two-story structure on Centre Street, the main drag in West Roxbury, was something of a Departmental dumping ground. Division 17 was staffed mainly by older policemen with a sprinkling of rookies, but there were about 12 ex-detectives there, broken for a variety of reasons and banished to the sticks. Though they were officially in disgrace, they constituted some of the brightest police minds in the whole city.

For the next three years, Division 17 was Eddie's home. During that time one of his cases, which started over a playground squabble, mushroomed into a legal circus that made the front pages of all the Boston papers for days. A matter that should have been settled at a PTA meeting ended up causing headaches at the State House and the Archbishop's residence.

On November 6, 1957, Barbara Ann Murphy, a strong-willed vice-principal at the Patrick Lyndon Grammar School in West Roxbury, enforced her peculiar brand of discipline. For years, she had been making youngsters who misbehaved write letters confessing their infractions and promising not to do so again.

On that day she coerced ten-year-old Deborah Goldstein into writing one such letter admitting that she had taken more than her share of turns in a schoolyard game, she had been in the basement music room without permission, and she had told a lie. Some of Debbie's classmates were also pressured into penning letters accusing her of cheating at games during recess.

Deborah was so upset at this treatment that the school nurse sent her home early. All she had to do was cross the schoolyard because the Goldsteins lived right next to the school.

For quite some time there had been a sort of feud going on between the Goldsteins and Miss Murphy. Five years earlier, the Goldsteins' boy Arnold had been so miserable in Murphy's fifth-grade class that they had him transferred to another school, even though the Lyndon was so close to their home.

Outraged at this latest alleged mistreatment of her daughter, Charlotte Goldstein stormed over to the school. Enroute to the principal's office, she burst into Murphy's classroom. With clenched fists, she vowed, "We'll get you crawling to us yet. . . . You've been kicked out of other schools, and we'll get you kicked out of here. I'm going straight to your principal."

In the office of George L. McKinnon, Mrs. Goldstein had little Deborah explain tearfully that the only reason she had written the self-incriminating letter was that Miss Murphy had bullied her into doing so. Principal McKinnon could easily understand Debbie's position because he too had often been intimidated by his fiery vice-principal. Fearing Murphy's wrath, Mr. McKinnon declined to get involved in the matter.

Refusing to accept this brush-off, Charlotte marched out to the playground — the site of her daughter's supposed "crime." Mrs. Goldstein disrupted the physical education exercises that Murphy was supervising and gesticulated to capture the attention of the children.

"Every kid here is going to hear what I have to say. Listen, kids, what you have for a teacher is a dirty, rotten, lowdown sneak!"

The vice-principal tried to wave the irate mother away, sneering, "Jews aren't needed here."

Charlotte Goldstein countered by shouting that Murphy was a "Jew-hater" who "shouldn't be handling children." When Mrs. Goldstein refused to leave the school grounds, Murphy threatened to call the police. Charlotte finally left, vowing that the vice-principal had not heard the end of the matter.

The next morning, Charlotte's husband Philip went to McKinnon's office, where he bumped into an ally, Mrs. Ruby Goldman. Mrs. Goldman's daughter Libby was in Murphy's class; Libby was distressed at having been pressured into writing a letter condemning her friend Debbie. Ruby had come to McKinnon's office intent on retrieving and destroying Libby's letter.

McKinnon gave the two parents permission to visit Murphy's class. In they burst, blustering mad.

"You made my child bear false witness against another child," Ruby scolded. "I object to this Gestapo method, and I want the letter back."

"You've been torturing the children until they lied about my daughter," Philip Goldstein, an auctioneer, bellowed in his most ringing professional tones.

Then turning to the class, he added, "You have rights. You are American citizens."

After a heated, unseemly exchange in front of the bewildered children, Murphy, Goldstein and Goldman repaired to the principal's office. There the Jewish parents continued to object to the way Murphy disciplined the children and insisted, "We don't want trouble — we just want the papers!"

When McKinnon didn't give them the satisfaction and support they demanded, they launched into tirades about the Nazis and the anti-Semitism. Finally Murphy had had enough and tried to bolt from the room. But Philip Goldstein blocked her exit, and Ruby Goldman laid a hand on Murphy's wrist to restrain her.

"You're my witness! You're my witness!" Barbara screamed to the principal as she wrenched herself free and shoved her way out the room, "Call the police!"

Eddie Connolly in a one-man patrol car was the unfortunate one whom Fate selected to respond to the call. When he arrived at the Patrick Lyndon School, there was not a soul on the playground.

"School disturbance?" Eddie murmured to himself. "I can't find a squirrel in the street."

At the school office he was directed to Miss Murphy's class. She related the story of how she had been assaulted on two successive days, first by Mrs. Goldstein, then by Mr. Goldstein and Mrs. Goldman. She insisted on pressing charges against the parents who "willfully disrupted the whole school."

Connolly made notes on the stories of Murphy and McKinnon. Before returning to Station 17, he dropped by the Goldsteins to alert them to the fact that they should get a lawyer, because they would shortly be summoned to appear in court to answer to Murphy's charges.

At the station, the desk sergeant directed Connolly to report the matter to the captain. Captain Francis Tiernan was rumored to have ice water instead of blood flowing in his veins. Curt, sharp, and remote in his demeanor, he did not want to be troubled with some parents that got into a tizzy about a schoolmarm.

"Don't bother me with stories about little kids and schoolteachers, Connolly."

"But, Captain, there's a religious angle to this . . ."

"Let Morrison investigate it then. Now get out. I don't want to hear about this nonsense ever again."

Sgt. Mark Morrison, a District 17 veteran who had little patience with Jews or any other ethnic group besides his own, was thus chosen to look into the matter. Morrison must have worked in the Quartermasters Corps in the Army because he always was wearing olive drab socks and boxer shorts under his uniform. He also liked distributing the issues of the ultra-right-wing American Front newspapers to fellow officers urging them, "Here, read about the niggers and the kikes, how they're wrecking this country." Morrison was hardly the optimal choice to investigate the emotionally charged situation at the Lyndon School.

In reviewing the series of events with McKinnon, Sgt. Morrison promised, "These Jews aren't going to drive the teachers out of this school!"

Eddie had the job of drawing up the official complaint for Murphy to sign. Connolly also had to hand-deliver summonses to the parents of all the children called to testify.

When the Jewish parents got wind of Morrison's bigoted remarks, they had local anti-defamation groups register vigorous protests with the police brass.

Francis Hennessey, the sole superintendent in those days, called Captain Tiernan and demanded the facts about the Lyndon School controversy. At first Tiernan was dumbfounded that the superintendent even knew about the affair and tried to pooh-pooh the matter. Hennessey was adamant and insisted that a written report be on his desk by the end of the day.

As soon as the Super hung up, Tiernan summoned Sgt. Morrison and Patrolman Connolly to his office.

"Give me a full report on that Lyndon School matter right now," he yelled, losing his usual icy calm.

"But, Captain . . . ." Connolly began.

"Shut up," Tiernan barked. "Just do as you're told."

"I did."

"You did what?"

"I submitted a full report to you two days ago."

"Get out of here then. Sergeant, turn your report in without delay."

A month later on Tuesday, December 3, 1957 Judge Andrew McDonnell interviewed dozens of children during a private hearing in his chambers. The next day he pounded the gavel to open the West Roxbury District Court proceedings that soon snowballed into a statewide uproar. The courtroom was packed with spectators: Christian parents and kids on one side, Jewish families on the other. Connolly watched over the children and saw that they each signed for their $3 a day in witness fees.

From the very beginning, the proceedings were fraught with tension. Mrs. Goldman got so excited that her nose bled, and she had to be ushered out into the anteroom for first aid.

Superintendent Hennessey ordered Captain Tiernan to attend the trial of the Lyndon School case every day from 8 am to 4 pm. Tiernan had to telephone Hennessey with a progress report each afternoon at 4 pm. Hennessey and Tiernan hated each other, and making the captain suffer through a trial in which he had no interest was just one more way the superintendent devised to torment his foe.

Connolly would smile every time his eyes happened to light on the rigid-faced captain, forced to sit through hours of endlessly repeated testimony about the most trivial details of this grammar school tiff.

When McKinnon was put on the stand, he admitted that though he had long disapproved of Miss Murphy's practice of having students write letters telling on one another, he had never dared to put an end to it. The principal made some vague allusion to a threat that Miss Murphy had made to "get" him if he crossed her.

Judge McDonnell interrupted the examination of the witness to pose his own questions.

"Are you a married man?"

"Yes."

"Then you are not afraid of women, are you?"

"I am not afraid of 99 out of 100," McKinnon said, "but Miss Murphy is that one."

The courtroom exploded into an extended gale of laughter, and it was quite a while before the judge could compose himself enough to call for order.

Though McKinnon had been called as a prosecution witness, his testimony was proving helpful to the defense. Besides condemning her method of disciplining and admitting that even he was afraid of her, the principal also denied that he had witnessed any assault and battery on her by the parents in his office.

Miss Murphy's attorney, Thomas White, then asked, "You did not approve of having this come to court?"

"It is very bad publicity for the school."

"Did you try to prevent the court action?"

"I called the station and was told that the entire matter was in the hands of Sergeant Morrison."

Judge McDonnell interrupted, "Your whole attitude so far in this case is an indication to me that you are a hostile witness and I do so rule."

One piece of schoolhouse evidence was trotted out to contradict other pieces of schoolhouse evidence. Defense attorneys presented Deborah Goldstein's report cards, on which Miss Murphy herself had given the fifth-grader A's for "respect for authority, respect for property, courtesy and cooperation." The vice principal's lawyers got McKinnon to admit that he had given Miss Murphy A's and A minuses for her performance.

Eddie Connolly had relatively little to report when he was called as a witness. So he was surprised when he felt a huge hand clasp him on the shoulder as he walked down the corridor during a recess. It was old Ice-Water himself.

"Hey, Eddie," Captain Tiernan congratulated him. "You did a good job on the stand. You really know how to testify."

From that day on, Eddie struck up a friendship with the supposedly unapproachable captain, a relationship that proved quite helpful to him in later years. But Sergeant Morrison did not fare quite so well.

Morrison came in for a real grilling by the defendants' lawyers, Nathan Hillman and Morris Michelson.

When asked if he made derogatory remarks about Jews, Morrison tried to claim that McKinnon had remarked "Those Jews are nice people," to which he had replied, "Regardless of whether they are Jews or not, they have no right to push anybody around."

However, McKinnon's secretary confirmed that he had actually remarked without any prompting, "Those Jews aren't going to drive the teachers out of this school."

Morrison became something of a hero to the *American Front*, which sent reporters from California to cover the events of the trial in detail.

Focus in the testimony began to shift away from the question of the propriety of the disciplining system to the question of prejudice. The Jewish parents testified that they had asked that Chanukah be recognized during the school's December holiday ceremonies and that Murphy had ignored their request, insisting that Judaism had no place in Christmas celebrations. By making Jewish children sing carols and participate in Christmas pageants, they contended, she was forcing alien religious beliefs on them.

In his summation, Defense Counsel Morris Michelson fulminated against Miss Murphy, whom he said was guilty of violating the Ninth Commandment "over and again by forcing the children to bear false witness against their neighbor.

"Furthermore," he said, "she is guilty of carrying on a campaign of malice, prejudice and vindictiveness against a little child. She even enlisted a policeman, who was filled with hatred against Jews, to aid her in her plot!"

Judge McDonnell cut him short by asking, "Are you addressing the court or the press? You cannot use this court as a mouthpiece to put these things over."

Defense Attorney White continued that theme when he said, "The defense case is a magnificent plot to blow up the city with anti-Semitism charges."

He pointed to the fact that Murphy had taught for 16 years with no complaints and ". . . then suddenly she becomes anti-Semitic in 1957?"

"This is not a question of a little child lying," he concluded, "but a case in which Miss Murphy did something to the Goldsteins' daughter so that they wanted to do something to Miss Murphy!"

All the overheated rhetoric and smoldering religious antagonism was not cooled by the judge's decision. Mr. Goldstein and Mrs. Goldman were found innocent of assault charges, but Mrs. Goldstein and Mrs. Goldman were each fined $25 for willful interruption of a school class.

Both women declared they would appeal, so instead of paying the $25 fine they were released on $100 personal recognizance. Speaking for the two still-angry mothers, Attorney Hillman declared, "The fundamental issue is whether the present type of discipline is going to continue in the school. We intend to present evidence elicited in this hearing to the School Committee so that proper measures may be taken to prevent this type of discipline from appearing again in the school."

Though the School Committee Chairman and others promised to investigate the matter, the Goldsteins and Mrs. Goldman aimed even higher. They approached Governor Foster Furcolo and asked that Eddie Connolly and Mark Morrison be dismissed from the Police Department. In light of all the front-page coverage that the story was getting, the Governor was forced to send someone to investigate the way that Connolly and Morrison had conducted themselves. Furcolo's legal counsel, Attorney Theodore Glynn, was assigned the thankless task; Glynn reported that the two officers had done nothing wrong.

Archbishop Richard Cushing was unhappy at the deteriorating relationship between Catholics and Jews in the city. He used his influence to get the Suffolk County District Attorney to nolle prosequi the whole matter so that it would be wiped off the books. He also got Benjamin Shapiro of the Massachusetts Committee of Christians and Jews to prevail upon the Goldsteins and Goldmans to forget their grievances in return for having the fines and convictions erased.

Thus ended the case in which Eddie was embroiled with the Archbishop, the Governor, and the teacher who made Jewish kids sing Christmas carols.

11

More Harm Than Good

Some perfectly legal arrests seem to do much more harm than good. That concept may puzzle the average citizen, but a veteran on the force can tell you that a good number of arrests are a big waste of the officer's time and the proverbial taxpayer's money.

How many times in a career will a cop risk life and limb to make a good arrest, only to have it "bagged" in court or thrown out on some legal technicality?

There are other legal arrests that exact an even higher price than precious hours wasted booking a suspect and making an appearance in court. Sometimes the price has to be paid in terms of suffering by the criminal or, worse, by those closest to him.

Every time an arrest ends in an unforeseen tragedy, an officer has to ask himself, "What if I hadn't brought this guy in? Wouldn't it have been better for everyone concerned if I had looked the other way . . . just this once?"

Among the routine correspondence that arrived in the Commissioner's Office one morning was a handwritten letter from an anonymous tipster, alerting the police to the activities of a bookie in Brighton.

"I, as a good citizen, would like to report that Ralph Zippi is operating a bookie joint under the eyes of the police of Station 14 who are getting paid off by this man to defy the law."

The letter gave the address of Zippi's establishment and plenty of dates and figures that seemed to support the informant's assertion. It included specific directions on where to find the bookmaker's "stash" or hiding place for the betting slips.

From the use of gaming slang and vulgar language, it was clear that the writer was a horse or numbers player himself and not some model church-going citizen. Very possibly this tip-off was coming from some disgruntled bettor who felt that Zippi had cheated him. Spitefully motivated or not, the matter had to be looked into.

The Commissioner's Office forwarded the letter to a Deputy Superintendent's desk along with an official "tab" to investigate and

report back to the Commissioner with the findings. The Deputy
decided to let Sergeant Detective John Byrne and Detective Eddie
Connolly of the Vice and Gaming Unit conduct the investigation and
gave them two weeks in which to make a report.

With the wealth of information in the letter, the arrest of Zippi
promised to be an easy way to boost the Departmental total one collar higher. Byrne and Connolly located the address on Commonwealth Avenue in Brighton. The gilt letters on the sign and
storefront pane dispelled any doubts in their minds: "Ralph Zippi,
Shoemaker. REPAIRS."

The two detectives sat in their unmarked car across the street from
the cobbler's and rechecked the description of Zippi in the letter: "59
years, balding, gray hair, bent, dark complexion, small frame, thin,
very thin."

Through the glass of the storefront, they could make out someone
sitting behind the counter, pounding away at the bottoms of shoes.
Though Connolly had 20/20 vision, he surreptitiously pulled a pair
of binoculars from the glove compartment to get a better look at the
interior of the shop.

There was no question that the man inside was Zippi. He fit the
description perfectly. Ralph was seated on a stool; the stained apron
around his neck hung loosely about his emaciated body. It seemed
that for every nail he banged into a sole he would spit a lunger into a
dirty pail by his feet.

It got pretty disgusting to watch him after awhile with all that
hawking.

Connolly made a wry face. "Let's forget this guy. He's got TB or
something. He's always spitting into his bucket. He's gagging and
choking. It's getting to the point where I feel like puking. Here, you
watch him for awhile, John."

Byrne took the glasses and studied the little Italian for a few
minutes. "Naw, that's just a smoker's cough."

The bookie action seemed to be pretty good. Women from the
neighborhood stopped in while running errands; there was a steady
flow of men from the adjoining tavern. Ralph would slip a sheet of
carbon paper between the top two leaves of a 3 by 5 pad of paper and
scribble the information down. He would give the customer the copy
and tuck the original slip in a rather original "stash": one of the
shoes in the rack of repaired footwear.

When the clock in the dashboard indicated 2:30, Connolly knew
that the action was bound to stop or at least slow down significantly
because the winning number came out at 3. They already had more
than enough to nail the shoemaker, so why wait?

"What do you say, Sarge, shall we wind this one up?" Connolly
asked.

"Okay."

"He's alone, so I'll go in by myself," Connolly said, shedding his coat. "Here, hold my gun."

Connolly wanted to enter in his shirt sleeves so as not to arouse any suspicion that he was a cop. A telltale bulge in the jacket of an unfamiliar person was enough to prompt a nimble-fingered bookie to destroy his stash before the slips could be seized as evidence.

"You follow as soon as I get behind the counter," Connolly said as he stepped onto the sidewalk and slammed the car door shut. Byrne concurred with a grunt.

Connolly crossed Commonwealth Avenue casually as if heading for the bar next door to the cobbler's shop. Instead of entering the ginmill, he merely waved at the barflies who nodded to him as he passed. Hugging the wall of the bar, he peered around the corner of the building at the shop. Then he strode up to the door, pulled it open, and moved swiftly behind the counter.

Connolly had grasped the shoe with all the betting slips before poor Ralph realized what was happening.

"Hey, you, get outta here! What the hell do you think you're doing?"

"Police," Connolly informed him simply. "You're under arrest."

Ralph apparently was about to make some sort of reply or comment, but he was suddenly caught up in a violent fit of coughing and spitting lunger after lunger into the foamy mess inside his bucket. When the coughing didn't seem to subside, Connolly became concerned.

"Shit," Zippi finally gasped between expectorations.

"Take it easy there," Connolly said. "You want a glass of water or something?"

"I'm alright," the little man sputtered, but the racking cough and spitting continued. "I just got a cough or a cold or something."

Zippi sank back down on his little stool. What little color there had been in his face had drained away, leaving him ashen.

Byrne burst through the door.

"You get him, Eddie?"

"Yeah, here," Connolly replied, shaking the contents of the shoe he was holding onto the counter for Byrne to inspect. While the sergeant sifted through the hundreds of slips each with notations on the horse and number players, Connolly looked doubtfully at the choking bookie.

"Did you search him, Eddie?"

"Not yet. Haven't had the chance. He's been sick."

Connolly tried to explain to Zippi that arrests like this were routine procedure; it was certainly nothing to get upset about. While he was trying to calm the man down, word of the arrest leaked to the tavern next door. Some of the patrons gathered outside; a couple were brave enough to step across the threshold.

A big Irish fellow with quite a few beers under his belt bellowed, "What the fuck are you doing to Ralph? He a sick guy. Can't you see that? He's got heart trouble, cancer and diabetes."

"Poor Ralph's dying," chimed in his companion, "and all these assholes can do is make him more miserable. Why don't you go out and arrest some real criminals? Everybody in this neighborhood is getting robbed, and all you can do is pick on a sick man."

"Get out of here before I lock you up with him," growled Byrne, who was a big-framed man himself.

The Irish tough and his buddy retreated a few steps to the crowd outside and began to relate in loud voices what had been said in the shop.

"Sergeant," Connolly remarked, "I think we're going to have trouble with those guys on the way out."

"No, you won't," the coughing man promised. "They're all decent guys. I'll talk to them."

Zippi kept the bar patrons at bay and coughed and spit his way across Commonwealth Avenue. He continued spitting into his handkerchief during the mile-long ride to the station.

As they helped Zippi out of the car and into the station, Connolly felt even sharper pangs of regret.

"I feel awful. We should never have arrested this guy. Like the Irish fella said, he's dying."

"Look," Byrne returned, "if some busybody wrote the Commissioner some bullshit about Zippi paying off some cops, what the hell do you think he'll write about us if we let this poor bastard go? That whole crowd from the bar saw us with all these slips. Anyone of them could be the snitch who wrote the letter."

Later that afternoon, the desk sergeant informed Connolly that Ralph would be sent to Headquarters to be photographed and printed. He would be bailed out when he returned; he wouldn't even be held temporarily in a cell. Most of the officers at District 14 knew about Zippi and his poor health.

"Connolly!" Zippi called as the detective was walking out of the station.

"Yeah?"

"I would like to thank you and the sergeant for treating me so well. I'm just a hard-luck guy. No hard feelings?"

"No hard feelings."

Connolly continued down the steps to the police car where Byrne sat waiting. The sergeant said, "Let's go back to Headquarters and answer this tab."

"Why not call it a day?" Connolly countered. "What a lousy week! Thank God, it's Saturday. I'm going to hate to have to face that guy in court Monday."

"Don't worry about him. He will be bailed out and home before we are. The court isn't going to do much to him; he's a sick guy. Besides, you know as well as I do that his boss will get a lawyer for him and pay his piddling $50. Hell, Ralphie will be back in action Monday afternoon. You'll see."

"I hope you're right. I just don't want to think about it any more."

After Mass the next morning, Connolly took it easy, going through the Sunday papers — the *Globe* and the *Sunday Advertiser*. Both publications contained a few paragraphs about an unknown male found floating in the Charles River by the Metropolitan District Police. They had taken the body to the Southern Morgue.

Monday morning at 8 am, Connolly showed up at the Vice and Gaming Squad office; he noted that Sergeant Matt King and Jerry Sullivan seemed rather glum as they sat in silence at their desks, taking sips of coffee out of paper cups.

"Hi," Eddie said, opening the evidence locker to get the shoe with the slips. "I got to go to Brighton Court. I'll take the green car. John Byrne said he'd —"

"Eddie," Matt interrupted. "Sergeant Crowley from 14 just called. You don't have to go to court today."

"Why not?"

"You were going about the Zippi case, right?"

"Yeah . . ."

"He was found in the Charles — drowned — early Sunday morning."

"Was he the one?"

"'Fraid so."

"Thanks, Matty." Connolly placed the evidence envelope back in the locker. "I think I'll go out for coffee."

With a bowed head, Connolly walked slowly out of the office. The question burned in his head: "Was a fuckin' bookie pinch worth a man's life?"

Every time Connolly passed the corner of Commonwealth and Washington, he couldn't help thinking about the considerate, skinny bookie . . . spitting, spitting.

Angelo Mastrichino had tried everything in the criminal line. No police officer would ever know all the breaking and enterings, the larcenies and robberies he had gotten away with. But he had done time; he'd been in the Deer Island House of Correction a couple of times, even done a stretch at Walpole State Prison.

When he wasn't in a cell, he was staying in some boardinghouse or shacking up with a hooker. He didn't seem to have a family or even a hometown, for that matter.

The first time that Connolly arrested Mastrichino was during a street drug roundup. From his observation post in the Tremont Street dental office, Tom Moran spotted Angelo making a buy from a dealer. Using the walkie-talkie, he sent Detective Emmett McNamara and Detective Connolly to tail Angelo in their unmarked car until he was out of the area.

As they cruised down the street, Emmett, a former prison guard, chuckled. "That Angelo. I'd know his walk anywhere. You know him, Eddie?"

"No."

"Well, he'll give you a lot of shit, even a fight. So we have to hit him hard before he can destroy the junk."

McNamara laughed again. "Wait till he sees me. I got a B & E warrant he didn't know he was carrying."

The car stopped about six feet to the rear of the subject. Like a rabbit, Emmett bounded out of the car. Angelo sensed something behind him; he turned and Emmett's powerful arms encircled him, trapping him in a necklock. Connolly banged into them, and all three fell onto the sidewalk, Emmett still holding the necklock and Angelo turning blue.

Connolly snapped the cuffs on Mastrichino's right wrist, then on his left.

"Mother-fuckin' cops!" he hissed. "Mother-fuckers!"

Emmett ground the left side of the man's face into the concrete with one hand while he fished around in Angelo's left jacket pocket where Moran had told him he would find the junk.

"Bingo!" McNamara said producing three small white glassine packages.

As Mastrichino, still cussing a blue streak, was pulled to his feet, the inevitable crowd gathered to gawk and comment.

"Handbag snatcher . . ."

"No . . . he looks more like a hold-up mother."

"Good work, officers!"

"Those fucking cops are alright . . . sometimes."

Emmett and Connolly ignored these remarks and dragged the squirming man towards the car. Their progress was interrupted by a spinster who presented herself in front of them.

"Be careful with that boy, officers. He's a human being, too. I want to know what he did."

"Are you his mother?" Emmett inquired.

"No . . ."

"Well, lady," he smirked. "He raped a three-year-old girl and her 86-year-old grandmother on the same day."

All the spinster's concern vanished in an instant.

"Cut off his balls!" she demanded, revenge flashing in her eyes.

"McNamara, you bastard," Angelo wailed as he was pushed into the police car to protect him from her wrath.

This arrest was only the first of many times that Connolly and the other officers at District 4 hauled Angelo in. As the years passed and Angelo was arrested dozens of times, the special relationship that sometimes springs up between an offender and an officer developed. Meeting on the street, waiting together in corridors, eyeing one another in joints, filling out forms together at the station — the cop and criminal come to understand one another very well. The two become familiar and friendly with one another, but they never become equals.

No matter how well an officer thinks he knows an Angelo, he can never let his guard down because the criminal can betray that trust at any moment. Nevertheless, a good cop will always keep his word, no matter how treacherous the person is he gives it to.

Finally, a day came when Connolly, Bill Gagan and George Bishop stopped Mastrichino on the corner of Washington and Northampton. A search of his person turned up a bundle of heroin and a set of "works" — needle, syringe and a beer cap to cook the dope in.

Later, without really knowing why, Connolly wandered down to the cellblock in Station 4 to have a chat with Angelo.

Angelo couldn't do much more than whimper. He was doubled up on the steel bunk, suffering from withdrawal.

"Angelo, how are you feeling?"

"Sick, oh, am I sick!" he whispered through clenched teeth.

"I'll get Doctor Lappin. I just saw him come in."

Connolly fetched the police surgeon, Matthew Lappin, who was at the front desk joking with the duty officers.

Connolly let Lappin into the cell.

"How much are you using a day?" the physician asked.

"Twenty-five bags."

"Okay, Eddie," Lappin said. "I'll take care of him."

Around 5 pm that day, just before Connolly left for home, he stopped by the cellblock to check on Angelo. The good doctor had done his job well; Angelo was sleeping like a baby.

The next morning before he left for court, Connolly dropped by again.

"Hi, Angelo."

"Hi, Eddie."

"How ya feeling?"

"OK, but I'm getting sick of this life, if you can call it a life. I never seem to be able to straighten myself out," he sighed. "How long have you known me?"

"Six or seven years . . ."

Angelo laughed bitterly as he reflected. "I've made so many good scores, and today I haven't got a dime . . . all I have is a habit. How can I go on?"

"Come on, Angelo, buck up."

"Eddie, I'm a parole violator on this arrest. That means I have to go back to Walpole or Norfolk for four or five years." He swallowed hard at the thought.

After a moment, he continued, "I'm not blaming anybody, Eddie. I know it's your job. I just blame myself. Thanks for everything . . . and say hello to Emmett for me. He's a good guy . . . even if he is a cop."

An officer came to remove him to court.

"Goodbye, Angelo."

"See you in court."

The arraignment was short and routine. The bail was set, but because Angelo had no money he was remanded to Charles Street Jail. The trial date was established. A parole officer lodged a parole violation warrant at the jail, so Angelo couldn't have been released if he had been able to come up with the scratch.

As the arraignment came to a close, Connolly and Angelo exchanged a long look before Mastrichino was led off. That was the last time Eddie ever saw him.

A few days later, Bill Gagan ambled into the detective room at District 4 with the news that Angelo had used his T-shirt to hang himself in his cell at Charles Street.

"Thanks for letting me know, Billy," Connolly said. "I always had a feeling that he would end like this."

"He was a junkie, a thief, a B & E man, and everything that was bad and wrong. But there was something about him that I liked. I could never put my finger on it, but it was something I liked.

"I often wondered where he came from, did he have a family, what his mother was like or his father. Once I compared his arrest forms. One time he said he was born in New York. Next time, Pittsburgh, Pennsylvania. Another time Milwaukee or some such place. No one ever could get out of him where he really was from.

"Billy, I can't help thinking that if we hadn't arrested him, he'd still be alive today."

Gagan said quietly, "Eddie, it's not your fault."

"I've told myself that a thousand times. I'll bet every cop asks himself that same question in similar circumstances, but it doesn't change the way we feel. Still, no matter how sorry we feel about a guy personally, we cops have to keep on doing the best we can."

"To Henry Street, 134," the dispatcher called over the radio, "Vacant house. Two men removing plumbing fixtures from the second floor."

Officers Joe Gambino and Eddie Connolly roused themselves to respond. Connolly pressed the button on the mike. "11-O car has the message. On the way."

"I'm surprised that three-decker wasn't stripped a long time ago," Gambino remarked as he stepped on the accelerator.

Three minutes later the squad car was parked in front of the ramshackle Henry Street home. Connolly headed for the rear of the building, hurrying along the long driveway that flanked the three-decker. Gambino had no problem gaining access from the front; the main door had been ripped off its hinges and flung onto the foyer floor. The heavy beveled glass that had once filled the oval in the door was now shattered into countless pieces.

Though Gambino tried to pick his way carefully across the glass, the crunching sound echoed up the stairwell. Through the open door in the vacant first floor apartment, he could hear Connolly trying unsuccessfully to tiptoe over the broken glass from the back door entrance.

The sound of hammers clanging against metal, which had been reverberating through the building when they first approached, suddenly ceased. The crunching of the glass had alerted the culprits that the police had arrived.

Gambino decided to throw caution to the wind and to rush into the second floor apartment when he heard a scuffling from the rear stairs and Connolly's voice calling, "I got one!"

Gambino charged through the long hallway to the kitchen and onto the back landing, where he saw his partner clicking the cuffs on a tall, thin, redheaded youth.

"What's your name?" said Connolly, not unkindly.

Despite the policeman's mild tone, the young man couldn't stop shaking.

"Billy. Billy Joyce."

Just then the sound of someone galloping down the front stairs, over the fallen door and out onto the street told the officer that Joyce's accomplice had managed to elude them by hiding on the third floor front landing and sneaking down when they were engaged with capturing Billy.

"Where do you live?"

"Roxbury."

"Come on, you know what we mean. Street and number."

"169 Bartlett Street."

"Who was with you?"

"Nobody."

"Then who was that hauling ass out of here a couple of seconds ago?"

"I dunno."

"You don't know, huh?" snorted Gambino. "Eddie, Roxbury's your home town too, ain't it? Is everyone there as stupid as this one?"

Connolly ignored the remark and continued his questioning.

"What were you two taking?"

"Just some old pipes," the redhead said in a low voice and gestured toward the kitchen. Gambino stepped back in and noted a pile of junk pipes and sheets of copper that had been ripped from a hot water tank.

"They got more in a pushcart outside," called Connolly. "I saw it out back."

"Just what were you planning to do with all this crap?"

"Sell it at Myers Junk . . . over on Harrison Avenue near Eustis Street."

"That's better. Now what was that other kid's name?"

"I don't remember."

"Maybe it will all come back to you when we get over to Station 11."

Billy was booked for larceny in a building, but because he was a minor the police were willing to release him on personal recognizance to his father.

It was awhile before Mr. Joyce, a hardworking warehouseman, could be located in Roxbury and summoned to the Dorchester station. After the long streetcar ride in the middle of his workday, he was in no mood for nonsense.

When he learned that Billy was taking all the blame by refusing to divulge his friend's name and address, he asked to speak to his son alone.

After a few minutes with his father, Billy dispensed with the heroics and agreed to cooperate.

"Tommy Ross was with me. He lives at 12 Lane Place, off Washington Street near Dudley Street terminal. Second floor."

Using Billy's testimony, a juvenile officer went to the Dorchester Court the next day and obtained a warrant for Tommy Ross, who, it turned out, was 18. For the theft of the pipes and warped sheets of copper, Ross was charged with straight larceny under $100, which according to Massachusetts law is a misdemeanor.

Once he got the warrant, Moe McCarthy, the juvenile officer, called Station 11, and soon Gambino and Connolly were heading to 12 Lane Place to arrest Tommy.

Most warrant arrests are routine. Police go to the subject's home and take him to the station for booking, photographing and fingerprinting. The bail is set, and the suspect either pays the bail and is released or can't pay and is confined in a cell at the station until court is next in session — usually the following morning.

Gambino wanted to get Ross out of the way as soon as possible; they had several more challenging things scheduled for that day. So as soon as they got to Lane Place and located #12, they rolled out of the car, hoping to be done within half an hour.

Number 12 was a rundown two-and-a-half story wooden structure. Painted on the gray clapboards over a rusted, hingeless mailbox was the name "Ross" in green letters.

The front door was unlatched; the staircase up to the second floor was tracked with mud, and a five-gallon fuel oil can blocked access to the second floor landing.

Gambino kicked the can aside and began pounding on the hollow door with the heel of his hand.

Connolly remained on the stairs between the ground and second floor landing and called, "Police! Open the door!"

After several minutes of persistent knocking and increasingly stern demands for access, the lock turned and the door swung open. Very slowly a mass of dark brown curls emerged, and then the head tilted up to reveal two wide, brown eyes set in the face of a boy who looked more like 16 than 18.

"What do you want?" he said, trying to sound tough.

"You, Tom Ross?"

"Yeah."

"We want you," Gambino smiled.

Tommy tried to slam the door shut, but Gambino's thick black shoe had been slipped over the threshold to prevent such a maneuver. Nevertheless, Joe yowled as the door crushed and twisted his foot. The surge of pain gave him the extra strength to heave the door in and send Tommy scrambling into the middle of the kitchen.

"I'm gonna get you, you sorry bastard!" Joe vowed.

By a kitchen table with three metal legs and a splintery gray board that served as a fourth, Tommy stood defiantly by a figure that sat slumped over to one side.

It was an old woman in an ancient wicker wheelchair. She wore a plain frayed nightgown under a blue flannel bathrobe. Her head and neck lolled to the left; her eyes were even wider than her son's and protruded from their sockets. Whether this was their natural condition or whether it was the result of her alarm, it was hard to say.

The woman made some ghastly gagging sounds as if she wanted to speak, but her illness had obviously robbed her of the ability to speak. Drool was sliding in long strings over her crooked, yellow little teeth. Tommy wiped the saliva away with a clean, but rather tattered dishrag.

The shaking of her shoulders indicated that she wanted to draw Tommy near and hug and protect him, but paralysis prevented her from doing more than quiver in agitation.

"Look what you've done!" the young man growled.

Tommy's eyes blazed with defiance, refusing to be ashamed of the pathetic condition of this woman and the squalor of the apartment.

"Tommy, take it easy now," Connolly said. "We just want to talk to you about a warrant we have for your arrest. You were stealing lead pipes and copper from a house on Henry Street yesterday . . . with Billy Joyce . . . now weren't you?"

"That fink Joyce, I'll kill . . . I don't know what you're talking about."

The tiny face of the white-haired woman wrinkled deeper with concern, jiggling back and forth. The drool was leaking even more quickly from the corner of her mouth.

"Ma, take it easy. I'm alright. They got nothing on me, the fuckin' cops." Tommy said, gently dabbing her chin dry. The contrast between the roughness of his tone and language and the tenderness with which he cared for his mother was touching.

"Can't you guys see my mother is real sick, and I'm the only one that takes care of her?"

"You're gonna have to find somebody else 'cause we've got a warrant and you're coming with us."

"I told you there ain't nobody else."

"Well, then," Connolly said, suppressing a sigh, "we'll just have to call an ambulance and have her sent to City Hospital."

On hearing this suggestion, the old woman started to sputter and cough, her eyes full of panic.

"No way," her son said firmly. "She would die. I'm the only one who knows what she needs."

Connolly hated the position he was in. He wished the call about the theft of the pipes had never come in. But he had to press forward.

"How about the neighbors looking in on her until you get bailed out?" he suggested.

"Bailed out?" Tommy snorted. "What do you expect me to use for money, huh? I haven't got a pot to piss in — or a window to throw it out of. What's the matter with you two? Are you blind? Can't you see that I don't make enough to give my crippled mother a decent meal? What do you think, I like living in this shithole?"

"Calm down, Tommy. I'm sorry, but there's just no way around it. You're coming with us."

The firmness and sadness in Connolly's tone finally convinced the young man that he had no alternative.

"I'll try the drunk downstairs. When she's sober, she sometimes does little things for Mom when I'm not around. It will only be till I get bailed out in the morning. Right?"

"Right."

Gambino went downstairs with Tommy to see if Bertha Fleming was in any condition to take on the responsibility for feeding Mrs. Ross and helping her to go to the bathroom. Connolly waited with the mother, whose expression of hurt and reproach was almost more than he could bear.

Tommy and Gambino returned. In response to an inquiring glance from Eddie, Gambino nodded that the arrangement had been made.

"I'm putting my mother to bed," Tommy announced. "Wait out here."

He wheeled his mother into a bedroom and closed the door. Though the two officers couldn't make out what he was saying, the tone of his voice was reassuring and confident.

He was in there a long time. When he came out, he carefully closed the door behind them. When Tommy raised his eyes to meet those of the men arresting him, they were glittering with resentment.

"That old lush better do what she said, or I swear I'll make you two bastards regret it for the rest of your lives."

"You'll be home in time to bring your mother her breakfast," Connolly assured him.

But the judge made a liar out of Eddie. After examining Tommy's probation record, the judge set his bail at $5000 and remanded the young man to Charles Street Jail to await trial.

Both Connolly and Gambino felt terrible that Tommy was being held on such high bail. They knew that there was no way that he was going to be able to find that kind of money, and they realized that they had to do something about Mrs. Ross.

Connolly described the mother's circumstances to Tommy's probation officer.

"Gee, that sounds pretty rough," the probation officer agreed, "but what do you expect me to do about it? Best I can do is to get hold of a social worker, and maybe she can put the kid's momma in a nursing home someplace."

At the trial things got worse. The owner of the three-decker that had been stripped by Billy and Tommy greatly exaggerated the extent of the damage to the house and the value of the pipes that had been stolen. He was obviously angling to get a hefty sum in restitution. Instead the judge found both boys guilty; Billy got a suspended sentence, but because of his record, Tommy was given six months in the House of Correction at Deer Island.

Soon afterwards Connolly was transferred to the Vice Squad at Headquarters. The problems of Tommy and his mother got lost in the hundreds of other cases Eddie was working on over the next two years.

Then one day, Connolly was standing outside a honky-tonk joint on Essex Street when the Ross boy brushed passed him.

"Hey, Tommy. How are you? Remember me?"

The annoyance at being stopped by a stranger gave way to a look of pure hatred.

"You fucking bastard. Of course, I remember you. You're the son of a bitch who locked me up for taking a few rusty old pipes. Sent me to Deer Island and my mom to a stinking nursing home. She wasn't even in that pit four months before she died."

"I'm sorry to hear that, Tommy. Really I am."

"You're sorry? How do you think I feel? I never got to see her since the day you hauled me outta my house. She died alone, without me, while I was in the can. And you, you cocksucker, you're the one who murdered her."

12

Counterfeiters with a Perfect Cover

Some people never learn. Being incarcerated didn't stop a pair of master writers and passers of spurious checks from plying their trade. In fact, being in prison gave this duo a perfect screen from the FBI.

An audacious and ingenious scheme was conceived by Paul Johnson and Lawrence Campbell, who managed to turn the correctional facility on Deer Island in Boston Harbor into the source of a flood of bad checks that turned up all over New England.

The investigation by Detectives Ed Connolly and John Doherty of the Robbery Squad that led to the exposure of the ring began appropriately enough at a Boston paper factory. It illustrated the \quirky nature of police work, where an inquiry into one crime can end up providing crucial information in a completely unrelated case.

There had been a payroll holdup just after Christmas, and Connolly and Doherty stood, all bundled up, on the loading dock questioning the employees for leads. Most of the workers were in a bad mood. Christmastime is the worst time of year to be short a paycheck. They all wanted the two detectives to do something fast to recover the money, but their impatience wasn't matched by any diligence in turning up clues.

One rapid-talking fellow named Sterns came up to the two policemen and said, "I got an idea who coulda done it."

"Who?"

"I'm going to marry a girl. Coulda been her brother."

"Why do you say that?"

"He's always in trouble. In and out of jail all the time."

"That's not much to go on."

"But just listen a minute," the little man chattered on, "I was talking to him the other night, telling him all about how we do things here. I told him about how we handle the payroll, and he said to me, 'That would be an easy holdup.' "

Connolly wanted to know, "How can we find this guy?"

Sterns was excited that he had captured the interest of the police. He felt that he had been indirectly responsible for the payroll robbery, and now he imagined that he was going to make up for his careless talk by engineering the apprehension of the culprit.

"Me and my sister and him are gonna be celebrating New Year's at Ort's Grill on Essex Street. Now this guy always — and I mean always — packs a gun. Just show up at Ort's Grill around midnight and you can grab him!"

Sterns beamed with pride at this plan he had concocted to trap his future brother-in-law. Sterns' story was all Connolly and Doherty had to go on, and it meant that their wives had to spend yet another holiday husbandless. Yet they didn't give a second thought to the festivities they would miss.

Around 11:30 pm on December 31, 1968, the two detectives found themselves elbowing their way through the giddy revelers up to the second story club. At 6'1" and 225 pounds, the muscular Doherty didn't have much of a problem. In his youth he had been a sparring partner for the Harvard College boxing team, so he wasn't about to be thrust aside by drunken patrons with silly little hats on their heads.

There was one problem negotiating the stairs. A toilet had been plugged up by some pranksters and had begun to overflow. The staircase had turned into a little waterfall. People were slipping and sliding and laughing hysterically at one another's predicament.

Finally the two waded their way up the stairs and with sodden shoes tramped into the main room of the club where the merry-makers were revving up for the magic moment.

Across the room Connolly spotted Sterns and his date along with Sterns' sister and the suspect. As soon as Sterns caught sight of the two policemen who were trying to act nonchalant, he began to make elaborate pointing gestures at his sister's beau.

There was no point in being subtle about the matter now, so they went over to the table and said to the suspect, "Police."

"I know you're police."

"You're under arrest for illegal possession of a firearm."

The man stood up, raised his hands and, with a smirk on his face, dared them, "So search me."

No gun.

In these pre-Miranda days, it was much easier to bluff your way with a suspect.

Undaunted by their failure to find a weapon, Doherty said curtly, "You're coming with us."

"For what?"

"You know for what. Now grab your coat, and let's get out of here."

Just as the New Year arrived in a crescendo of clattering, hooting and rejoicing, Connolly and Doherty pulled the man from the arms of his protesting fiancee and escorted him down the waterfall into a car and back to the station.

Once they had him sitting down, they asked him, "What did you have to do with it?"

At first he maintained, "I don't know anything about it." But when he saw the determined, impassive faces in front of him, he conceded, "Well, I know a little."

"We know the whole story so you might as well come clean."

"I guess you're right," the man confessed, playing with a still-coiled streamer that he had brought with him from the club. "I shoulda known that you wouldn't have picked me up if you were just guessing. But you cops are all the same, always picking on me."

He then launched into a long tale, the gist of which was that, as a young man, he was constantly being leaned on by a particular policeman whose beat ran through his neighborhood. The policeman was forever bringing him in on truancy charges and eventually got him sent to the Lyman State Reformatory, where he really fell in with a bad crowd and learned all kinds of criminal tricks. Thanks to the neighborhood cop, he became a housebreaker and a cheat.

For a while Connolly and Doherty humored him and let his tirade against the police run its course, but eventually, they brought his attention back to the matter at hand.

"Let's talk about current things."

"I know how they get the checks out of Deer Island. I'll tell you the whole story."

Connolly and Doherty concealed their surprise as well as they could as their man began spilling the particulars on the check-forging gang that was operating out of the House of Correction. Doherty just bit a little harder on the cigar that was always jammed in the side of his mouth. Connolly looked down at papers on the desk so that his eyes wouldn't reveal his shock and elation.

They had gone fishing for information about a paper factory payroll holdup and stumbled upon a detailed confession about an interstate operation, in which bad checks were being passed all over the East Coast and as far west as St. Louis. With the names and addresses provided, the Boston Police together with the FBI were able to expose the members of the ring.

Apparently the scheme was conceived by Paul E. Johnson, a 23-year-old man from Everett with a long record of passing checks that he sometimes forced people to cash at gunpoint. In June, 1956, Johnson had escaped from a maximum security lockup at Boston Municipal Court, where he had been arraigned on charges of check forging and carrying a gun.

When he was recaptured several weeks later, he began serving a term at Deer Island. There, Johnson fell in with another master check man. Lawrence E. Campbell, 44, was a notorious South End character who earned himself the nickname "Paper Hanger" because of his ability to make and foist off worthless checks. He had been in and out of prison for the past ten years for forging, among other things, medical prescriptions and social security cards. He was currently serving an 18-month sentence for larceny.

Recently Campbell had replaced a civilian employee who had been running the prison's ancient hand press on which cards and other forms for institutional use were routinely printed. When he entered Deer Island, Johnson had brought with him two stolen checks: one from a New England airline and the other from a world-wide steamship line. Using Johnson's checks as models, Campbell set up type to duplicate the originals.

But Johnson needed help from someone with access to the outside — an easily corrupted screw. He found the man he needed in guard James Griffin, a fellow resident of Everett who was looking for a way to supplement his $81.25 a week paycheck.

Griffin smuggled in blank check paper stock and delivered it to an intermediary, who passed it on to Campbell. When "Paper Hanger" had run off a good quantity of checks, they were wrapped up as packages and sent back through the intermediary to Griffin.

The guard then smuggled the checks out of the prison and delivered them to relatives of Johnson's. When Johnson was released on December 27, he was free to retrieve the packages of checks from his folks and organized a band of men and women to help him to spread the bogus checks.

Johnson was careful; he didn't get too greedy. None of the checks that he wrote was for more than $100. Nevertheless, as the checks began to bounce, the airline and steamship companies became more and more concerned and presented the FBI agents they had called in with a stack of about 70 bad checks.

The agents immediately recognized a resemblance between this rash of phony checks and a 1949 case that they had cracked in which counterfeit social security cards were used to pass off the checks. The man behind the social security card ploy was "Paper Hanger" Campbell. Initially, the FBI was stymied when they discovered that Campbell was still serving an 18-month stint in Deer Island, but a little further investigation and the information from Connolly and Doherty revealed that Campbell was operating a press and was linked to Johnson and the outside world through his own guard-and-inmate courier service.

Once the pieces were all in place, the authorities moved in on the inmate, the guard, the check passer and his four assistants, including an attractive brunette who was trying to earn money to get back to St. Louis.

"Paper Hanger" was moved away to an isolation cell while the investigation proceeded. The guard Griffin called in sick, but this weak maneuver did not prevent Penal Commissioner Edward Friel from suspending him. Griffin had to face a Civil Service trial board as well as regular court proceedings.

13

Good Gypsy, Bad Gypsy

Sergeant Connolly released the trigger and shook the nozzle.

"Don't want to waste a drop of gas," he thought. "Taxpayers got enough expenses with this crazy department."

He replaced the nozzle on the pump at the entrance to the garage of Station 4 on Warren Avenue in the South End. He was scouting the street for a place to park when he spotted a swarthy man in a wide Panama hat, green coat and yellow pants waving wildly at him and calling, "Hey, Sergeant . . . Help!"

The startled sergeant walked a few paces down the inclined driveway to meet the dark-complected man, who charged blindly through the traffic to meet him.

"My wife has been raped!" he gasped as out of breath he stood before Connolly.

"Where is she now?"

"In my store on Tremont Street," he answered, still panting, "She was savagely raped and beaten."

"By who?"

"Johnny Oliviera. He comes from New York City. He's a gypsy like me. He's my cousin."

"How long ago did it happen?"

"Last night. Around two in the morning."

"It's almost noon. Why didn't you call the police before now?"

"Sergeant, you know gypsies don't call the police. We take care of things in our own way."

Connolly's eyes narrowed.

"What's you name?"

"Walter Oliviera."

"Okay, I tell you what, Walter. I'll get an ambulance, and we'll take your wife to the hospital for treatment and examination."

Oliviera looked puzzled and a little uneasy.

"What examination?"

"Examination to see if she has been raped," said Connolly, getting a little impatient with this character. "You know, the doctor has to look into her privates to see if there is any sperm up there to show that intercourse has taken place recently."

"Oh, yeah. I understand. Now I know what you're talking about. But, Sergeant, can't you just arrest Johnny? I don't want no doctor looking at my wife's insides. Can't we just skip that part?"

"No way."

Walter considered this piece of news in silence for a moment.

"Give me a description of Johnny. Does he have a car?"

"No. He came from New York by plane yesterday. He's 26 years old. Black hair and brown eyes like all gypsies. He's a little bit shorter than me, and he's real skinny."

"What was he wearing?" Connolly asked, scribbling the description on a rumpled pad that he found in his pocket.

"He's a real flashy dresser."

Connolly contemplated the man's green jacket and yellow pants, but refrained from making any wisecracks.

"I think he was wearing a really sharp purple linen suit," Walter continued, "with white shoes and a flowered shirt."

"OK, Walter," Connolly said, flipping his pad shut and stuffing it into another pocket, "we'd better pick up your wife and get her over to the hospital."

"That's alright, Sergeant. I can get her. It's just across the street. I'll get her. You stay right here. I'll be right back with her in five minutes."

"Look, Walter. I'm not hanging around on the street waiting for you. I gotta park my car before I cause an accident in this garage. Then I'm heading for my office. I'll be on the second floor. Just ask for the Detectives' Room."

"Detectives' Room," he nodded with a nervous grin.

"Make it snappy, will you? I have to type out a report on this matter."

"Don't worry. It won't take me long. I'll get Matilda . . . that's my wife's name. We'll be right back."

"Before you go, one more thing. Where do you think Johnny is now?"

"Probably at my cousin's store on Mass. Ave. near the railroad bridge. You know, the gypsy store."

Oliviera charged across Tremont Street towards his store; Connolly climbed back into his cruiser and headed for a spot that he noticed had opened up during the conversation. Minutes later he was in the Detective's Room preparing the report and putting a wanted out for Johnny Oliviera.

It was 12:24 pm when he sat down at an empty desk to type the report. By 1:00, however, there was still no sign of Walter or his wife.

"What the hell happened?" Connolly thought. "Maybe he met up with Johnny and got into a fight. Next thing you know, we'll have a stabbing or a shooting or some damn thing. These gypsies are serious about their women being violated."

When his watch showed 1:20, Connolly decided to get a car and a crew together and head over to the Tremont Street shop to see what new crime of passion had been committed. He was trotting down the stairs when he nearly collided with Walter, who was sweating even more profusely than the first time he had met him. The gypsy's shirt was soaked through and clung to his chest in several spots.

When Walter finished wiping his brow with a huge, grimy handkerchief and replaced the Panama on his head, Connolly noticed a woman trailing a few steps behind Oliviera. The region around her left eye was beginning to swell, and blood was seeping out of a cut in her upper lip.

"This is Matilda, my wife," Walter said cheerily, waving his hat in her direction. When Connolly studied her, he saw that she was a few years younger than Walter, but considerably heavier. She packed about 200 pounds on her five feet. Her loud, low-cut blouse plainly revealed that much of her weight was contained in her flabby breasts.

As another officer passed them in the congested stairwell, Walter suggested in a low voice, "Sergeant, let's go where we can talk in private."

Connolly led the couple to the Detective's Room, which was always vacant in the afternoon, and closed the door.

"What took you so long?"

"I wanted to make sure that everything was alright with Matilda," Walter replied, casting what he hoped looked like a solicitous glance at his unhappy-looking spouse.

Oliviera fished around in his pocket and dropped a crumpled bill on the blotter.

"Here, Sergeant. Here's fifty bucks for your trouble. Johnny, he's up at the Mass. Avenue store, and Matilda is ready to be examined."

Matilda looked even more uncomfortable than ever.

"Keep your fifty," Connolly growled. His suspicions now became a conviction that all was not kosher with this case.

"Sergeant, please arrest Johnny before he goes back to New York," Walter pleaded. "He's a bad gypsy."

"Let's talk about something else first. What took you so long to go across the street and get your wife?"

"Well, Sergeant, I had to get her ready for the doctor to examine her?"

"What do you mean, 'ready'?"

"I had to give her a quick lay . . . to get some sperm inside her for the doctor to look at."

"What about that black eye? How come her lip's still bleeding if this rape happened last night?"

"We'll say Johnny did it. You want a hundred, sergeant? OK, you got it. Believe me that Johnny is a bad gypsy. Anyhow, Matilda will tell the judge that it was Johnny who hit her."

"Walter, you are a first-class motherfucker," Connolly exploded. "I got a room downstairs for you. You'll have plenty of time to think of how you're gonna explain to the judge the difference between a good gypsy and a bad gypsy."

Connolly marched the protesting man down to the desk to be booked and placed in a cell; then he helped Matilda find a phone to arrange the bail.

As she was about to leave, she turned to Connolly, her earrings jingling softly.

"Walter is a good gypsy," she said tearfully, "and that Johnny is a bad gypsy."

Connolly watched her leave the station and considered for a few minutes.

"Maybe I'd better take a ride to Mass. Ave and check out that bad gypsy after all . . . now that the good gypsy is behind bars."

Outside Station 4 at night.

14

Puppy Love

"I don't believe it!"

"You'd better believe it 'cause it's true!" Sergeant Connolly whispered.

Patrolman Sandy McPherson stood there in the lobby of District 4, studying Connolly's face to determine whether the story he had just heard was merely some sort of obscene practical joke that the sergeant was trying to pull off.

"Look, you don't have to take my word," Connolly continued, speaking in the same hushed tones. Then he waved his thumb in the direction of a woman leaning against the smooth marble wall not five feet away. "Does she look like a person that would make up a story like this?"

McPherson murmured, "I dunno . . ."

"Hey, lady," Connolly called, raising his voice to address the prim-looking older woman with sharp features, "I mean, Mrs. . . . uh . . ."

"It's Miss Irwin."

"That's right. I remember now," Connolly said. "I hate to ask you to do this, but would you go over the story you told me so this officer can get the details firsthand from you?"

"I heard you speaking to him, Sergeant Connolly. Officer, I hope you don't think I would ever use the kind of language that the sergeant used with you!"

"Certainly not, ma'am," McPherson said, bobbing his head.

"Well," said Mrs. Irwin, the disapproving frown on her face softening a bit, "I live on West Newton Street, between Tremont Street and Shawmut Avenue. The block is now inhabited mostly by Hispanic persons."

"I know the area," McPherson said, nodding.

In the Gay Nineties when the South End had been a fashionable place to live, the three-story red brick townhouses in the blocks that Miss Irwin had mentioned were elegant dwellings. However, until recently the area had been in decline, and the fine homes had been converted into apartments and rooming and lodging houses for low-income, minority families.

Miss Irwin cleared her throat, hesitating before she came to her point.

"I have a neighbor . . . Ellie Kelly. She lives at #94. She's a heavy drinker. Always in trouble with the neighbors — both white and Hispanic . . . because of her acts, unnatural acts, every evening."

"Tell the officer what kind of 'acts,' Miss Irwin," Connolly coaxed trying to suppress a smile at her discomfiture.

"Well, every evening about five o'clock she sits on the top step of her front stairs with her dog . . . ."

"Tell the officer what she does with the dog."

She closed her eyes, turned her head to the side and made herself say it, "She has sexual intercourse with the dog . . . in front of everybody. The P.R.s are all at the windows, yelling at her. The traffic is backed up in the street with people watching. She doesn't care who sees her!"

"It's hard to believe," McPherson said.

"It's disgusting, That's what it is. It would make a respectable person sick to their stomach to see that kind of filth."

"But are you sure about what you saw? Maybe she was just playing with her dog . . . you know, wrestling," Connolly said, setting her up for the self-incrimination he knew would come.

"Of course, I'm sure. I watch her every day of the week. I know the difference between patting a dog and . . . and . . . sexual intercourse."

"I should hope so, Mrs. Irwin."

"Miss Irwin!" she reminded him sharply.

Miss Irwin was becoming suspicious that the two officers were laughing up their sleeves at her.

"Now," she sniffed, "what are you going to do about this disgrace?"

"I tell you what, Miss Irwin. The next time your friend is . . . "

"Ellie is not my friend," she insisted indignantly.

"The next time your neighbor is out there with her dog, you call the station directly, and we'll get right over there."

"I most certainly will call, and I'll expect you to come right away, or I'll call the *Globe*."

Out the door she sailed without a good-bye or a thank you.

"We appreciate your cooperation," McPherson called after her.

"Just jealous," Connolly commented. "She needs what the dog is giving Ellie Kelly."

"Probably gets her cookies off just watching."

"Still we're going to have to do something about this Kelly broad and her canine stud one of these nights."

Two days later Miss Irwin rang District 4, triumphantly announcing, "Ellie Kelly is engaged in sex!"

The clerk who answered the phone replied, "Aren't we all sometime someplace?"

"Don't get fresh with me. All you police think you are so funny. You would rather make smutty jokes than lift a finger to protect the morals of the people who pay your salaries. So stop that sniggering and put me through to Sergeant Connolly this instant."

The clerk faked a contrite tone of voice. "I'm really sorry about that, Miss. I'll get the sergeant for you right away."

He flicked a switch so his message would go booming over the intercom system throughout the building. "Sergeant Connolly, pick up line three. Personal call from a lady who wants to talk with you about sex. Sergeant Connolly, line three."

By the time, Eddie punched the flashing button on the phone, Miss Irwin had had more than enough of police humor.

"Yes, ma'am. I'm on my way," he said and tossed the receiver back into its cradle. He grabbed his cap and ran out the front door. Eddie McMahon and Donald Varnerin, two night officers who had just come on duty, were standing by their car in front of the station.

"What is it, Sarge?" Varnerin called.

"Take me up to 84 West Newton Street in a hurry," Connolly said, breathlessly, yanking a rear door open.

"What you got?" asked McMahon as he slid into the driver's seat, "A shooting?"

"No, a dog screwing a woman."

"A what?"

"You heard me. A dog screwing a woman. Let's go."

With Eddie McMahon at the wheel, Connolly in back and Varnerin riding shotgun, the cruiser pulled up in front of 94 West Newton Street within three minutes.

Like most of the houses on the block, #94 was shabby with neglect, but retained the elegance of its original design. The wide flight of brownstone steps was graced by an ornate wrought iron railing, and the carved entrance door to the hall was flanked by two thin windows, which had been covered with metallic contact paper.

A crowd had gathered at the foot of the stairs to enjoy the spectacle. The Puerto Ricans were laughing and making coarse remarks in Spanish. Traffic in the street was almost at a complete standstill, with both drivers and passengers craning their necks for a better view.

On both sides of the streets, curtains had been drawn back, and two to four heads jockeyed for the best position at every window. Some women were trying to pull their boyfriends or husbands away from the scene, but most of the men were cheering and joking with one another. Miss Irwin kept her window shut and glared down at the policemen as they tried to get out of the cruiser.

"Better get another car over here," Connolly said, and Varnerin radioed in the order. Patrolmen John Molineaux and George Bishop were dispatched immediately.

As the officers made their way through the throng, they too became the butt of the crowd's humor.

"The pigs want to get rid of the dog so they can get a little action."

"Ellie wouldn't look twice at any of them. They ain't hung like that hound of hers."

The sight of Ellie Kelly sprawled on the brownstone landing was anything but sexy. She had hiked her ratty shift up under her breasts; from lower torso to toes she was stark naked. She wiggled her sooty feet in air as she clasped the panting dog. The handsome black and brown German shepherd mix had a hard time keeping his balance as his front paws were planted on her huge, wobbling beer belly; his hind legs were shuffling constantly on the steps as he tried to steady himself.

The animal's bright red penis pumped in and out of his flabby mistress while the creature turned its head excitedly from side to side to observe the noisy crowd that was cheering him on.

Connolly tugged the 60-pound mutt from Ellie's embrace, while the other two officers pulled her dress down and tried to get her on her feet.

"Show's over," they called to the crowd. "Go home."

Immediately a chorus of boos and catcalls rose up.

Ellie was stinking drunk and didn't take kindly to this coitus interruptus. She flailed away at the officers and raked her nails across their cheeks and the fronts of their uniform jackets.

"Leave me alone, you bastards. I'm not finished yet. You have no right to bother me. I live here."

Her canine lover came to her rescue. Still huffing and puffing and still fully erect, the shepherd kept snarling at the policemen and making feints at their pant legs.

John Molineux finally wrestled the snapping animal into the area between the outer and inner doors of the house and sprayed Mace in the dog's face, but the chemical only seemed to enrage him even more. John narrowly escaped into the building; the wildly barking shepherd had trapped him indoors and effectively cut off rescue by his partners, who were struggling with Ellie and the angry crowd outside.

Ed McMahon radioed the Animal Rescue League to come to dispose of the now-savage dog, while Connolly and the other men from Station Four hustled the equally overexcited Kelly woman into the back of the wagon. The crowd deeply resented the interference of the police in this neighborhood ritual, and they showed their displeasure by hurling bottles of various sizes and brown shopping bags of garbage along with verbal abuse in English and Spanish at the officers.

Finally a team from the Animal Rescue League appeared with their van and dog-catching equipment. The AR men had quite a time getting the loop around the mongrel's throat; one man was bitten rather badly. Nevertheless, they did manage to capture and confine him, still barking violently, in their van. So the dog was whisked off to the animal shelter, and Ellie, to her cage in District 4.

Connolly sympathized with the poor dog, that, after all, had merely been the instrument of Ellie's lust and exhibitionism. He called the shelter and made sure that no attempt was made to destroy the dog until the matter had been decided by the court.

Upon arraignment in Boston Municipal Court, Ellie Kelly was committed by Judge Roberts to Bridgewater State Mental Hospital for 30 days observation, but her canine accomplice was sentenced (without benefit of a trial by a jury of his peers) to death.

15

Thou Shalt Not Kill Thy Father

Police officers Joe Pocaro and Ed Burke in the 4-R car were cruising up Shawmut Avenue in the South End enjoying a warm spring day in 1965. Many local residents and street people were out basking in the sun. As the cruiser whisked by Blackstone Park, the winos sprawled on the benches gave a nod of recognition to the officers. Addicts stared dully into space, dreaming of their next fix.

Suddenly the police radio crackled into life. "4-R car, 4-R car, man with shotgun at 518 Shawmut Avenue . . ."

Pocaro, the observer in the car, acknowledged the call and at the same time snapped on the blue light and siren. Burke remarked, "It's the next block, Joey."

The cruiser bounced off the curb as the car jerked to a halt on the left side of the road. Burke and Pocaro bounded out of the vehicle and onto the sidewalk. With guns drawn, the men charged into the building and began galloping up the narrow staircase three steps at a time.

Screeching around the corner of Massachusetts Avenue into Shawmut right up to 518 was Eddie Connolly, their sergeant-detective in District 4, along with Detectives Gagan and Hoban. Dressed in plainclothes, they rolled out of their unmarked car, hurried up the stoop and ventured into the semidarkness of the stairwell, noting the smell of smokeless powder that permeated the dead air.

Halfway up the stairs, the officers slowed down, gathering themselves into a crouch behind the rickety bannister. They peered into the darkness, straining to detect the least sound. Then there came the low moan of a dying man, a sound that was unmistakable to the policemen who had heard it so many times before.

Since the steep stairs offered no cover, Pocaro began to pull himself up onto the top landing, but his hand brushed against the sticky wetness of the body that lay there groaning.

"This is the police. Come out with your hands up!" Burke barked as he hit the landing and hugged the wall for the little protection that it offered.

Connolly knelt near the dying man whom, even in the darkness, he made out to be black and elderly. The victim's short corduroy jacket didn't conceal the enormous bare paunch that hung over his stained pants. The floor was littered with chunks of plaster that had fallen from the ceiling and made little crunching sounds as the officers crept closer.

All three police .38 specials were cocked and aimed at the door to the single apartment on the landing.

"Come out with your hands up!"

"Please don't shoot," came the response from behind the door. The voice was fragile; it was the voice of a female, white, young and terrified.

"Open that door and keep your hands up!" Connolly shouted.

It was stiflingly hot in the hallway, and the gasping man on the floor was still oozing a tremendous amount of blood that felt thick and gluey under the officers' shoes.

The sounds of activity that filtered up from the floors below indicated that more reinforcements from District 4 were arriving.

Connolly called down to the lead man below. "Don't come up yet. Have the ambulance to stand by. I think the victim was hit with a shotgun. It's pretty messy up here."

As he was talking the door opened, spilling sunlight onto the landing. The moaning had subsided, but blood continued to flow from what was left of the 60-year-old black man's face and chest.

"Now, come up!" Connolly yelled into the stairwell. The silhouette of a young woman trembled as she stood framed in the bright light of the doorway.

"Don't shoot me," the female's voice pleaded. "Please, don't shoot me."

"We won't," Burke promised.

"Not you," she whimpered. "Him."

She gestured to a young black man standing in the room off to the left, with a shotgun in his hand. At that moment Big Jim Welch and John Caulfield along with the ambulance crew were just reaching the landing. Welch, a 25-year veteran of the force, threw all 265 pounds of his weight into a charge that sent Connolly, Burke, Pocaro and the girl all tumbling into the apartment. The only one left on his feet was Welch; right behind him was Caulfield, a quiet man, another officer with 25 years of experience to his credit.

Before the young black man could raise the shotgun, Welch threw his best Sunday punch, and Caulfield snatched the weapon out of his hand.

Before the three officers and the woman had gotten back on their feet, Welch had the suspect handcuffed and lying on the floor.

"Hey, Sergeant, here's your man," Welch laughed. "John and myself were on our lunch break when we heard the call. Is it alright if we go back and finish our sandwiches at Harvey's . . . or do you need any more help?"

"No thanks, Jim and John," Sergeant Connolly replied sheepishly as he watched the two leave the apartment and step over the body in the hall.

"By the way," Welch called over his shoulder. "This dead guy's name is Gus. The guy with the shotgun is his son, Terry. I used to walk this route, and I know both of them. I never knew them to be in trouble. Most likely it's a fight over the white broad."

The ambulance crew had stopped working on Gus, and Dr. Matthew Lappin pronounced him dead.

"You better call the Homicide Squad," the doctor ordered. "I'll get a hold of the ME"

"OK, Doc," Connolly answered, but glancing around the apartment he saw no phone. He left Burke and Pocaro to guard the scene and take custody of the premises, while he and Lappin went in search of a phone.

As they crossed Shawmut Avenue to a local variety store at the corner of East Springfield Street, Connolly sighed, "Doc, we may have trouble making a call here."

"Why?"

"You'll see."

An old black man, who seemed half asleep as he sat on an empty milk crate, recognized Connolly from 20 yards away. He scrambled into the store, slammed the door, and locked it with such force that the glass shattered and fell in pieces onto the sidewalk and the shoes of Connolly and Lappin.

The black fellow was pushing his body against the door to reinforce the lock.

"Open this fuckin' door," Connolly shouted.

"I can't," the man called back.

"You better, or I'll blow the lock off and you with it."

"Gabe wants to know if you have a warrant," the doorkeep countered.

"Tell Gabe to open this door, or I'll make a parking lot out of this whole corner!"

"Who's Gabe?" the doctor wanted to know.

"What the hell do you think they're selling here? This is a bookie joint, and Gabe is the friendly neighborhood bookie," Connolly informed the physician. Then raising his voice, he called into the store, "I have a murder across the street. This is the only public phone around, and I'm going to use it."

"Oh, it's you, Sergeant Connolly. We didn't recognize you at first without your uniform . . . ."

"Sure you didn't. That's why you asked me if I had a warrant."

As they waited while the door was unlocked and slowly opened, Connolly joked, "Time to put your gas mask on, Doctor."

"What?"

"You'll see."

As the two men entered, they could barely distinguish the canned goods, pies, cakes and other items through the clouds of smoke.

"What's burning?" Lappin coughed.

"Bookie slips."

"Where's the phone?"

"The farthest place from the door . . . in back of the store . . . somewhere behind this electrically controlled gate . . . There it is. Behind the counter, next to buckets of burning papers."

A large, impeccably dressed white man stepped out of the back room and courteously tipped his stylish, wide-brimmed hat to Connolly, "Hello, Sergeant."

"This is Gabe — our local Mr. Nicely-Nicely. Gabe, this is Dr. Lappin, the police doctor. We have a fuckin' murder cross the street, and we need a telephone to notify a lot of people including the DA and the ME."

"I can't have people just barging in here without . . ." Gabe began.

Connolly's voice rose sharply, "You're denying the police the use of the phone, and you committed arson!"

"But, Eddie," Gabriel answered in a genuinely polite tone, "with all the robberies in the area, I have to be cautious about strangers . . . ."

"Fuck you," Connolly growled. "Besides, I'll have you indicted for interfering with a medical doctor in the performance of his duties."

"Right, Sergeant," Lappin nodded, suppressing a smile.

Beads of sweat appeared under the large brim, and Gabe ceremoniously gestured to the telephone.

"Come on, Doc. Let's make our calls and get the hell outta here. Too much damn smoke."

After placing the necessary calls to the Medical Examiner, the District Attorney and others, Connolly and the doctor left the store and discussed the operation as they walked back to 518 Shawmut.

"What a strange setup he's got there," Lappin said, shaking his head, "A well-stocked store, a deli case full of cold cuts and yet he's booking numbers and horses to make a living."

"The bookie business is all profit or all loss—most of the time it's all profit," the sergeant explained, "Gabe has been a bookie for 20 years. He's been arrested. People who work for him have been arrested time and time again. But the courts let them off with a fine and they're back in business."

"A nice guy like Gabe," he continued, "all the people in the neighborhood here love him. They play their numbers and the horses; he doesn't cheat them. Hell, they even borrow money from him. Most cops know who he is and what he is, but it's hard to get evidence against him. Everytime I ever went in there, there was always smoke. He trusts no strangers and no cops. Not even for a phone call."

The sight of double-parked police cars on the narrow street had drawn a gaggle of people.

"Hey, Sarge," a young clerk from a Mass. Ave. hardware store called out. "What you got — a shooting or a cutting?"

"No comment, Lewis," Connolly replied tersely as he disappeared into the building. "Read it in the *Record*."

When they reached the top of the stairs, there was a man dressed in black with a clerical collar and a straw farmer's hat intoning prayers over the body.

Under his breath Pocaro informed the sergeant, "There have been four colored ministers up here since you left. This one makes number five."

"Five?" Connolly said. "This guy has to go to heaven."

Inside the apartment on a bed with a filthy, rancid mattress sat the son Terry and his girlfriend, Sharon. The floor in front of their feet was strewn with empty wine bottles and crumpled newspapers. As soon as Connolly walked in, Terry decided to make conversation.

"Sergeant, I'm going to marry Sharon, so I have to protect her at all times. You know that, Sarge."

"Terry," Connolly replied, "we are waiting for the homicide people from headquarters. If you want to make any statements, they will record it. You understand that you're under arrest."

Terry nodded. "I know I'm in trouble. I shot him."

In walked Sergeant Detective Jack Barry of the Homicide Squad. His sparkling blue eyes and baby-smooth complexion complemented his quiet, effective manners. His years of topnotch police work lent him an air of authority without his seeming bossy.

"Hi, Jack," Connolly said.

"Hi. I saw him on the way in. The ME been here?"

"No, but Dr. Lappin pronounced him."

Behind Barry trooped Detective Joseph Daily and Police Stenographer George Godfrey; the room was now getting crowded. Detective Frank Carpenito, the police photographer, stayed out in the hall, waiting for the Medical Examiner to arrive, complete his examination and officially order him to photograph the scene and the body.

Soon Dr. Richard Ford arrived, a tall man who habitually wore a cowboy hat. He bent over the corpse and gently probed the skin around the jaw and chest. Detective Frank Bailey, the department ballistician, handed him a wheat light, a large lamp, which Ford accepted without looking up from the body.

The doctor stood up and signaled Carpenito to start taking photos from various angles while he waited out of view of the camera. Then the ME was on his knees again and with the help of Daily and Bailey, he turned the big-bellied Gus on his side. Underneath the victim they discovered a tiny jackknife with an open one-inch blade, which glinted briefly as Carpenito flashed a picture of it.

The Dr. Ford gingerly placed the knife in a plastic bag, tagged it and handed it to Detective Jim Bickerton for evidence.

Meanwhile Sgt. Barry had informed Terry of his rights, and the stenographer stood at his elbow recording each question and answer in his notebook.

Terry stated that his father was drunk and had made several attempts to get into the apartment and bother his girlfriend. Finally, the old man managed to snap the chain lock off the door and barged in, brandishing the preposterously small one-inch blade.

Terry had simply pulled the 12-gauge shotgun from its hiding place behind the bed and fired a single shot at his dad, hitting him in the chest and the jaw. Gus stumbled backwards into the hall where he collapsed.

Connolly was intrigued as to how this neatly dressed but rather common-looking Jewish girl came to be living in a tenement.

"What are you doing here?"

"Well, this is my boyfriend . . ."

"How did he become your boyfriend?"

"My psychiatrist told me to get out and meet people. I stayed at home too much, he said, and that I should meet more people."

By now it was clear that the young woman was not mentally stable.

"How did you meet Terry?"

"I was walking down the street one day. I said hello to him and he said hello to me, and we started talking. He asked me if I wanted a cup of coffee. I said yes. He said that he lived close by so we went to his house for the cup of coffee."

"And this is the place he brought you to?" Connolly asked, gesturing to the floor covered with empty beer and wine bottles.

"Yes, and I've spent the last couple of days here with him."

"What's your psychiatrist's name?"

She told him.

"Do you think he was right to tell you to meet people?"

"Oh, yes. I like to meet people. I like to talk to them."

"Well, you know, you don't talk to people and meet them under these conditions . . . just living in a house with a strange man all of a sudden . . ."

"But Terry is very nice to me. It's his father who gets mad when Terry brings me in this room. His father wanted to come in this room with me, but Terry said no. He was just protecting me."

"Give me the telephone number of your father."

Sharon's father met them at the station, accompanied by a lawyer. The father was extremely worried when he heard the situation she was in. Connolly advised him to get the girl to a doctor right away to make sure she hadn't contracted a venereal disease.

"The next thing to do is to straighten out that psychiatrist of hers. A backward girl like her shouldn't be given that kind of advice. You can take her home now, but we may need her tomorrow morning for the arraignment."

The next day Terry was arraigned in Boston Municipal Court before Chief Justice Elijah Adlow. As an indigent, Terry was represented by a court-appointed lawyer, and the case was postponed.

A week later, the case came to trial. Connolly and Barry outlined the case to Judge Adlow for probable cause to hold Terry for the Grand Jury. The government witnesses, the photographer, the ballistician, and the Medical Examiner all testified. Terry and Sharon told their stories.

Finally Judge Adlow rose and went to the table where the evidence was displayed. With one hand he hefted the 12-gauge shotgun; with the other he held the one-inch jackknife.

Adlow meditated for a while, then looking from the Assistant District Attorney to the defense attorney, he remarked, "This was a family squabble . . . not a murder! No probable cause. Defendant dismissed."

Connolly exchanged glances with Barry. They knew better than to get excited about what they might imagine to be a miscarriage of justice. Their job was to apprehend suspects and deliver them to the court's doorstep. There was no percentage in getting involved emotionally in the outcome of these matters.

Out in the corridor, Connolly heard Terry's voice. "Hey, Sergeant, wait a minute . . ."

"What is it?"

"When can I get that shotgun back? My daddy gave that to me."

"Drop by the station tomorrow," Connolly said curtly and pushed his way into the crowded elevator, not bothering to look back.

16

"Who Could Do That to Their Own Baby?"

The men of the Drug Control Unit did not interact solely with adults. A plainclothes detective's job is not all shoot-outs and shakedowns, pimps and prostitutes, dope peddlars and underworld czars as much of the public imagines it is.

Sometimes the Drug Squad ran across people who did terrible things to their own offspring — sexual assaults, maimings, murders, and other heartless acts. Like any other compassionate human being, Eddie Connolly could never fathom how mothers and fathers could be so cruel to their own flesh and blood. Over the years, though, he learned to act swiftly when there was the least suspicion of child abuse.

There are hundreds of personal tragedies involving children that never become a story in the morning paper or a spot on the 6 or 11 o'clock telecasts. Even the media people have the decency to spare some families the indignity of ballyhooing the mistreatment of a tiny child.

When the phone rang, the chatter and the story-telling didn't stop. Bob Ryan reached over with his right hand and brought the receiver to his ear and used the index finger of his left to block out some of the noise.

"Drug Control."

At 250 lbs., 6'2" Bob was the big man of the unit. An ex-Marine, he had scars all over his body, mementoes of the action he had seen at the 38th parallel in Korea, but he was not one to brag.

Bill Currier, a New Hampshire farm boy who had 20 years experience on the Vice and Narcotics Squad, and his fellow detective Arthur Linsky were telling Eddie Simmons about a screw-up they had been involved in the other night. They kept right on laughing their way through the story as Ryan scribbled an address on a notepad.

"Whatcha got, Ryan?" Lieutenant Connolly asked.

"Complaint about possible drug trafficking over at Lenox Street. You wanna come along?"

"Sure, Why not? I ain't got nothing better to do."

"We'll all go along," squad boss Frank Coleman said. So the whole gang of them piled into three cars and headed for the housing project.

When they found the right entryway, they started to quiet down. Up the cramped stairwell the six men walked single file.

Second floor, Apartment 204 to the left. Bill Currier gently turned the knob, but no luck, the door was locked. Like most housing project doors, this one was steel-encased with two or three deadbolts on the inside to keep out the crooks and the cops.

It appeared they would just have to wait until someone exited. They felt kind of foolish, a half dozen men crowding on the landing and sitting on the stairs. They all prayed no one on the upper floors would want to use the stairs because the presence of so many white men would be sure to arouse suspicion. It would be easy enough for a neighbor to alert the occupants of 204 that a bunch of guys with crewcuts were camped outside their door.

Fortunately, it wasn't too long before they heard the bolts slide back. The men instinctively moved and poised themselves to pounce. As soon as the young male had the door halfway open, Ryan and Currier slammed passed him into the apartment. Eddie Simmons was right behind them. Coleman and Connolly were left with the job of picking the man off the floor and searching him.

Coleman threw him up against the wall and found a few decks of heroin and a set of works in his right pants pocket.

In one of the bedrooms, Currier and Ryan discovered a prostitute and john between some green-striped sheets.

"Out of the sack, you two," Ryan ordered.

"What the fuck do you think you're doing busting into my bedroom like this?" Katie fumed.

Her trick was completely naked, but he crawled out from under the covers. He seemed very embarrassed at his predicament and looked longingly at the tangle of clothes he had shed on Katie's tangerine-colored throw rug. While Currier was going through his pockets, the john tried to shield his genitals with his hands, but Ryan said, "Show us your arms."

An inspection of the john's anatomy showed no sign of tracks. Currier threw his clothes at him. "Put your pants on and get the hell outta here!"

They turned their attention to Katie, who had wrapped herself in a ratty-looking quilted bathrobe. She was demanding to be searched by a matron and threatening to sue.

Meanwhile, Simmons had discovered two men and a woman in the kitchen. They were bent over the gas-burners of the stove, cooking up heroin in bottle caps. There was plenty of evidence to arrest these three, but the men decided to go through the rest of the apartment for more evidence. All they could come up with was two bundles of heroin, 50 decks. It was nothing much, just what you might expect to find in a trick pad.

However, in a tiny, stuffy back bedroom, Simmons found two more addicts obviously in the throes of withdrawal. Their noses were running. Their brows were beaded with sweat. Their diapers and sheets were smeared with diarrhea. One baby was white and seemed to be about four months old. The other infant was a light-skinned black, a little younger.

Questioning revealed that the white child belonged to the girl in the kitchen, the occupant of the apartment. She was pretty, but the toll that the drugs were taking on her face and body was very apparent. She had no idea who the father of the child was. She had been using drugs heavily when the child was born, so naturally the baby came into the world an addict like his mom.

The baby was absolutely filthy. The load in its diapers indicated that he had not been changed in at least a day.

"You don't keep these children very clean," Connolly commented.

"I'm busy a lot," the mother replied, nervously taking a deep drag of a cigarette.

When Bob and Eddie tried to clean the little ones up a bit, they discovered cigarette burns all over the child's stomach and thighs.

"What's this, burning your own baby?"

"It was an accident."

"Get off it."

"My hands shake a lot. When I change the kid's diapers, I keep dropping my cigarette."

"Sure."

"First you bitch at me for not cleaning the kid up. Now you're hollering at me because I try to do it. You just can't win with you guys."

The black infant had been left with her by a couple of junkie friends who purchased the baby from its natural mother in front of the City Hospital Methadone Clinic for a bottle of methadone.

"Why did they buy the baby and then leave it with this bitch?" Connolly wondered aloud.

All Simmons could say looking at the two mistreated children was, "Who could do this to their own baby?"

Connolly and Ryan scrounged around for the least dirty sheets and blankets they could find. Then each man took a baby in his arms down to the cars. They were driven by Currier to Boston City Hospital. There the babies were treated for the burns and the withdrawal symptoms.

The wagon carted the adult addicts to District 2, where they were booked on various minor drug violations.

Thanks to excellent, compassionate treatment at City Hospital, the babies were weaned from their drug habit and put up for adoption by the state agency. Both kids eventually found decent homes.

Though there was not much anyone could do about straightening out the lives of the addicts and whores, at least the life of one black baby and one white baby had been saved by the timely response of the Drug Unit. Little achievements like that went along way toward encouraging the men as they doggedly fought the ever-increasing drug traffic in Boston.

An even more horrifying incident occurred a few years later in a project across town. Conditions in the South Boston apartment were cramped: three small rooms and a bath — hardly enough for Lillian, her husband, Earl, and their two small children. Lillian had been born in rural Virginia and only gotten as far as the sixth grade in school. She was bitter and unhappy about the lack of space and the lack of peace and quiet that she had enjoyed when she was young.

So every day, while Earl went off to work in a shoe factory in Roxbury, Lillian would sit and sob for hours. Her crying and neglect, of course, set the kids off too, so the neighbors had to put up with hour after hour of wailing from Lillian's apartment.

Several people had made attempts to become friends with her and find out what was wrong, but she rebuffed and ignored them. The neighbors became concerned that the children were kept indoors all day and were never taken out for fresh air, sunshine and exercise.

Finally, the incessant crying became unbearable. The neighbors alerted the police, who in turn notified the child welfare agency to look into the conditions in the home.

Before the investigation got underway, the neighbors called the police again, frantic with worry now that the crying had changed to chilling screams and hideous ravings.

In response to the call to DEvonshire 8-1212, the dispatcher sent uniformed officers from South Boston's District 6 to handle the problem. Overhearing the emergency call, Detectives John Doherty and Eddie Connolly also decided to respond.

When the squad car and the detectives' unmarked vehicle met at the scene, a woman, her face tense with concern, directed them to the third floor. Anyone with ears could tell it was the source of all the screaming.

Doherty was the first to reach the top landing. He attacked the door with one powerful rap. When there was no response instantly, he hit the wooden door with his massive shoulder, splintering the door as it flung open. Doherty was in first, followed by Connolly and the men in uniform.

Everyone's stomach churned in disbelieving horror at the carnage in the kitchen. The walls were spattered and splotched with red. The four-year-old sat in the middle of the floor, covered with blood, his tiny frame shaking uncontrollably with terror.

Lillian stood by the stove in her blood-soaked nightgown, screaming inarticulately. From her hands hung the legs and torso of what had been a naked baby boy, his head battered to almost nothing, blood still running from the hole where the neck was. She continued to bash the corpse against the wall, against the stove, against the table.

As she was swinging to strike the seated child with his brother's remains, anger overcame the officers' initial revulsion, and the two detectives sprang into action. In an instant Doherty had wrenched both the woman's arms behind her back as she squirmed, snarled and snapped at his face. Connolly, his skin prickling and shrinking back in horror, forced his hands to wrest the corpse away from his mother's clutch.

One of the patrolmen recovered sufficiently to have the presence of mind to fetch a blanket from one of the bedrooms and help Connolly wrap the headless body in it.

The other officer removed the four-year-old to the police car where neighbors brought damp towels and dishcloths to wipe the blood off his face and hands.

Lillian was thrown in the back of the detectives' vehicle and brought to Station 6 to be booked for murder. A doctor was summoned to examine her; he determined that she was mentally unstable. The baby's body was sent to the morgue only after the Medical Examiner viewed the scene and ordered the disposition of the corpse.

In the 60's, stories like this were considered too unspeakable to be reported by the press. At the hearing, the judge ordered Lillian into a mental hospital. Custody of the surviving son was given to Lillian's sister in Virginia.

Three or four years later, Lillian was released from the state hospital as sane. When she stood trial, she was found not guilty of murder by reason of insanity at the time of the crime. She promptly engaged the services of attorney Joseph McDonough to regain custody of her son.

Several attempts to reclaim the boy legally in both Massachusetts and Virginia courts failed. So she and Earl left Boston for a while and took a trip to Virginia. One afternoon they abducted the boy from the sister's home and took him back to Boston.

Connolly appeared in Civil Court as a witness for the sister in Virginia who wanted to thwart the new custody proceedings. Apparently, the old adage of "possession is nine-tenths of the law" applied, for Joe McDonough won the case, and the boy was handed over to his parents.

The three of them took off for New Hampshire, where Earl had found a position with another shoe factory up there. Connolly couldn't help wondering how the boy made out in life, after being battered with his brother's body, then forced to live with the "mother" who did this to him.

Sergeant-Detective Ed Connolly pins a Boston Police badge on his son William and welcomes him to the Department on June 20, 1966.

Daughter Irene admires the medal her father received at the Policeman's Ball May 10, 1959 while mother Irene looks on approvingly. (M. Leo Tierney, *Herald*)

Eddie counts the money seized during a 1973 drug raid in Roxbury.
(Ray Lussier, *Herald*)

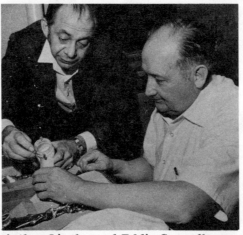

Arthur Linsky and Eddie Connolly examine manila envelopes containing cocaine and heroin, seized during a DCU
bust.   (Globe photo)

MEMBERS OF THE DRUG CONTROL UNIT

Tribute to Lieutenant Connolly, Red Coach Grill, December, 1975 on the occasion of his leaving the Drug Unit: *(left to right) First row:* Bill Currier, Bob Mack, Mario Potito, Tommy Maher, Reni Kennedy, George Peters, George Woods, Joe McKenna, Eddie Clark, Courtland Ballard. *Second row:* Willis Saunders, Al Frost, Walter "Mitty", Robinson, Arthur Linsky, John Gannon, John Burke, Ed Connolly, Joseph Jordan, Dennis Casey, Arnold White, Jack Parlon, Vinnie Logan. *Back row:* George Costigan, Jerry Dailey, James Chassion, Joe Smith, Peter O'Malley, Richard Ross, Herbert Spellman, Vincent Hayes.

Seeing the President and Mrs. Reagan off at Logan Airport.

Outside Our Lady of Good Voyage, Superintendent Ed Connolly poses with Mounted Officers Russell Fisher (l) and Tom Foley (r) after attending a special liturgy honoring the patron saint of policemen.

(Gene Dixon, *Herald*)

17

Operation One Block

At the end of October, 1967, the men at District Four began to notice an increase in the drug activity in the South End. Many young white people from sections of the city like East Boston were seen cruising through Hispanic and black neighborhoods, openly seeking drugs.

When Patrolmen Thomas Moran and Peter McDonough arrested a man on Tremont Street with 25 bags of heroin, everyone knew the situation was getting out of hand. As Sergeant Earl Crocker told the press, "When a uniformed patrolman in a marked car can make arrests on heroin, something's got to be drastically wrong."

Division 4 Captain Edward A. Doocey asked Detective Sergeant Connolly, Patrolman Moran, Sgt. Crocker and Detective Arthur Linsky of the Vice Squad to plan an undercover operation to clean up the area. Doocey ordered his patrolmen to ease up so that the covert narcotics investigation could proceed freely.

By the week of November 20, the details for "Operation One Block" were taking shape — a precedent-setting project involving the use of what was at that time high-technology equipment and a tremendous amount of unpaid overtime.

All day Wednesday, November 22, Thursday (Thanksgiving), November 23, and Friday, November 24, Tom Moran and Arthur Linsky observed the activity on the 600 block of Tremont Street in the South End. This area, bounded by West Canton, Dedham and Dartmouth Streets, seemed to be the center of a $10,000-a-day trade in narcotics run by Spanish-speakers.

The cops' outpost was the front windows of a second-story office and laboratory of a dental technician, known as Uncle Louie. Surrounded by bunsen burners, bridgeworks, braces and other dental paraphernalia, Linsky and Moran observed and recorded the drug sales from behind the shades, using binoculars.

Other officers on the opposite side of the road and on adjacent streets posed as streetcleaners, ambling along with their wheelbarrows and hokey-pokeys. They too noted the descriptions of the dealers and sellers as well as the make, model, and license plate number of the clients' cars in order to link buyer and seller. Sometimes they brushed so closed to a dealer that they could read the denominations of the bills being pulled out of the buyer's wallet.

Detective Francis P. Carpenito, a photographer from the Identification Unit, took black and white 8mm film of the deals being transacted on the sidewalk. One vantage point for filming street transactions was from a specially outfitted truck. Some smooth-talking cop had cajoled a used car dealer into donating an old brown Whiting's Milk truck to the cause. Holes were drilled into the back and sides of the vehicles. The eye level apertures were for the movie cameras; the lower ones served as urinals for officers confined inside for many hours at a time.

A driver would park the vehicle in a good spot in the morning and walk away. The cameramen inside would film all day long. They had to be quiet because an amazing number of nosy people came poking around, trying to find out what was in the apparently abandoned milk truck.

Meanwhile Patrolman Peter Ryan of the Intelligence Unit shot movies from another above street-level post. By the time the operation was finished, "there was enough film for a documentary."

While Moran and Linsky were gathering evidence to enable them to get search warrants for the houses of the suspected pushers, Connolly was marshalling the forces of the Department for the sweep planned for Saturday the 25th.

Given the almost constant flow of curbside business, Connolly knew that he would have to have dozens of officers to apprehend and book the customers and the dealers. He went around to the men in Division 4 and persuaded two captains and 27 officers to volunteer for the assignment. From the Vice Squad he got Captain Joseph M. Jordan and 22 of his officers; from the Identification and Intelligence Units, Eddie got the photographers he needed. In those pre-Union days, officers were willing to work overtime without any extra compensation. About half the men were night officers working the Saturday day shift on their own time.

A large number of men were needed for this operation because the planners decided that it was necessary to put three or four men in each car. All the driver could be expected to do was maneuver the vehicle. The other two or three officers had to be fast on their feet; they had to leap from the unmarked car, rip open the doors of the suspects' car, and immobilize all the passengers before any of them could dispose of the dope.

It was fairly easy to get willing and able men, but the success of the operation also depended on getting the unmarked cars belonging to the superior officers, for theirs were the only police cars at the time that had a radio with the frequency that could communicate with walkie-talkies. Connolly went to each of the men individually to borrow the vehicles for the Saturday sweep.

"Don't smash it up now," they would joke.

"Not too bad," Connolly would reply.

Each night after their regular tour of duty the core group met in the Detectives' Room to fine-tune plans for the 25th. Once Connolly had convinced all the superior officers to lend their cars, Sergeant Crocker decided where the unmarked cars would be deployed outside the immediate area of the 600 block. He also typed a master plan so everyone could carry a reminder of the details of the operation in his pocket.

On Friday evening there was a meeting for all those assigned to observation posts during the next day's push. Mimeographed maps of the area as well a sheet of instructions were distributed for the men to consult during the coming afternoon. Among the instructions was the reminder: "Remember we would rather miss a few arrests than foul up the whole operation."

The men in the observation posts had to be in their assigned spots by 7 am on the morning of the 25. As soon as the courthouse opened, Linsky was knocking on the judge's door asking for search warrants for 620, 622, 627A and 639 Tremont Street, as well as 69 Montgomery Street, using the evidence he and the other officers had amassed during the last couple of weeks. The bulk of the rest of the personnel involved reported for a final briefing at 11 am.

The notoriously inaccurate New England weathermen had warned that it might snow, but the cloudy sky seemed for once to confirm their predictions. If the snow did actually start to fall, the operation would have to be called off because the obscured visibility and the inevitable traffic jams would have made surveillance, filming and, most importantly, pursuit and apprehension too difficult.

After the group had listened to the latest forecast on a radio, someone voiced the obvious, "If the weather is as bad as they say, we're in trouble."

"In more ways than you think," Connolly replied. "I could never get the co-operation and volunteers again. These guys would be bullshit coming in on a day off for nothing. The bosses would drop us, too. We'd never see those cars again . . . so let's keep our fingers crossed, pray for good weather and get out there before all the junkies sell everything they got today."

Putting the snowclouds out of their minds, the team agreed to go ahead with Operation One Block. The men left Station 4 and then drove the cars with the administrative frequency band directly to their stakeout positions on streets adjacent to the 600 block to await directions from Connolly over the radio.

Everyone was in place by noon, biding the half an hour till the official 12:25 start of Operation One Block. The plan was to spend the
afternoon nabbing the customers, and at the end of the day move in
on the homes of the dealers.

The dental office observation post was referred to as OP-1. From
there Moran and Linsky used the walkie-talkies to alert the officers in
the unmarked cars as to the descriptions of customers. Connolly and
Sergeant Crocker coordinated the movements of the street apprehension teams.

"This is OP-1. We have a sale going down at the corner of Pembroke
and Tremont." Moran excitedly rubbed the bright red whiskers on
his chin with his knuckles. He felt like a sports commentator describing the play-by-play as he watched the action on the street through
his binoculars.

"A Spanish male, about 22 years, 5'2", thin, green and yellow
jacket. He's the seller. Buyer is a white male, about 18 to 20, black
leather jacket with a fur collar — that's a gray fur collar, jeans, long
hair, black. He's got it . . . he's putting it in his right jacket pocket.
He's taking off in a hurry, hauling ass up Pembroke, outta sight. He
may have a car. Anybody see him?"

"Vice 6-car is at Warren and Pembroke," Connolly informed him
over the radio. Eddie tried to raise Willis Saunders, the black officer
driving the 6-car, "Willis, have you spotted him?"

"We have him. He's getting into a blue Ford with a banged-up
front. He's starting up, coming right at us," Willis responded.

"Let him get out of the area first," Connolly reminded him. "8-car,
move in with the 6-car. You help them out."

The 6-car, and a little later the 8-car, fell in behind the sky-blue
Ford, tailing it until it was well out of the "buy" zone. When the Ford
stopped for a red light on Columbus Avenue at Berkeley Street,
Willis braked as well. Eddie Ivanowski and Ralph Regan bolted out
into the street, jerked the driver's door open, and hauled the operator
out. They had him sprawled over the hood without his feet ever
touching the pavement. Swiftly their hands ransacked his pockets.

Regan alerted Moran and Connolly of the capture. "We scored. One
white male, six decks of smack. Going into 4."

It had only been five minutes after the official starting time, and
already the first arrest had been made. One of the men in the 8-car
got into the prisoner's Ford and escorted the 6-car to Station 4. The
customer with the long hair was booked and photographed with the
men from the 6-car. Ivanowski put his initials and the date on each of
the packets seized. The prisoner was taken on to Headquarters and
then back to a cell at 4.

Connolly kept the 16 unmarked police cars parked or circulating
in such a carefully worked-out pattern that no buyer could walk,

drive, or take a cab or bus out of the 600 block without being tailed instantly by one or more cop cars.

"We have a buy going down." Moran was gearing the team up for another pinch. "Two blacks just got out of a cab . . . it's a yellow checker taxi, double-parked on Tremont. Hispanic male is the seller . . . there's money being passed . . . they have the goods. The guy with the white pants is dirty . . . Back into the cab, cab going out Tremont towards Mass. Ave. Both blacks in their 20's, maybe 25, 27. Mr. Whitepants has a long black rain-or-shine coat. The other fellow is a good 6'2", a mean-looking mother, brown three-quarter length coat. The taxi number is 543, painted on the trunk. Didn't get the plate number."

"Four-car at Mass. Ave. and Tremont, got that. We're taking them," called Detective Bill Rowe, a Vice Unit veteran. He was riding with Sergeant Larry McNamara and Detective Arthur McNamara, two of the five McNamara brothers who, like their father and sister, were all police officers.

"That cab just passed us," Rowe continued, "We'll follow it out toward Ruggles Street."

The yellow checker cab pulled up in front of the Spa Restaurant. Mr. Whitepants was paying the fare. Before he or his friend knew what was happening, they found their arms pinned to their sides by the McNamara boys. A quick frisk produced 75 decks of heroin in three bundles of 25.

Rowe clicked on his walkie-talkie. "Car 4 to OP-1. Two prisoners from that cab. Three bundles of H. Heading in to 4."

"OP-1 has that," Linsky acknowledged.

"Good work," Connolly broke in. "Car 10, you cover Mass. Avenue at Tremont while the 4-car is off the air."

Bobo, otherwise known as Officer Tom Connolly, radioed back, "Ten-car has that."

As the day warmed up and the threat of snow faded, more clients wandered in, and more collars were made. Only three of the 55 people arrested were "walking buyers"; the rest transacted business through an open car window or jumped out of their double-parked vehicle to exchange $10 for each packet of "horse," some in shadowy doorways or in the relative seclusion of a phone booth, but most right in the middle of the sidewalk.

Detectives Bob Hayden, Bob Costello and Bill Keough stopped a car with four East Boston teens in it. One of them tried to chew and swallow several decks of heroin. Bill had to force the boy's jaws open and scrape his fingers past the gagging kid's tonsils to retrieve the evidence.

The Eastie punk was furious and took a nasty bite out of Keough's hand.

"You're gonna need rabies shots for that one," Hayden remarked as they headed for the hospital.

Later on that afternoon, Willis Saunders also had to visit the emergency room because of human bite wounds.

Sergeant Russell Childers chased one fellow on foot for blocks. When he was captured, the client still had the packages of H on him, even though he had had plenty of time to ditch the heroin before anyone laid a hand on him. When Childers got to the station, he found that there was no room for his prisoner.

The cells had filled up with people so fast that the guardroom had been commandeered as a holding area. Many of the junkies had not had their "wake-up" shot yet and were already shivering and puking all over their irritable cellmates. Two men had to be rushed to Boston City Hospital because of the severity of their withdrawal pangs, and several others were treated in their cells.

The search of one suspect turned up a transistor radio case that had been gutted and used as a convenient container for a syringe, needle and other items in his portable hypodermic kit. Another fellow that Connolly searched had, in the same pocket as his decks of heroin, a police "bluebook," the publication the Civil Service issued at that time for those who were preparing for the police exam.

"What are you doing with this?" Connolly asked.

"Studying to be a policeman."

"You'll never make it."

The more people that were detained, the greater the danger of word getting back to the 600 block before the all-important arrests of the dealers had been made. For this reason, some people had to be held at the station even though they were not being charged with possession of heroin. Nobody was taking any chances of the dealers' being tipped off.

Childers radioed Connolly with the news that Station 4 was past capacity. When Commissioner Edward McNamara heard of the unprecedented number of arrests, he remarked to his chauffeur, "The Feds must of been behind this operation. Our guys aren't this good!"

Deputy Superintendent Jordan was more willing to give credit where it was due. He contacted the newspapers and television stations and encouraged them to "give this story top coverage."

The media representatives began monitoring the conversations on the administrative channel very closely, and Connolly reminded the officers at headquarters to keep the reporters the hell away from the 600 block. He promised that they would be filled in on all the details later at Station 4 in plenty of time to write the whole thing up for the Sunday editions of their papers.

Around 4:45 the dealers seem to have depleted their supply; the arrests of the clients ceased, although the booking of those detained continued for several hours afterwards. There was a special elation in the hectic squadroom as the undercover officers, unshaven and in beat-up clothes, filtered back to the station to see for themselves the magnitude of their achievement.

Armed with the warrants that Linsky had obtained on the basis of the previous week's surveillance, police hit the supply houses in the South End as well as Santiago's Restaurant at 1453 Columbus Avenue and another Hispanic eating place at 627-A Tremont Street. All the suspects were arraigned the following Monday in Boston Municipal Court, except for the Columbus Avenue arrestee who was charged at Roxbury District Court.

The ages of those apprehended ranged from 18 to 37; only two of the 55 were female. Most of the people came from Boston neighborhoods: 17 from East Boston, 14 from the South End, five from Roxbury, and three from the North End. The rest came from neighboring towns and cities like Medford, Winthrop, and Peabody. The haul included a couple who had been living in a trailer park in Salem, New Hampshire.

In commenting to the press, nighttime Vice and Narcotics Unit Chief Lieutenant Joseph P. Rowan made the overly optimistic remark, "We put heroin out of business in this city — at least for a good while." The comment may have been just what the citizens wanted to hear, but was far too rosy to jibe with reality.

Detective Linsky made a controversial statement that got him into hot water: "We could have made at least another 50 arrests if we'd started in the morning, but we weren't after the junkies. Our main concern was to get the bums who were selling the stuff.

"As it turned out, the arrests show that the Puerto Ricans have taken over the heroin market in the city with the best bag in town."

The implications that Puerto Ricans in particular were pushing the purest heroin earned Linsky a reprimand from City Hall. While his observation was essentially correct, it came at a time when Mayor White was instituting an exchange program with officers in Puerto Rico, and there was a big effort in the department to get officers to volunteer to take a basic Spanish courses so that they could communicate more easily with the 18,000 Hispanics in Boston. Community Relations head Captain Jeremiah Sullivan indicated to angry Puerto Rican community leaders that in the view of the Boston Police Department no single ethnic group was responsible for the heroin traffic in the city.

When Connolly's men returned the cars with the special frequency, many of the superiors officers were upset at the damage that had been done when the undercover men forced buyers' cars to the side of the road. What they saw as "huge dents" and "crumpled fenders," Connolly dismissed as a "few barely noticeable scratches and nicks." Whenever the brass telephoned to complain, Connolly simply failed to return their calls.

The *Boston Globe* took note of the operation in a Tuesday editorial entitled "A tough job well done," in which the Boston police were praised for their "magnificent planning and equally magnificent execution." The editorial concluded by saying, "But a $10,000-a-day traffic in narcotics has been broken up in the largest and certainly the most successful narcotics raid in the city's history and congratulations and commendations to the Boston Police Department surely are in order."

The arraignment proceedings also kept the story in the eyes of the public. The big drug bust was bristling with human interest angles for the papers to play up. Among those trying to get into the courtroom, police recognized a man for whom they had a warrant in connection with the Saturday drug sales and arrested him in the corridor. The mother of a young defendant became hysterical when her son appeared in the docket; she fainted and had to be revived by the court physician.

In the case of Mrs. Veronica Woodburn, Judge Elijah Adlow dismissed charges of being in the company of a person in possession of narcotics when it was revealed that Mr. Woodburn was one of the defendants charged with illegal possession of heroin. "You can't find a woman guilty of being in the company of her husband," the judge declared.

Fred Higgins, the father of a 19-year-old Everett man, demanded that the judge do something for his wayward son. "I've been trying to get him into a hospital and I can't. It's a shame when I can't get my son into a hospital in Massachusetts."

Adlow replied, "Don't blame the state of Massachusetts that the hospitals are crowded. You just take better care of your son."

All the defendants pleaded not guilty; the cases were continued until December 12, and the suspects released on bail totaling $63,000 — all except John Santiago, a Roxbury man, the only one charged with unlawful sale of a narcotic and illegal possession of a gun. Eventually 36 of the defendants were found guilty of various charges involving narcotics.

There were many references made by prisoners to "Coco" and "El Viejo [The Old Man]" — the beginnings of an investigation into the Hispanic drug trade that would take Connolly, Moran and others more than a year to wrap up.

With the rash of stories and photo spreads on the November 25 bust, one might have thought that it would be difficult to buy any heroin for the next month or so. However, the very next Saturday, Connolly and company moved about six blocks down Tremont Street to a predominantly black neighborhood where the junkies were coming for their supplies. With the assistance of Captain Bill Gross, 35 State Police narcotics officers and the same set-up, the operation netted 86 suspects in four hours on one corner. So for several months on and off, the city and state narcotics team worked to scour the South End.

"We may not be stopping a French Connection here," Connolly reflected, "but the people of the South End are grateful that the cops are setting up things like Operation One Block. If this trafficking was allowed to continue, many of their kids could end up junkies.

"It took so many good men on their day off to arrest so many bad men who didn't care what day it was, so long as they could make a buck selling heroin."

18

El Viejo

Sweeps like the one on November 25 became routine, but most of the fish netted were small fry. Nevertheless, questioning these minnows revealed valuable information about the barracuda. One element in the narcotics picture had changed. The Hispanics seemed to be wresting control of the heroin traffic from the blacks, thanks to superior connections with international smugglers in the New York Spanish community.

The local Puerto Ricans arrested for pushing often referred to "Coco" and "El Viejo" as being the kingpins of the drug trade. Eventually with the assistance of Kenneth Acerra, a Puerto Rican officer, Connolly and Moran discovered that "Coco" and "El Viejo" were one and the same person.

Through informants it was not difficult to learn the identity of "The Old Man." Octavio Rivera was only 49 but looked older. Apparently, he made weekly trips from New York to Boston with large amounts of heroin, which he would cut and distribute to about ten men who acted as his lieutenants in the drug trade.

In early 1968, Connolly and Moran stopped Rivera on suspicion every now and then, but every time they frisked him, he came up clean. They resigned themselves to waiting until they could catch Rivera with the goods on him, but The Old Man was a crafty one.

He even managed to get a Hispanic lawyer who frequented Station 4 to put in a good word for him whenever the attorney bumped into the officers who were determined to put the elusive El Viejo out of business.

"I understand that you have been bothering Mr. Octavio Rivera, claiming he is involved in drug dealing or some such thing."

"Oh, you mean Coco?"

"I don't know anyone of that name. I'm talking about Mr. Octavio Rivera. I happen to know that he is a very honest and respectable citizen, and if you don't want to get the Hispanic community on your back, you'll stop harassing this poor man."

But Georgie was telling a different story about Rivera - not that Georgie was the world's most reliable source. A Puerto Rican addict,

5'2", 120 pounds, he wore a simpering smile and was forever trying to ingratiate himself with those he thought could give him dope.

He usually wore some kind of hat that was too small for him on the back of his head. Like most junkies, Georgie was always sniffling and shivering from the cold.

The oozing, festering sores on Georgie's arms made an unappetizing spectacle, but that didn't seem to deter Tom Moran from taking this thief/stoolie/drug addict home to eat at the same table with his seven children.

No one else in his right mind would leave Georgie alone in a room for five minutes, much less invite him over for the weekend; he would undoubtedly take everything that wasn't nailed down. Nevertheless, Moran would have the little Puerto Rican sleeping over at his home in Dorchester.

"How can you do that to your wife?" Connolly would ask.

"Peggy? Oh, she likes him."

"Nobody likes that syphilitic stoolie."

Tom's habit of hosting disreputable houseguests like Georgie may have contributed to the breakup of his marriage. Another factor that strained the domestic felicity of the Moran household was the fact that Tom, like the other men involved in drug control, frequently had to kick in money from his weekly pay to make narcotics buys and to pay off informants.

To get Georgie to squeal on Rivera, the men had had to fork over $200, a sizeable chunk out of their checks. They didn't like to think that money that should have gone toward buying their children new clothes was going to feed a junkie's habit, but if they ever expected to get El Viejo, they knew that somebody would have to be paid off.

The department would certainly never advance them any money and likewise never seemed to reimburse them for these expenses either. The men were also reluctant to get money from the Feds who usually insisted on taking over the case. Government officials had different ideas about how to treat an informant and wouldn't allow the Boston police to sit in when they debriefed a stoolie. Also, the Feds also didn't show the same concern for the informant's safety after they were through with him that the men of the DCU did.

No, it was better in the long run to pay these slobs out of your own pocket; that way you'd have a shot at keeping them around for years.

One the funniest facets of people like Georgie is their vehement denials that they are stool pigeons. Whenever they left the station after trying to peddle some information, they would complain to their cohorts on the street, "The cops pinched me again, but they don't have nothing on me. I didn't tell the cops a fucking thing."

Of course, if two of these types happened to be at the station selling their wares at the same time, they would glare at one another indignantly and immediately start accusing one another of being a lousy fink.

In any case, for $200 Georgie had told Connolly and Moran that Rivera would be returning to Boston to an apartment at 677 Dudley Street sometime before the end of the week. El Viejo would be bringing in four ounces of pure heroin to be split, bagged and distributed to dealers within a matter of hours after his arrival.

With the assistance of Federal Narcotics Agents Peter Gruden, Matt Seifer, Bill Ferris and Dick O'Connor, the Boston officers monitored Rivera's comings and goings for months and learned that he owned a number of vehicles and had several plates at his disposal. It was Georgie, however, who assured them that this time Rivera would be operating a 1965 Buick sedan with the New Hampshire registration HZ-757.

Since there was no way of knowing exactly when El Viejo would show up, Connolly and Moran prepared for a long stakeout. Across the street from the apartment building at 677 Dudley, which had formerly been the Gladstone Hotel, was a parking lot adjoining the El Sombrero nightclub. On the afternoon of Thursday, November 21, 1968, Connolly drove up in a beat-up green Oldsmobile, for which he had paid $500. From a phone booth he called Moran at home.

"The Old Man's not here yet. You go get something to eat. We got time yet. He'll need time to cut the stuff up."

"No," Moran said. "Pick me up now."

It was a five-minute drive to Moran's home on Harbor View Street. On their way back to the El Sombrero lot, they alerted Sgt. Earl Crocker, who had been working with them on the Rivera case, to cover the back exit of 677 Dudley Street while they watched the front.

Connolly pulled the Oldsmobile between two cars already sitting in the lot. He leaned over and lay on the front seat; Moran was crouching in the back. In these less than comfortable positions, they watched the light fade from the sky, popping up every now and then to see if the Buick had appeared.

The later it got, the more activity there seemed to be in the lot. Men came reeling out to urinate. A girl would slip into a car with one man. When they were finished with their backseat lovemaking, she would go back into the El Sombrero to look for another customer.

Arguments between angry patrons more than once developed into full-fledged fights. Knives flashed, reflecting the garish nighttime neon lights. At one point it looked as though murder was really imminent, and the cops were just about to reveal themselves to prevent a death. Fortunately, officers from District 2 arrived to quell the disturbance before Eddie and Tom had to blow their cover.

The presence of the men from Station 2 bothered Connolly's conscience a bit. Ordinary police protocol demanded that he inform the

District 2 captain if he were planning a stakeout in the captain's area, but Moran, Connolly and Crocker had agreed that the importance of collaring this major dealer demanded the utmost secrecy.

In the wee hours of Friday morning, Moran took the Olds to the Victoria Diner to get some sandwiches while Connolly hid between some cars parked for the night.

All day Friday the men lay in the car, speaking rarely. Once in a while, one of them would dart out to take a leak, but most of the time, they played the waiting game. They spent another night watching men pissing against the wall, hookers plying their trade and fellow cops breaking up fights. Moran and Connolly allowed themselves only catnaps, but never at the same time. Especially during the early hours, dozing off for even an hour could mean the loss of their quarry.

The minutes dragged on interminably, and they wondered whether they had been duped by Georgie, whom they knew had absolutely no integrity. But finally, on Saturday afternoon around 3 all the waiting paid off.

Connolly was on the lookout.

"Moran! Moran!"

"What?"

"He's here."

"It is the Old Man."

Peering between the headrests, Tom watched El Viejo climb out of the Buick with the New Hampshire plate HZ-757 and head into the building.

"He's got nothing," Moran groaned.

"Take it easy."

"He can't have four ounces on him. Where could he hide it? He just had on a shirt and a pair of pants."

About fifteen minutes later Rivera reappeared with another swarthy fellow. Rivera started to unlock the trunk.

"Here it comes," Connolly cried.

The two men took a stereo set from the trunk, and together they carried it into the building.

"Why go to all that trouble?" Moran wondered.

"Just in case someone like us is watching."

"Let's get him."

As soon as Rivera and his accomplice boarded the rickety grillwork elevator with its open cage, Moran and Connolly slipped into the building. They gave the Puerto Ricans enough time to get to the fifth floor and then started up the stairs that wound around the elevator shaft.

The policemen had secured a search warrant for Suite #505, trusting Georgie's information that Rivera had leased the apartment under the alias of Martinez.

Without bothering to knock, Connolly and Moran pulled out their guns and burst through the door of #505. At first they were startled to find no Rivera, no stereo, and most importantly no heroin. There were just Hispanics sitting around smoking.

It was not hard to deduce that these men, all from the Hartford, Connecticut area, were waiting for El Viejo to cut the heroin and to allot each one his share to sell in the Nutmeg State.

As much as he hated to do it, Connolly gave the order, "Call District 2."

Moran put in an urgent call for reinforcements, and within minutes a gang of detectives from Station 2 came through the door. The four Hartford men were thoroughly searched and put under arrest.

Once again the middlemen were getting in the way of the capture of the main man, El Viejo. All of the men disclaimed any knowledge of Rivera. So the interminable stakeout seemed to have led to another dead-end.

But out in the corridor, a female resident of the building beckoned to Moran and Connolly; they recognized her as another one of their army of informants.

"Here, take our cuffs," Connolly said to the officers from 2 as he and his redheaded partner skipped out to confer with the woman, who was anxious not to be seen by any of the Hispanics in #505.

"He's in #510," she whispered and showed them where the corridor twisted around to Rivera's second apartment on the same floor.

"Right there. That door there."

They nodded their thanks and drew the guns out of their holsters once again. She scurried back to her flat, slipped in and threw the bolt on the door.

They had no warrant to search #510, but too much time had been frittered away already. Together they kicked the door in on Rivera and a companion who were clearly not expecting visitors.

"¡Policía!" the Old Man exclaimed, but there was no one left to heed his warning or come to the rescue.

Both men went for Rivera, but being slight and unarmed, he didn't put up much resistance. Keeping a firm grasp on El Viejo, Connolly reached over and yanked out the needle that the female accomplice had apparently just stuck into her arm moments before the two had rammed through the door. The young lady who was interrupted in mid-jolt proved to be 27-year-old Carmelina Cintron, a girlfriend of Rivera's.

On the table were three plastic bags each containing an ounce of heroin, as well as 238 decks that had been put together from the fourth ounce. On the dusty surface of the large mirror on the table were the measuring spoons, a scale and a makeshift sifter improvised from a nylon stocking stretched over a coat hanger pulled into a diamond shape. Next to a container of quinine for "cutting" or diluting the heroin were scattered about a thousand unused glassine bags.

Also on the table sat the stereo unit, which had served to conceal the heroin, upended and partially disassembled. The street value of the horse on the table was nearly $80,000. There would be no problem with evidence to arrest Rivera and Cintron with possession of heroin with the intent to sell and conspiracy to violate narcotic drug laws.

The press made a big hoopla about the year-long investigation that culminated in the arrest of El Viejo. The *Record American-Sunday Advertiser* named Thomas B. Moran, Sergeant Earl B. Crocker and Sergeant Detective Edward F. Connolly "Policemen-of-the-Month." Besides getting their picture in the paper, each man received a check for $50 and an engraved citation signed by Police Commissioner Ed-

Officer Thomas B. Moran, Sgt. Earl B. Crocker and Sgt. Det. Edward F. Connolly (l. to r.) display checks that they received for winning *Record American-Sunday Advertiser* Policemen of the Month Award for the capture of alleged kingpin of dope-pushers.

mund L. McNamara and *Record-American* publisher Harold G. Kern.

Commissioner McNamara also granted each man two days of relief in recognition of their many extra hours of duty. However, since the men were so busy with other cases, none of them was able to take two days off.

All the commendations and backslapping didn't seem to mean much in light of what subsequently happened to the dealers they had expended so much effort to apprehend. After the four Hartford pushers were booked, they were immediately let go due to insufficient evidence.

Rivera was in jail over the weekend. On Monday he and Cintron appeared before Judge Eisenstadt of Roxbury District Court. Both were held for the Grand Jury, but even though Eisenstadt set his bail at $50,000 double surety, the sum was petty cash to a big-time drug dealer like El Viejo.

He plunked down the 50 grand and promptly flew back to Puerto Rico. For the next five or six years, whenever Connolly got word of a recent sighting of Rivera in some Puerto Rican city, he would pester the FBI to apprehend him on a fugitive-from- justice warrant, but nothing ever came of it.

19

The Hooker Who Snitched On Everybody

Any experienced policeman will tell you that detective work is 95% information and 5% legwork. Perhaps the most productive informant the city of Boston has ever seen was Suzy Q, an unbelievably gutsy hooker who was responsible for turning in over 200 drug dealers to Lieutenant Connolly's Drug Control Unit.

The DCU was subdivided into three squads: one under Sergeant Frank Coleman, the second under John Doris, and the third under Henry Rinaldi. There was a friendly rivalry between these squads to see who could bring in the most pounds of dope at the end of each shift. When necessary, they could all cooperate to put a particularly pernicious crook out of business.

One thing that the squads did not like to share was their informants, and detectives would rather go to jail than reveal the identities of their sources on the street to a judge. But the relationship between the men in Doris' squad and Suzy Q far exceeded the normal bounds of loyalty.

Detective John Shepard was the first to spot her. One winter night in 1970, he and John Doris were parked in an unmarked car opposite Big Jim's Cafe — popularly known as the "Heroin Stop and Shop." A tough-looking woman in her early 20's sailed out of the joint — 5'6", 135 pounds. Seeing the men slouched in the car across the street, she shoved a packet she was holding in her hand down the front of her pants.

This guilty gesture prompted Shepard and Doris to collar her. They intended to take her over to the House of Detention behind the Suffolk County Courthouse. There, a matron would search her to determine if the packet she had so hastily put away did indeed contain a contraband substance.

Once they had her in the car, they were able to get a better look at her. Her features and figure weren't half bad, but her clothes were soiled. Her long chestnut hair didn't hold the wave that she tried so hard to put in it. Her teeth were unusually bad, bordering on the grotesque, and her breath as foul as her language.

She said her name was Margaret Susan Quinn, but she preferred to be called Suzy Q, a name which, she informed them, she had tattooed on her left thigh. She obviously needed a fix pretty badly. But even though she wasn't feeling well, she was a fast enough talker to convince the two officers to take a long shot.

"Let me go this time, and I'll roll over one of the motherfuckers who are dealing around here."

Rather than take her to the House of Correction, Shepard followed an impulse and agreed to the trade-off. Before she got out of the vehicle, she had made arrangements to set up a dealer that the DCU had wanted for a while.

This incident was just the first in a series that lasted five years. Whether it was her neglect of her appearance or her sharp tongue, Suzy wasn't able to support her habit just by whoring, so she had to supplement her income by selling information to the DCU on a daily basis. Shepard and Suzy fell into a routine that never changed.

Every evening right around 7 when his shift reported for work, Suzy would call Shepard at an unlisted number and arrange to meet him, usually in the lot of a gas station at the corner of East Berkeley and Columbus Avenue. Half an hour later, Doris and Shepard would be waiting in the car; Suzy would slip into the back seat and sell absolutely reliable information about whomever she happened to have picked up news.

Suzy Q quickly became an unofficial but crucial member of the team. Every single day that Shepard was at work, Suzy would call and then meet him to set up a successful bust. The basic rule with informants was to pay them only if the leads they provided panned out, but Suzy was so consistently accurate that they sometimes paid her upfront. They knew that the $10 or $15 they would scrape together to pay her for the tips would probably be spent on drugs, but they never offered her narcotics in exchange for information.

The more she became part of the family, the more concerned everyone became for her health, especially Shepard. He would bring hand-me-downs from his daughters for her to wear.

One night she sighed, "I'm starving."

"No wonder. You never buy any decent food."

"Then why don't you buy me a meal somewhere?"

Shepard really did feel sorry for her.

"I'll take you to the Victoria Diner under one condition. Please control that mouth of yours. Everybody at the Vic knows me, and I don't want you embarrassing me. So no swearing."

Suzy Q agreed, and before long they were sitting across from each other in a booth in the late-night eatery. Suzy ordered a salad and a steak and wolfed them down as if it were her last meal before she was sent off to the electric chair.

Despite her uncouth table manners, Shepard was relieved that she hadn't said anything untoward, but she was just setting him up.

In an unnecessarily loud voice she called out, "Hey, waitress, what you got for fuckin' dessert?"

The waitress turned red and hastily handed her a menu. After glancing at the choices, she made a selection. When the order did not arrive after a minute, she shouted, "Where the fuck is my apple pie?"

As the mortified Shepard looked apologetically at the offended waitress, Suzy grinned maliciously. On the few other times that Shepard would take her out to eat, she never failed to create a scene with her deliberate use of obscene language.

But a little embarrassment was a small price to pay for their invaluable informant. On days when she couldn't come up with a set-up for a drug dealer, she would provide information on other felons. One day she announced she could tell Shepard who had killed a woman whose body was found in the Charlesgate area. Apparently, some men had come to her with the ID and checkbook of the deceased and asked her to try to pass off the checks.

The paradoxical but undeniable regard that the men of the DCU had for this courageous character was never more evident than during the mind-boggling tangle of events that led to her getting knifed.

In mid-December, 1971, Suzy mentioned to her DCU friends that "one of the banks near Headquarters" would soon be hit. She promised to let Shepard know as soon as she got the particulars.

On December 20, 1971 around 1 pm, Shepard was in Superior Court when he caught sight of Suzy, flushed and out of breath; she had run all the way from Dartmouth Street to tell him that the robbery was about to go down at the Pioneer Financial on East Berkeley.

By the time Shepard got to a phone to alert Headquarters, the heist was already in progress. Three men with sawed-off shotguns had

The Victoria Diner as it looked before it was remodeled. "The Vic" is still popular with Boston cops as place to get good food late at night.

made their way into the bank, shot out the security cameras and forced the tellers to turn over a mere $550.

Apparently their scheme was conceived with more gall than brains, because their getaway car was a heap that wouldn't start when they came barreling out the door of the bank. The mastermind of the operation, a hotheaded blond, put a shotgun to the driver's head, vowing to blow his brains out if he didn't get the car going in a hurry. Fortunately for the man at the wheel, the blond had only three bullets in his shotgun at the start of the robbery and used them all to blind the cameras. So there was nothing but a click when the ringleader pulled the trigger.

Finally, the engine turned over, but the car only sputtered along a short distance before it died for good in the middle of Arlington Street. The men fled in different directions, abandoning the car and creating all kinds of traffic problems.

That night when Shepard and Suzy Q had their customary rendezvous, she coolly informed them that she had one of the robbers in her basement apartment on 36 Dartmouth Street.

"He sent me out to get some wine."

"How much does he want?"

"A quart."

"Look, here's some more money. Get him two quarts, and make sure he drinks both of them."

Suzy hurried off to the corner package store and returned to her basement flat. Shepard and Doris moved their car so they could watch the stairs leading down to Suzy's below-ground dwelling. About an hour later she was back at the window of the unmarked car.

"He's drunk and asleep on my bed," she reported.

"Good, we'll go and get him."

"Wait a minute, just let me run back to make sure that everything's alright."

As she was descending the stairs to reassure herself that her guest was still asleep, she was accosted by two black men who hustled her downstairs.

This development made the detectives in the car uncomfortable. As the minutes ticked away, they became more and more apprehensive that she might be in some kind of danger, but eventually the two men came out, and shortly afterwards Suzy was back.

"Did you see those two colored guys that were just here?"

"Yeah."

"Grab 'em."

"What for?"

"They've got 21 stolen diamonds on them. One of them fuck-faces is a maintenance man in the Jewelers' Building. He robbed the place he was supposed to be cleaning up. Anyway, they want me to fence the ice for them."

For the moment the slumbering bank man was forgotten, as the police roared down the street after the diamond thieves. These two were nabbed and taken down to Station 4 for booking. When all those formalities were taken care of, they went back to Suzy's.

Sure enough, the trigger-happy blond was still there, sprawled on her bed. His naked torso revealed a muscular physique.

"Put your shirt on, buddy," Shepard said as they roused him out of his stupor. "You're coming with us."

They hauled the fair-haired thief in, but he denied being involved in any robbery and didn't have the money on him. Shepard and Doris began to suspect that Suzy might have had something to do with the robbery. After all, she had warned them about it long before it happened. Besides what was this guy doing half-naked in her bed?

Back at 36 Dartmouth Street, they questioned the devious Suzy Q repeatedly about being involved, but she insisted she didn't know where the money was. She did, however, offer to tell them where they could find another one of the holdup trio for a small fee.

"This one could be dangerous. He escaped a couple of days ago from Deer Island, and he may have a gun on him."

As usual she provided a detailed description — a 20-year-old with well-groomed black hair, big ears and bloodshot eyes.

"He's sitting in the Hayes-Bick right now, having a cup of coffee."

The Hayes-Bickford Cafeteria had one entrance on Park Square and another on Boylston Street, so the men split up to cover both exits. When Shepard spotted the man sitting alone at a table, the suspect sensed danger and ran for the other door. Doris was waiting for him.

A search of his person turned up no clue to the location of the money, and he too swore he had nothing to do with the robbery. Nevertheless, they arrested him, if for nothing else than having escaped from prison.

While it was true that the third robber was still at large, Shepard and Doris became more and more convinced that Suzy had taken the money from the blond man in her apartment.

But the police were not the only ones who came to that conclusion. Two men from the "South End Clan," a crowd that Suzy Q ran around with, decided that they would steal from Suzy the money that she stole from the men who had stolen it from the bank.

On December 22 around 3 pm, Suzy was in her apartment cooking and shooting up some nembutols, which she had just gotten from her doctor. Sharing in her windfall was Robert Hoffman, a postal clerk who had been keeping her company while her husband was serving out his term in the New Bedford House of Correction. Among friends, Robbie Hoffman was known as the "Dude" because of the wild-colored clothes he wore.

Joey O'Brien from the D Street Projects in South Boston and Malcolm Sheridan from Roslindale, two of the Clan, were there too. When she thought the visitors had gone, Suzy absentmindedly pulled a stocking with $300 of the Pioneer Financial job money rolled up in it out of a hiding place in an easy chair.

"What you got there?" Sheridan asked coming back down the stairs unexpectedly.

Suzy turned her back to him and tucked the roll of bills into her favorite spot, the front of her jeans.

"Nothing, nothing," she replied.

Sheridan looked at her for a minute and then went up the curving back staircase without saying a word.

About an hour later, Suzy was slumped over the table in her little kitchen alcove in a nembutol-induced stupor. She heard someone coming through the entrance at the top of the stairs. Anyone could walk in anytime because Suzy had kicked the door in one night when she had lost her keys and had never had the lock fixed.

Robbie, dressed in purple pants with pink pockets and a lavender shirt, went up the stairs to investigate. The next thing Suzy saw was Robbie tumbling down the stairs, clutching his chest, crying, "I've got a bad heart. I've got to get to the hospital."

Suzy always prided herself in being able to snap out of any narcotic daze. The sight of her boyfriend having what she thought was a heart attack jolted her back to reality. But then she saw Sheridan with a blood-stained, thin-bladed knife in his hand. He stepped over Robbie Hoffman, who had collapsed at the foot of the stairs, and walked over to Suzy and jabbed the blade into her breast.

Suzy wondered if this were really happening or if it were a bad reaction to the pills. She fell back on her bed, trying to clear her mind. Suddenly Joey O'Brien appeared and started going through her pockets and undoing the front of her jeans. He wanted the bank money.

Suzy was resisting, so Sheridan went over to Robbie, raised the knife as high as he could and plunged it into the wounded man's stomach. Then Sheridan turned and sneered, "How do you like this?"

Suzy pleaded with O'Brien just to take the money and get out; all she wanted was to get Robbie to a hospital. Then she grabbed her straight razor with a white plastic handle and flashed it in the face of the intruders. Unexpectedly Suzy felt a jolt of pain in her back as someone stabbed her again.

O'Brien was bent over Robbie's body.

"The Dude is dead. Shit. We better get out of here."

Joey galloped upstairs and out of the apartment. Sheridan wasn't giving up. He had gone this far and wasn't leaving without the money. Though Suzy Q was bleeding heavily from the wounds in both her front and back, she kept Malcolm at bay with her razor, then edged towards the stairs. Since she didn't have a phone in the apartment, she had to get upstairs to someone who did.

She made it to the stairs and was dragging herself up, when Sheridan lunged at her. Somehow she found the strength to deliver a vicious kick right between his eyes. Malcolm yowled, dropped his knife and reeled back down into the basement apartment.

Suzy made her way along the street-level hallway to David Beach's apartment. When her frantic knocks got no response, she summoned her inner resources once again and kicked in his door. She fell onto his bed and fumbled for the phone.

She wasn't sure what number she was dialing. She just kept screaming over and over "Suzy Q . . . Dartmouth Street . . . Drug Control." Finally, the exertion proved too much, and she slumped into unconsciousness.

When the cops arrived, they found blood splotched all over the walls and floors of the first floor and basement apartment. Robbie was dead on arrival at Boston City Hospital, but Suzy Q still had her hands clenched around the straight razor and the $300 bankroll when she was rushed into the operating room.

Shepard and his wife were just settling down to get a head start on wrapping some of the Christmas presents for their six children when he got the word that Suzy had been knifed and was on the danger list at the BCH.

She was still being sewn together when the DCU detectives met at the hospital. The doctors allowed Shepard, Doris and Smith to put on masks and sterile gowns and to enter the operating room to question Suzy while the surgeons finished stitching her up.

"Suzy, who did it?"

She was only semiconscious; not only was she groggy from the anaesthetic, but she was suffering withdrawal symptoms because the hospital had declined to oblige her with a fix. But it would take more than a couple of stab wounds, an operation, withdrawal pangs and the murder of her boyfriend to rattle Suzy Q.

"It was Joey O'Brien and Malcolm Sheridan."

She gave them Joey's address in the D Street Projects and told them Malcolm lived somewhere in Roslindale. Shepard and company went back to the Identification Bureau and found that both men had records. The DCU detectives brought mugshots back to the recovery room for Suzy to identify.

She looked extremely pale and haggard. She could barely keep her eyelids open wide enough to inspect the pictures.

"That's the cocksuckers," she rasped finally.

From Sheridan's record the officers were able to determine that he had a sister in Roslindale. This sister agreed to cooperate and revealed that Malcolm had planned to spend Christmas Eve with another sister who lived in Brighton. So while Santa was stuffing the stockings of good little boys and girls, the DCU men maintained a stakeout of the Brighton apartment until 7 am, but to no avail. Malcolm had somehow gotten wind of what was going on and never showed.

This was not the first nor the last time that the DCU men missed a holiday at home because of an emergency case. Besides, Suzy Q may have been a black sheep, but as disreputable as she was, she was a member of the DCU family.

Shepard and company broke the surveillance to attend Mass with their families on Christmas morning, but resumed the investigation later that afternoon.

Though the clues were leading nowhere, the entire DCU rallied to make the South End hotter than it had ever been. Connolly and all the rest of his force leaned hard on every junkie they knew, vowing not to let up until the killers were caught. Drug Control men were in all O'Brien's and Sheridan's favorite bars in the Combat Zone and Park Square and in reputed hangouts like the Greyhound Bus Terminal.

The pressure got so intense that Malcolm began to fear that if any of the DCU men sighted him he would be gunned down on the spot, so he surrendered himself to a policeman he was friends with in District 2.

When Malcolm was transported back to District 4 for questioning, he was dreading the revenge that he expected the DCU would wreak on him. He confessed to the two stabbings, although he claimed that he didn't think he had killed either Suzy or Robbie. He also exonerated O'Brien, who was still at large, from any blame in the actual knifings.

Once Malcolm was in custody, Suzy revealed that he had robbed a Dr. Frederick Brown of Jamaica Plain earlier that month. On December 10, Sheridan, calling himself Steven Fillmore, had come to Brown's office seeking a prescription for barbituates. Sheridan had then used an imitation black .45 automatic to coerce the physician into handing over a gold Elgin wristwatch, $60 in cash, some narcotics and the doctor's own .38 Smith & Wesson snub-nosed revolver.

"Look, you're in for one beef," Shepard told him, "I happen to know you're the one that hit the doctor in J.P. You might as well make a clean breast of it. You're the one who fired that bullet into his floor, aren't you?"

"How did you know about that?"

"Never mind. Just tell us what you did with his gun."

"I threw it down in some bushes by the tracks on Lamartine Street."

So the DCU had not only identified the killer of Suzy's unlucky boyfriend, but they had unexpectedly solved the robbery of the doctor, not to mention the diamond heist. Though the serial numbers on the $300 Suzy had in her stocking did not match any of the numbers of the bills taken from the Pioneer Bank, the detectives who knew her realized that she was smart enough to exchange the money soon after she took it from the blond.

A Grand Jury found probable cause for Sheridan, but not for O'Brien. Later, however, at a May 17, 1972 trial, both men were sent to Walpole Prison for ten to 20 years for manslaughter.

Suzy's near brush with death had shaken her enough that she finally agreed to a proposal that Shepard had been nagging her about for a long time — submitting to a drug rehabilitation program.

Once she consented, there remained the problem that all the facilities in the city were overcrowded. Lieutenant Connolly called up his friend, Father Henry Kane, who coordinated the Mayor's Council on Drug Abuse, and the Redemptorist priest pulled a few strings and got Suzy admitted immediately to the Boston State Hospital in Mattapan.

Amazingly enough, being in a drug rehab center did not hamper Suzy from calling in leads to Shepard about drug activity on the street. However, the men from Doris' squad had to visit her every day and slip her a roll of dimes so she could make her phone calls, as well as candy and gum, which were forbidden at the hospital.

One night Detective Joe Smith was smuggling in Suzy's phone money and supply of sweets when another patient at the hospital recognized him as a cop. The patient turned on Suzy, accusing her of being a police plant; she lashed back with her usual ferocity. Smith slipped away as quickly as he could, but the commotion kept building until the whole drug rehab unit was in an uproar.

The next morning Father Kane got Lieutenant Connolly on the phone.

"I want that woman the hell out of here."

"Right away, Father."

One snag: Suzy had no clothes but a hospital gown. She told the men at the Drug Control Unit what she wanted. So they went over to Jimmy the Thief's and bought her a shirt, dungarees, sneakers and a jacket. They took the garments down to her, let her climb into them, and brought her back to her old haunts.

And Suzy Q got right out on the street, selling her body to lonely men and information to the DCU.

20

"Find the Cop Who's Dealing Dope"

Lieutenant Connolly and the men of the Drug Control Unit kept hearing a lot of rumors about a cop selling heroin. There were never any specifics, but the word kept coming from enough different sources that they reluctantly concluded the story might be true.

Even though they had absolutely no details, it was easy to picture what was going on. Some officer was shaking down dealers for money and then taking their dope and letting them go. He was in a position to keep putting the squeeze on dealers, who would be unable to complain to authorities because that would mean admitting that they themselves were selling narcotics.

A cop selling drugs was anathema to the men in the DCU. Here they were putting their lives on the line every night, doing everything in their power to stop all the drug trafficking, and this one man was undermining their credibility and the credibility of all honest Boston policemen. It took only a few rotten apples like this one, and soon dealers and informants would begin believing that all policemen were corrupt.

If the story ever got to the media, things would be much worse. The *Globe*, the *Herald* and the local TV newscasters would have a field day. As it was, the kids of cops had to take all kinds of abuse from classmates on the schoolbus or in the schoolyard. Officer's wives had to put up with little digs and innuendoes while sitting under the dryers at the beauty salon or shopping for groceries at the Star Market. If a story like this ever became public knowledge, their lives would become even more miserable.

Connolly and his men had to get this dope-dealing cop and forestall all the unfavorable publicity. Besides, it was a matter of pride: the Boston Police Department cleans its own laundry.

As top narco man, Connolly felt the burden the most heavily. Though his best drug enforcement guys like Walter Tower and Steve Murphy reported hearing the same rumor, Eddie wanted to check it out with the Feds.

Connolly contacted Ross Kinderstin and Chris Egan of the Drug Enforcement Administration. The local DEA men could report only that they too had heard that a Boston cop was dealing heroin, but they had no leads to offer.

The only thing the men in the DCU could do was wait, knowing that sooner or later someone's snitch would give them the big break they needed. Meanwhile they kept plugging away, making arrests, seizing drugs and appearing in court with their ears cocked for any whisper about the pusher-cop.

Then early in May of 1974, Arthur Linsky and Bill Currier reported that they had heard some talk about a black policeman who was snorting heroin. Word had it that he hung out at the Music Bar, a dive on Columbia Road in Dorchester.

"How about selling?" Connolly pressed them. "Have you heard anything about this cop selling?"

"No," Bill admitted. "When I first heard about it, I figured him for a hired cop."

The three men considered this possibility that the informants had mistaken a security guard for a cop. Boston had dozens of security firms that dressed their staff in uniforms that resembled the BPD's.

"Let me get back to my man," Currier added after a moment. "I'll put him right on it."

"Thanks, Bill."

But a few weeks passed, and Currier still had not connected with his informant. The weeks stretched into months and then a year. The men on the DCU had so many immediate crises to deal with every night — busting joints, collaring dealers, playing footsie with the DEA — that the vague rumors about a cop selling dope were kept on the back burner.

Eventually, another lead materialized. One night Tower, Murphy and Jimmy Jones crowded into Connolly's office, ushering in a uniformed officer.

"Lieutenant, this is Rick," Jones said, jerking his head towards the man in uniform. "He works in Roxbury. He has a story to tell you. But first he has a request."

"What's all this about a request . . . a story?" Connolly replied testily. "Let's have it without the bullshit."

"Rick wants on the DCU for the story he's got to tell," Tower explained.

"What kind of story?" the lieutenant said skeptically.

"A cop selling . . . the cop you've been looking for. He has it."

As much as Connolly's adrenaline surged at the offer, he stuck to the basic rule with informants, whether they are a runny-nosed, scabby junkie or a brother cop: no promises.

"No deals. Just tell the story."

The short, slim rookie considered for a moment. He was burning with ambition, but he was bright enough to know that he would have to play things Connolly's way if he wanted to join the men on the DCU.

"Well," Rick said, plunging into the story. "His name is Ernie Stone, a big black, works nights with me. He walks most of the time, but you can never find him on the street because he's never there. He always at the Music Bar, selling dope . . . or guns."

"Where's he get the dope and the guns?" Connolly demanded.

"Where do you think?" Rick replied. "He steals it or takes it off the dudes on the street. He's as strong as an ox and as big as an elephant. Everybody's scared shitless of him."

"He's a user?"

"Snorts the white stuff, sir. He's got a wicked habit."

Connolly half-closed his eyes as he searched his memory.

"I think I know the guy. I remember when he was in the Academy. I thought he'd go to the top," Connolly said, "Yeah, he got shot a few years back. I know him now."

Connolly got up from his desk and walked around for a minute. Then he turned and addressed the rookie. "OK, Rick, I'll get you into the DCU, but you just feed the information on this one. You're not to work on Ernie personally. Some people around here wouldn't understand. Even a bad cop, some people defend."

Rick was not fazed by the indirect questioning of his integrity. He had got what he had come for: a promise of a berth in the DCU.

Of course, Rick had not offered them any solid proof, but there was no reason to doubt his story. He indeed worked a two-man patrol with Ernie Stone. At the start of a tour of duty, Stone the veteran would leave his rookie partner to walk the tough two-man beat alone. Ernie would slip a sportscoat over his uniform and head for the Music Bar to sell dope with his partner, a person whose identity was still not known.

Night after night Sergeant Coleman and Lieutenant Connolly staked out the Music Bar from a van or from an apartment they rented across the street.

Almost every night Ernie would show up, carrying his attache case, always wearing a suitcoat or jacket over his uniform. Very seldom did he patrol his assigned sector. On one occasion he had to do so because the word was out that the sergeant was checking posts.

When he was assigned to a cruising car or wagon, he always had an excuse to stop into the Music Bar several times on a tour of duty. He would tell Rick that his girlfriend worked there as a barmaid and that some bastard had threatened her. It was only natural that he would want to drop in frequently to make sure that she was alright.

Connolly felt sure that the attache that Ernie was always carrying contained damaging evidence. Perhaps that was where Stone stashed his heroin. Eddie and his men were always on the lookout for a chance to get a peek in the bag.

Whenever Stone was in court testifying on a stolen car or breaking and entering case, the DCU men who were around waiting to testify on other matters would keep their eyes on the briefcase, but Ernie always took it with him.

Then one morning at Roxbury District Court, Ernie was suddenly called in, and he left his briefcase and coat on a bench in the hall.

Connolly and Sergeant Burke snatched it and ducked into an empty room. Burke jiggled a paperclip around in the lock, and the attache case sprang open. Inside they found some papers, an orange, and two pairs of socks, one clean, the other dirty. Cursing they hustled like hell to replace the coat and bag before Ernie came looking for them.

One night Coleman and Connolly were informed that Ernie was planning to meet a dealer at the Music Bar and then go to an address on Cabot Street on the other side of Roxbury to make the buy. Luckily, that same night they were joined by two Boston DEA agents, Ross Kinderstin and Dick O'Connor, who brought along a young black agent, whom they introduced as "Russell."

Russell was one of the DEA's top undercover operatives. He was on loan to New England DEA Director Ed Cass especially for the Ernie Stone case. Months earlier, Connolly had gone to Cass for assistance. Eddie needed a black undercover operative from outside the Department. There were relatively few blacks in the Boston Police Department, and they all knew each other very well, since they were all members of the same black police associations.

Cass had given his word that he would bring someone in when he could, but Connolly eventually concluded the DEA director had forgotten about the DCU's request. But now here was a topnotch agent to fulfill that promise.

Intelligent and well-educated, Russell could talk and act like any of the denizens of the Music Bar who hadn't made it out of grammar school. Russell was simultaneously working on multi-kilo cases in New York and Philly, and so his time in Boston was necessarily limited.

Since it was impossible for any white DCU men to hang around inside the Music Bar, Linsky managed to develop a black hooker-junkie into a cooperative informant inside the Music Bar. The CI agreed to introduce Russell to Ernie so that the agent could make some hand-to-hand buys. For three years Connolly had been on the case of the drug-peddling cop, and now this second break made it look as if Ernie's dealing days were numbered.

From their post inside the van, Connolly, Coleman and the DEA agents observed Russell saunter into the Music Bar, and before long the CI was introducing Russell to Ernie. Outside, Currier, Simmons and Linsky were parked further down Columbia Road near Richview Street. Other DCU officers had Ernie's Cadillac under observation.

Russell bought a round of drinks for Ernie and his partner Jimmy. Ernie started snorting heroin in plain view, but made no attempt to sell Russell any. Stone was too busy sucking a snowstorm up his nostrils to pay much attention to his new friend.

By 11:30 he was really high and decided it was time to depart. Ernie waved a cheery "So loooong" to the Music Bar patrons and stumbled through the cloud of smoke and out the door.

He was laughing and staggering, unable to locate his car. Finally, with the assistance of his man Jimmy, he located the Cadillac. Once behind the wheel, the dope-crazed cop rammed the car into action. The wheels were spinning, and the Caddy jerked squealing out into the middle of Columbia Road.

Connolly snapped on his walkie-talkie, trying to raise Linsky and Currier: "9-2 to Narco 3-4. Caddy, blue, taken off like a flash outta hell down Columbia Road toward Quincy Street."

"Narco 3-4. We got that," Simmons said in response to Connolly's call. "He just roared passed us. We're on him."

Seconds later, the speaker on Connolly's walkie-talkie was sputtering again. "Narco 3-4. He's traveling about 70 mph. Just hit a parked car and kept right on going."

"9-2. We're behind you. We're heading to Cabot Street."

"Narco 3-4. Our friend Ernie is flying tonight. He just sideswiped a white Buick at Warren and Quincy. When he turned into Warren, he went through a red light. He's gotta be crazy!"

Coleman was driving Connolly to the address where the buy was supposed to take place; the feds were following in their own unmarked car. Coleman shot through a yellow light at Warren Street and Martin Luther King Boulevard. As the DEA men passed under the light, it turned red.

A marked car spotted them go through the red, chased them and forced them over to the side of Warren Street. Connolly was listening with one ear to reports of the trail of destruction the blue Caddy was leaving behind and stared with disbelief as their chase was called to a halt by patrolmen who picked this of all times to get tough about beating the lights.

"Frank, turn around."

"What?"

"You won't believe this, but a cruiser got the Feds stopped for a traffic violation."

Coleman whipped the unmarked car around and headed for the flashing blue lights of the patrol car. Linsky's car kept asking why they hadn't all met up yet.

Connolly jumped out of the car and walked up to the officer who was about to write up a moving citation.

"Lieutenant Connolly, Drug Control. They're with us."

"Oh, OK, Lieutenant," the officer said. "Go ahead."

Linsky's voice came on the air. "That car, 9-2, has stopped in front of 26 Cabot Street. We're parked behind Salades Restaurant. We can eyeball the apartment from here. One man went inside. The other guy is still in the car."

"We'll be there soon," Connolly responded and hung up the mike.

Within minutes, Coleman and Connolly were studying the blue Cadillac. Slumped over the wheel with his jaw hanging down was Ernie Stone. For the next three-and-a-half hours, three DCU cars and one DEA vehicle had the passed-out cop's Caddy under observation.

During that time, the restaurants and bars in the area closed. When they turned off their lights and neon signs, Cabot Street became considerably darker.

Coleman restlessly looked at his watch. Sensing that the men in the other cars might also be growing impatient, Connolly got on the radio.

"We won't go in unless Ernie goes in," Connolly reminded them firmly. "Jimmy may be cutting it up in there with someone else."

"We got that, Lieutenant," a voice acknowledged over the car radio.

Then another voice chimed in. "Yeah, he might be getting laid."

"Wise guy, get off the air," Connolly said dryly, knowing the other men couldn't see the grin on his face.

Shortly after 4 am, the slamming of a door aroused the drowsing narco men. Jimmy had left 26 Cabot and was walking toward the Caddy. He tried to open the door on the passenger side, but it was locked. He rapped on the window with the big, flashy ring on his right hand, but Ernie was dead to the world.

Jimmy came over to the driver's side and started calling, "Ernie. Hey, Ernie, wake up."

When he got no response, he began calling and cussing even louder and started to thump on the hood of the car. The DCU and the DEA were laughing like crazy at Jimmy's predicament.

Finally, all the commotion he was creating woke one of the neighbors.

A woman stuck her head out of the window and yelled, "Hey, nigger, get the hell outta here. Stop making that fucking racket, or I'll call the cops. You're waking my kids."

A grey-topped black man padded out to his front porch. "Hey, drunk, shut your mouth or I'm calling the white cops and I hope they beat your black ass. Now, screw."

Things were heating up; Jimmy had had enough. He gave the windshield a final pound and hollered, "Ernie, you're an asshole."

Then he walked out to Tremont Street, waving his arms to hail a cab. As soon as Jimmy got a taxi, Connolly raised the others on the radio. "9-2 to Narco 3-4. Follow him out of the area and take him off when you're well out of this neighborhood. We'll drop this. Ernie more than likely will be sawing logs for hours. We'll see you guys back at the office."

It had been a long night. Coleman, Connolly and the men from the DEA and DCU were glad to be able to pack it in at last.

The sun was just breaking in the east and frosting the dusty panes of the office windows with an orangey-pink glaze when Linsky, Currier and Simmons walked in with Jimmy in tow.

"What have you got?" Connolly asked.

"Five bundles of smack and this," Bill Currier said, presenting the lieutenant with a double-barreled derringer. "It's fully loaded."

"Where'd you find him?"

"In a cab near Grove Hall."

"Before we go home, we got to book Jimmy in District 2. Then get him printed and mugged. By that time it will be court time. We'll let Arthur take him to see the judge at 9. We'll lodge him in District 2 after going to ID"

The men nodded that they understood.

"So long. I'm going home," Connolly added, reaching for his jacket. "Nobody else is going to say it, so I will 'Thank you. Good night . . . I mean . . . Good morning.'"

As he had countless times before, Connolly got into his car and headed home just as the rest of the city was rousing itself. A few delivery trucks were out. The sun was rising over the harbor as he hit the expressway. The heavier traffic was in the northbound lanes, suburbanites coming into the city.

Driving towards Milton, Connolly thought about his men and the guys from the DEA. He pondered questions that he had kicked around a thousand times before, "I wonder if anyone cares about a group of men, black and white, all good guys, working 16, 18, 20 hours to arrest a bad cop. No overtime, no complaints. Nobody's name will be in the papers. I care, but I don't think many other people will even know about this."

Lieutenant Connolly took the exit for Milton. "Why did Ernie become a cop? He was shot once in the line of duty; he was a hero. Now he's a bum. Why did he go bad? Why does it have to be one of us?"

It wasn't long before Russell was able to make a buy, but it was from Jimmy, who was out on bail awaiting trial but still selling. Ernie took the money, but Jimmy passed the dope. They could get Ernie on a conspiracy, but Connolly was hoping to really nail Stone during a second buy.

Then time ran out. Ed Cass informed Connolly that Russell had to get back to New York right away on a much more important case than a dope-peddling Boston cop.

Without Russell as a witness, Connolly and company didn't have much of a case, but Ernie didn't know that. He was confronted with some of the evidence that had been gathered. Instead of bringing the matter into court, he was allowed to resign and plead guilty on a lesser charge. He was given three years suspended sentence and probation.

From the day he left the courtroom, nobody from the DCU saw Ernie anywhere in the city ever again. Some rumors had it that he went for treatment for his heroin habit; others said that he got a job like Russell's working for the Drug Enforcement Administration.

One thing Connolly and the men at the Drug Control Unit knew. It had taken three years, but Ernie Stone was no longer a Boston cop. Whether the DCU had been screwed by the Feds was another question.

21

"Bus' em Back to Africa!"

Normally police officers wouldn't think of questioning the orders of a judge, but when the ultrasensitive issue of desegregating the Boston Public School system boiled over, many cops flatly declared themselves opposed to the court's decree.

In response to a suit filed by the NAACP, Federal District Judge W. Arthur Garrity ruled on June 21, 1974 that Boston's public schools were indeed racially segregated and ordered the city to remedy the situation, even if it became necessary to bus children from one district to another. The NAACP suit charged school officials with systematic segregation and maintaining a "dual system."

About a third of the city's 96,000 schoolchildren were black, but 82.2% of these children were attending schools with black enrollment majorities. These same schools tended to be more poorly equipped and to produce students with lower test scores than schools with predominantly white populations.

Judge Garrity ordered the city to reduce the number of black majority schools from 68 to 44 in accordance with state-mandated plans. While black leaders and parents applauded the move, School Committee Chairman John Kerrigan criticized the plan and called Garrity's competence into question.

One of the most questionable parts of the plan was the pairing of white South Boston and black Roxbury. Harvard Law Professor Louis L. Jaffe, the major architect of the Phase 1 desegregation plan, warned that the people of South Boston "are intensely hostile to blacks" and advised that that area not be included in Phase 1. The State Board of Education, however, seemed to want to make an example of Southie, the home of some of the Boston School Committee members who had worked hardest to preserve the status quo.

In the months prior to the fall opening of school, resentment in Boston's white communities was building. The protest marches and violence that erupted were not solely attributable to racism. Many parents were legitimately concerned about the safety of their children.

Many parents in Boston's white neighborhoods — Charlestown, South Boston and Hyde Park, for example, — resented the fact that

their children would be used as pawns in remedying the racial im-
balance situation. Some of the youngsters, both black and white,
would have to waste hours on the bus crossing the entire city.

White police officers who were also fathers knew just how
dangerous parts of Roxbury could be, and they didn't want their
children going to school in what they considered an unsafe
neighborhood. Editorials in *Pax Centurion*, the organ of the Boston
Police Patrolmen's Association, openly opposed the desegregation
plan. Funds from the BPPA treasury were used to mount a legal
challenge. Colored ribbons — green for Southie, purple for Hyde Park
— fluttered from the handlebars of certain police motorcycles, showing those officers' solidarity with white neighborhood groups determined to overturn the judge's decision.

Impassioned vows that busing would never be implemented were
heard at rally after rally. Police Commissioner Robert di Grazia knew
that an unprecedented show of police force would be needed to contain the volatile situation; in fact, "Operation Safety" became the
biggest security operation in the city's history.

Addressing a meeting of city, metropolitan and state police as well
as school officials, di Grazia outlined his plans. He confidently
assured the crowd that "this busing situation will be over in two
weeks."

"Not in two years!" Lieutenant Connolly called out.

Unlike di Grazia, who had recently moved to the city, Lieutenant
Connolly knew how deep feelings ran in many neighborhoods.

Because there was no way that the regular day shift could handle
the trouble that was anticipated and still tend to their regular duties,
di Grazia ordered the entire night shift and day-off crew to report for
work on September 12, 1974, the first day of the first desegregated
schoolyear. Lieutenant Connolly's Drug Unit, along with other plainclothesmen in the Vice, Robbery and Auto Squads, were told to get
into uniform or jumpsuits and helmets and report to the various
schools around the city. The Massachusetts State Police and the
Metropolitan District Police were also requested to stand by.

Though Mayor Kevin White and Commissioner di Grazia spread
the word that the police were to keep a low profile, the violence in
some parts of the city made it imperative for the officers to become
very visible.

Around 7 am on that first Thursday morning, Lt. Connolly and the
men from the DCU joined about 600 other cops on the streets in front
of and surrounding South Boston High School. The old yellow brick
structure stood atop Dorchester Heights, the hill from which General
Knox fired cannons at the British during the Revolutionary War.
Soon, another protracted battle would be raging on the very same
hilltop.

Sidewalks, fences, and boarded-up windows on houses were scrawled with vicious graffiti: *Bus' em back to Africa; Welcome Boneheads; Klan Kountry; French-fried Niggers For Sale.* Workmen were hastily summoned to the school to scrub away a freshly painted warning, "Niggers Go Home," from the door of the school before the students — and the TV cameras — arrived.

Though Eddie thought the whole project was wrongheaded and extremely wasteful of taxpayers' money, he was determined to fulfill his responsibilities. He was fairly sure that all his men would do the same in spite of their own misgivings. A couple of weeks earlier, rumors were circulating that the Boston Police Patrolmen's Association had informed its members that they did not have to make arrests ordered by their superior officers to enforce the desegregation plan because Judge Garrity had not clarified that it was in their power to do so. Lieutentant Connolly was confident that the DCU men would do what he told them, but he wasn't going to take any chances.

The lieutenant kept hammering the same message into every man's head: "Whatever your personal feelings are relative to busing, you have to put them aside. Your duty as a police officer comes first — to protect everyone, no matter what their color is."

As the long yellow buses rolled by, some taking a few black kids into Southie and others taking even fewer local kids out, Connolly noted the same expression on the young faces: uncertainty tinged with fear. Motorcycles rattled alongside, in front of, and behind their buses. Policemen dressed in combat gear had infiltrated their neighborhood streets on foot, in patrol cars and on horseback.

Each teen on a bus couldn't help wondering why he had been banished from familiar surroundings and condemned to a future at a strange school with strange kids, schools where, if rumors were to be believed, they would get the shit knocked out of them. Black boys imagined what they would do if confronted with a lynch mob. Every Southie girl who was slated to be bused was assured she would end up "raped in Roxbury," and no decent white guy would ever dream of marrying her after that.

The children themselves were not really to blame for the violence that broke out; it was the adult population that had skipped work to gather in thousands to watch, to yell their disapproval and, in some cases, to interfere with the implementation of Judge Garrity's desegregation plan.

The neighborhood streets, which normally would be populated at this hour with dogs sniffing at one another or an elderly lady hobbling to the corner variety store, were now choked with throngs of truants and red-faced adults, brandishing signs on sticks or hefting stones with which to shatter the windows of the passing buses. The milling around inevitably led to some pushing and shoving between the officers and the restless crowd.

Out of the 1744 students enrolled at South Boston High, a mere 124 showed up for classes. Twenty-one school buses had been hired to bring the 581 black students to the school, but most of the vehicles were empty. Only 56 black youngsters ventured into hostile territory that morning. As the buses passed through the streets of Southie, dropping kids off at the high school or the Hart Middle School, irate residents hurled stones, bottles, beer cans and crude racial slurs at the innocent passengers.

The police restricted the crowd of about 500 to the sidewalk on the opposite side of the street from the school so that the Roxbury teens could get off their buses. They couldn't stop the hecklers from using bananas as props as they imitated the antics of chattering chimpanzees and armpit-scratching apes, then pelted the Roxbury students with the bruised fruit. A watermelon rocketed over the fence and splattered into the schoolyard.

Listening to the crowd chanting "Die, niggers, die!" a Jesuit priest remarked in dismay, "If what I've been seeing isn't hate, then I don't know what hatred is."

Even when all the pupils were safely inside, the police had to contend with members of the crowd throwing things at blacks coming in and out of the building. Rev. John Banks of Roxbury was hit in the face with an egg. Dean Yarborough managed to escape a volley that included a tomato, a golf ball and assorted soft drink cans.

Connolly was ordered to have his men remove the spectators and hecklers from G Street and Eighth Street, just below South Boston High School. Among the crowd were a good number of housewives and mothers who were counting on the fact that the policemen would not dare touch them because they were female. As Connolly's helmeted troops approached the protestors and ordered them as politely as possible to "move on," the women replied with jeers and catcalls, dubbing the police "black baby-sitters."

"Stop pushing, you nigger-loving cop!"

"Don't you put your filthy hands on me! I'll have my son beat the livin' shit out of you if you lay so much as a finger on me!"

Trying to make himself heard over the din of the crowd, Connolly told the DCU men, "Keep moving them down the hill!" Noting that Connolly was the man in charge, a disheveled-looking old Irishwoman in her 60's deliberately stepped in his path. She rapped sharply on the plastic shield of his helmet and spat her insult in his face.

"Hey, you. I hope when you get home you find your wife in bed with a nigger."

"What did you say?" Connolly demanded, throwing up his visor.

"You heard me. I hope when you get home you find your wife screwing some blubber-lipped nigger!" she screamed.

"Well," Connolly said in the meekest voice he could manage, "If I catch those two in bed one more time, either them or me is going to have to leave that house."

Flabbergasted by this unexpected response, the old harridan allowed herself to be pushed back into the throng that was slowly being herded down to the beach at the foot of the hill.

One officer, Joseph Sirignano, was struck in the chest with a stone and had to be rushed to the hospital; he was treated and released the same day.

When there was a lull in the scuffling and jeering, Connolly pressed an ear to his walkie-talkie to get a sense of what was happening in the rest of the city; it was nothing like what was happening on Dorchester Heights. Even in Southie, despite all the ruckus and the sea of angry people, only four young men were ultimately arrested for disorderly conduct.

Since there were too few students to conduct normal classes, it was decided to let the kids go home early. The police brooked no interference with the black teenagers boarding the buses. Only two vehicles were needed to take the 56 kids out, quite a contrast to the morning parade of 21 buses.

While the escape from the school was effected neatly, trouble lay ahead as the nervous, inexperienced bus drivers raced down the steep slope of the hill in attempt to get out of Southie as fast as possible. The policemen lining the streets just shook their heads, fully expecting to see the pair of yellow buses tumbling into Dorchester Bay.

Overanxious bus drivers who were taking the ninth-graders from their classes at the L Street Annex turned the wrong way and drove right into an ambush. The buses were stoned; eight black students and a bus monitor were injured by the flying glass.

That evening Kevin White was invited to a meeting of black parents at the Freedom House in Roxbury and to a gathering of white parents in Southie. While Mayor White — or Mayor Black, as the anti-busing forces sometimes liked to call him — chose to go only to the Roxbury meeting, State Representative Ray Flynn, who eventually succeeded White as mayor, railed against the police presence in South Boston.

Flynn condemned the "extravaganza of police and horses and motorcycles" as "degrading" and "an outrage." He asserted that "when the police show up here with riot gear, horses and dogs, word gets around South Boston that something big is happening at South Boston High School. That's when all the trouble starts."

About the same time that Flynn was criticizing the police presence in Southie, Eddie was leaving his house, having changed out of his uniform and into civies. He headed back to Headquarters to begin his regular shift on the Drug Control Squad. For him as well as for most of his men, it was just the beginning of years of double duty. Sure, it was real nice to get the overtime, but it also drastically cut the hours he had to spend with his family and in the sack. Gradually, he became accustomed to sleeping only four hours or so a night.

On Monday, the third day of school, Detective Francis E. Creamer was dispersing teenagers from in front of the South Boston District Courthouse. Kids had gathered around there with big plans for storming and "recapturing" the high school. A brick hurled by a member of the crowd struck Creamer squarely on the chest. The 48-year-old officer collapsed onto the pavement and lacerated the left side of his scalp.

Two fellow officers rushed to his aid, called the 1500 wagon to take him to Boston City Hospital and gave him mouth-to-mouth enroute to the BCH. Nevertheless, Creamer went into cardiac arrest, and on October 7, he died — the only person to lose his life as a result of Boston's busing furor.

Connolly had known Creamer in the Robbery Squad. When he heard the news, he thought, "The first casualty, and it had to be one of us. Not from a gunman's bullet or some punk's knife, but from breaking up a band of good citizens who wanted to stop some little kids from learning their school lessons."

On the fifth day of school, David Duke, the Grand Dragon of the Ku Klux Klan, addressed a large crowd in an all-white section of Dorchester adjoining South Boston. He fired up the bigots in his audience by saying, "We are going to win a great victory in South Boston for the white race. The Federal government is taking little white children out of their homes and sending them into black jungles; the Federal government is taking the money out of your pockets to finance the production of thousands of little black bastards. . . . We don't believe that Negroes fit into modern society."

Representative Flynn and other South Boston leaders repudiated Duke's statements and refused his support. Duke met with some South Bostonians at the Czech Club on Columbia Road, but his views proved too extreme, and the men from Southie literally ran him out of town, depositing him outside the city limits. Nevertheless, the mere presence of the Grand Dragon in the vicinity further muddied the reputation of South Boston in the eyes of the nation.

Because Connolly was in the middle of all the skirmishes and stonings in the first weeks of busing in South Boston, he knew how distorted the accounts of events were in the press. Most of the Boston media complied with Kevin White's request to downplay or ignore any negative or potentially inflammatory incidents. On the other hand, the national magazines and television reporters failed to understand what was happening to the people of South Boston and unfairly dismissed all of Southie as a nest of diehard racists.

Southie was portrayed as a zone where no blacks ever set foot unless surrounded by a motorcade of cops. Eddie reflected that it had not been too long ago when South Boston had been a place where blacks and whites mingled freely and easily. For example, blacks used to go sunbathing in droves at Pleasure Bay, on the tip of the South Boston peninsula. A black family picnicking on the beach would send a kid to borrow some mustard from a white family near-by — no problem. However, the national attention focused on the embattled community branded every South Bostonian with the biased nature that was characteristic only of a few of its leaders.

The cost of implementing the desegregation order was staggering, and by far the biggest item in the budget was police pay. The tab for the first month, September 12 to 30, 1974, came to $1,361,836.33 in police salaries.

The Boston Police Department started spending an average of $100,000 a day on overtime; that figure did not take into account the expenses for feeding 1000 men on duty. In addition, the State Police were shelling out $20,000 a day, and the Metropolitan District Commission, $16,000 a day. The final estimate of the cost of keeping the BPD on double shifts for the first school year under Phase 1 was $7,153,800. Experts predicted that the price tag for police presence in the school for the following school year would top $10.7 million.

In the first months of busing, the number of police called into South Boston varied greatly from day to day. When things calmed down a bit, Connolly was assigned to another part of the city, Hyde Park. Instead of assisting in a massive security plan controlled by other people, Connolly and the troops from the Drug Control Unit had to manage the security of Hyde Park High as they saw fit.

School
Busing

Lt. Connolly arrests an unruly youth outside Hyde Park High on the day of the Crowley stabbing, October 15, 1974

(Paul Connell, *Globe*)

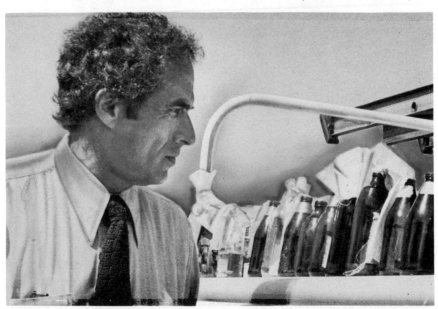

Police Commissioner Robert di Grazia examines molotov cocktails confiscated near Hyde Park High.

(Dick Thomson, *Herald*)

Outside Hyde Park High, Lt. Connolly dismisses the school detail for the day.

(Paul Connell, *Globe*)

Paul Barry, Boston Public School Department security officer, inspects damage to a school bus, stoned along Babe Ruth Boulevard in South Boston (9/12/74).   (Dennis Brearley, *Herald*)

After all the students are safely on their way home, the cops can leave Hyde Park High. (Stanley Forman, *Herald*)

Police motorcyclists escort school buses out of South Boston. Classes were dismissed early on October 2, 1974 because of the trouble that broke out in the morning.

(M. Leo Tierney, *Herald*)

The Tactical Patrol Force (TPF) members throw canisters of tear gas to disperse a rock- and missle-throwing crowd on East Sixth Street in South Boston (2/15/76).

(Ray Lussier, *Herald*)

South Bostonians march down Broadway to protest school desegregation on October 4, 1974.
(Stanley Forman, *Herald*)

Riot helmets are not needed on a rare quiet morning at South Boston
High during the early days of busing (8/18/74).   (M. Leo Tierney, *Herald*)

In the wake of the Michael Faith stabbing, South Bostonians and
Boston Police clash in the streets (12/12/74).

(Ray Lussier, *Herald*)

22

Molotov Cocktails at Hyde Park High

Connolly was sent to replace Superintendent Paul Russell and to take responsibility for the security inside Hyde Park High School. Located on the southernmost tip of Boston, Hyde Park was at that time a predominantly white residential area. Most of the 1400 kids that attended Hyde Park High walked to class.

Unlike the situation at South Boston High, which had been essentially all white before busing, the integration at Hyde Park High only meant doubling the existing 20% black population to about 40%. However, the fall of 1974 brought not only desegregation, but also the acquisition of a ninth grade, housed in the Annex a few blocks further down Metropolitan Avenue. There was a higher percentage of blacks among the 1100 new freshmen than among the 1680 upperclassmen who went to classes in the main building.

Between 37 and 40 school buses arrived each morning, escorted by police cars and motorcycles through streets lined by men on foot. Those students who came by public transportation found Boston Police officers at the stop when they alighted. A few incidents did flare up at the MBTA station, but the BPD along with the T police were there to check any disturbance before it got out of hand.

In contrast to the rock-throwing, abusive throngs in Southie and Charlestown, protesters in Hyde Park never numbered more than 20 or 30. Parents would gather in a very orderly fashion on a corner near the school. Though they would stay there all day with signs, they never presented a real problem to the police.

Connolly surveyed the fortress he had inherited from Russell. The three-story structure was built as a huge triangle with long wide corridors. In one part of the basement was the shop area where the vocational courses in woodworking, machine and drafting were taught. Since most of the kids taking class had elected these practical courses, they were not as rambunctious as Voc Ed students sometimes are. Besides, the teachers in shop ruled with an iron hand.

The basement also contained a lunchroom which, large as it was, could not accommodate all the students at one sitting. So the kids had to eat in three shifts . . . with 20 to 30 policemen, school aides, teachers and submasters, monitoring the situation to make sure no one started a fight.

Though the idea was to desegregate the school, the kids inevitably gravitated to tables where other members of their race were eating. Blacks congregated in certain areas; white kids staked claim to others. The few Chinese and Hispanic students sat alone, ostracized by both factions.

During Connolly's first week at the school, there was a brief free-for-all in the cafeteria with plates of spaghetti splattering everywhere, trays and chairs flying through the air, and the lunch-room generally being turned into a shambles. Though food fights were rare, one or two were more than enough.

Eventually, Headmaster John Best decided to eliminate the lunch period completely. The kids came to school in the morning and went straight through six periods. They were dismissed in a staggered pattern; often blacks were allowed to leave early on the buses while the whites stayed in the building.

Trouble tended to break out when the classes were changing. The bell would ring and the silence of the halls would give way to zoo-like chatter as the students straggled to their next classroom. One student would bump against someone going in the opposite direction, and a brawl would be touched off. To stave off these encounters, Connolly stationed a policeman every 20 feet in the corridors, whenever possible next to an alarm box. In the boys' bathroom, a couple of officers and a male aide saw to it that no problems arose.

Despite all these precautions, it was easy for one person to lash out with a comment and for someone else to reply with a haymaker. Both boys and girls threw themselves into a fracas without the slightest hesitation.

One day, Connolly was talking to Superintendent-in-Chief Joe Jordan about the situation in Hyde Park.

"Mr. Superintendent, I think I can solve our problem. It's so simple. It's been right in front of me all the time. Every day I look at it. How come I didn't realize it sooner?"

"What's that?" Jordan returned lazily to undercut Connolly's big build-up for his brainstorm. "What do you want to do . . . close down the school?"

"No, we should try one-way traffic. Everyone travels in the same direction. That way nobody can cross paths or bump shoulders with a fellow coming the opposite way."

"Let's think about this a little more."

"The kids will be bullshit if we implement the idea," Connolly admitted. "It would mean that they'll have to walk a bit further to get where they're going, but maybe it would do them good. Work off a little more of that steam."

With Jordan's approval, Connolly presented his idea to Headmaster John Best at their regular early morning conference in Best's
office.

"Let's give it a shot," Best said enthusiastically. "We'll have a
teachers' meeting and explain the idea to them. Then we'll give them
the rest of the week to prepare the student body for the change. We'll
try your idea out next Monday."

Several days of announcements in class had alerted the kids to the
new rules, but when Monday arrived they acted as if they had never
heard of the idea before.

"Clockwise, clockwise," Assistant Headmaster Jeremiah Botelho
kept calling as the kids streamed through the front doors. "To your
right."

"I'm goin' to my locker. It's right around the corner," a tall black
basketball player announced as he tried to brush past Botelho,
heading left.

"Don't you know your right from your left?" the assistant headmaster snapped.

"You expect me to go all the way around just to get to my locker?"
the hoopster demanded, towering over Botelho.

"Bright boy, Jones," Botelho smiled. "To your right!"

"Shit!" Jones growled, but obeyed.

All morning long, the police and administrative staff talked
themselves hoarse, rerouting the traffic.

"I just wanna go to the office."

"To the right."

"My class is right there. Ten feet away."

"To the right."

After an exhausting morning, the students grudgingly began to
observe the circular traffic flow pattern. Eddie was pleased that at
least initially the incidence of corridor clashes dropped dramatically.

At the least indication of physical contact, the police would move
in and get the situation under control. Connolly had a strict rule that
anyone involved in a fight would be arrested. He and eventually the
students learned that the arrest meant little, because the kids were
soon out on bail. The court would usually dismiss those involved in a
hallway tussle, but if the incident involved a weapon or an assault on
a teacher, the consequences were likely to be more serious.

In any case, the main point was to get the parents down to the station to bail out the young offenders. Connolly and the others hoped
that the parents' annoyance at being dragged away from work or
household chores would result in some meaningful and effective
punishment administered at home.

There would be long periods of serenity when the school would
seem to have subsided back into its pre-busing calm. Then, without

explanation, fights would break out in two or three different locations simultaneously. Connolly would have to summon the Tactical Patrol Force and other outside units for assistance. The patrol wagons would pull up to the side doors of the building. Officers would hustle the cursing teenagers out, load the wagons up and cart them to Station 5. There the adolescents would be booked, and their parents notified to come in. Students would be released into their parents' custody and ordered to appear the following morning in court to answer charges.

Shortly after Connolly assumed command at Hyde Park High, there occurred an act of violence that was by far the most serious incident since the school had opened in 1928.

On Tuesday, October 15, things got off to a bad start. Mr. Richard Costello, a teacher, saw a white girl being chased out of the girls' lavatory by a gang of black girls. He caught the leader of the gang by the waist to detain her; suddenly a trio of black males were raining blows on Costello's face and head and stole his wallet. His head injuries were so severe that he had to go home.

The assault on the teacher led to disruptions all over the building. Later that morning, a white sophomore named Joseph Crowley and a friend were walking by the same restroom when they found their progress stopped by a catfight in progress.

When Crowley saw a white girl outnumbered by blacks, he tried to intervene. All of a sudden, he felt a sharp pain in his abdomen. He pulled open his leather jacket and saw the blood seeping through his shirt.

He turned to his friend and said, "I've been stabbed. What should I do?"

A teacher gave Crowley some first aid and summoned an ambulance to take the boy to the Carney Hospital. The school flared into an uproar as exaggerated stories about the knifing spread. Eventually, three white boys and three white girls were also sent to the Carney for treatment of minor injuries.

Captain Joseph Rowan and the entire 125-man Tactical Patrol Force had to be summoned to restore order. They came on horses, cycles and two special buses stationed at a nearby shopping plaza.

After conferring with the police, school officials announced at 10:45 that school would be closed for the rest of the day. The faculty decided not to keep the school closed the next day, but did demand that the police station at least 50 or 60 men inside the building.

Though no arrests were made inside the building, Crowley's 14-year-old sister was caught hysterically throwing rocks at the busloads of black kids.

In his understated style, the headmaster tried to downplay the incident when he talked to the press, "It appears that a few apparently minor incidents touched off an awful lot of involvement by a number of students here which degenerated into a pretty close to riotous situation.''

John Best went on in a franker style to admit "Last Friday was a good a day as you could have and we thought we had turned the corner. There is no question that today's incidents set us back. It was very discouraging to us and to 90% of the students."

Parents were exchanging rumors that Crowley had died. His wound was merely a deep slash and not puncture, but the fact that he had to be kept overnight made the incident the worst so far in the busing saga.

That same day Massachusetts Governor Francis Sargent ordered 450 Massachusetts National Guardsmen to report to their armories to stand by in case they were needed to intervene in a desegregation tumult. Many Bostonians felt this hasty measure was an insult to the efficiency of the Boston Police Department. The mayor was "outraged"; and Commissioner di Grazia called the alert "too drastic" and warned that it would cause attendance to drop.

For next two days, the white Hyde Park High students staged a boycott of classes, and attendance was down to 30%. Teachers searched students entering the building more carefully to prevent a repetition of the stabbing incident.

On Friday, only the perspicacity of some officers in the street averted a potentially catastrophic situation. Around 12:30 on October 18, Patrolman Harold Prefontaine stopped a 1966 blue Rambler station wagon driving along Metropolitan Avenue to allow two small children to cross safely at the intersection.

The operator failed to stop until Prefontaine ran up to the front of the car and held up his hand. The patrolman ordered him to pull over and surrender his license.

While examining the driver's papers, Prefontaine spotted a broom handle and a club on the floor of the front seat. Sergeant Leo MacDougall and Patrolman Edward Holland of the TPF approached the car and observed a passenger in the backseat hastily covering some bottles with a brown paper bag. The officers got a whiff of what seemed to be gasoline or kerosene.

They ended up charging the Hyde Park High truants with possession of an "infernal engine," to wit, Molotov cocktails. Closer examination revealed ten Michelob bottles: four still unopened, two empty, three filled with gasoline and recapped and one open bottle with gasoline and a cloth wick hanging out.

In addition there was one Narragansett Lager Beer bottle containing gasoline. Two light bulbs had been sawed off midway down the metal base. These too had been filled with gasoline and had white cotton cloth draped over the edge as wicks.

At District 5 one of the boys confessed that they made the Molotov cocktails in a wooded area nearby, and they had planned to use them to firebomb buses traveling from Hyde Park High to American Legion Highway.

To avoid a repetition of the Crowley knifing, Connolly and Best agreed to have metal detectors installed. Each morning as the students climbed the front stairs and entered the main doors, they had to pass through one of six metal detectors. On rainy days students stood cursing in the drizzle waiting to get in. School security personnel would check purses, bookbags and bundles for weapons. The frisking turned up weapons like clubs and pipes, but outside the school the police found knives, obviously discarded before the student had to pass through the metal detectors.

Thereafter, whenever news filtered back to Best and Connolly that someone might have smuggled a knife or gun past the metal detectors, they would wait until after school and conduct a thorough search of all the lockers. Though this procedure was not terribly legal, it was necessary to ensure the safety of the kids. The students never caught wise to the fact that their lockers were being surreptitiously inspected, but then again the administrative bloodhounds rarely turned up more than moldy sweat socks and long-forgotten book reports.

Slowly white attendance rose back to normal, but shortly after Christmas break an even worse hurricane of violence tore through the school.

Early on Thursday morning, January 9, 1975, a white boy was about to enjoy a candy bar he had just pulled from his locker. A black classmate tried to snatch it away. A fistfight broke out on the first floor, and the melee spread throughout the entire building.

Connolly notified Headquarters that he needed help pronto, and in minutes busloads of TPF men were on their way from the Bayside Mall lot where they were waiting in readiness.

At the height of the uproar, more than 225 policemen were in the building trying to restore order. Students tried to grab the cops' guns; in one case a student was successful, but the officer managed to retrieve his weapon.

During the fracas, an angry kid yanked at Connolly's walkie-talkie, but the leather strap that hung around Eddie's neck held fast.

Lieutenant Connolly ordered the paddy wagon to pull up to the Central Avenue doors, and 15 young hell-raisers — 13 black and two white — were tossed in back. Suddenly, the firebrands lost their sizzle.

"Kids are funny," he remarked later that day. "They sure were quiet once they got into the wagon. I guess they had their fling, and it was all over."

To prevent a reoccurrence of the gun-snatching incident, Eddie told all officers to unload their weapons at the early morning rollcall in the cafeteria and only reload when they left the school. He also advised them to keep their guns in their pockets.

With 225 policemen going at it with hundreds of kids, it was inevitable that some of the adults in the school would also get roughed up. Many religious, parent and minority groups had insisted on having observers in Hyde Park High to report back firsthand on the conditions on the school. Needless to say, having everyone from the Quakers to the US Department of Justice marshalls underfoot all the time merely aggravated the problems of keeping order, and added to Eddie's feeling that the whole school was becoming one big surrealistic circus.

Perhaps the most annoying aspect of the presence of these outsiders was that some of them were drilling kids in "how to straighten out a policeman." The students were coached in how to get an officer's badge number and name, to note his appearance and the place he was standing, and to establish the exact time the incident occurred by looking at a clock.

These overrehearsed teens hoped to intimidate cops with their star witness skills, threatening to bring up officers they didn't like on charges of racism.

Eventually, Best banished all these meddling outsiders from the school, a move that eventually cost him his job.

One particular lady had tried to interfere when a black girl was being arrested and ended up on the floor. She complained to the press that such incidents would not occur if the same details were sent every day to the school.

Connolly agreed that the officers who came on a regular basis before Christmas had developed a good rapport with the monitors and kids. It was not unusual to see a cop sitting by a student in the hallways, tutoring him or her in math or English. There were friendly pick-up games of basketball or touch football.

But lately, Eddie explained, the officers had been serving on a rotating basis, and he had no control over who was sent or even how many men were sent on any given day.

Eventually, this uproar too subsided for a while, only to flare up once again. The incidents at Hyde Park High started getting more outrageous.

It was Wednesday, February 12 — the beginning of Lent. It might have been the fact that it was Ash Wednesday, but a group of black girls decided to torch the American flag in the auditorium and reduce it to ashes.

White kids, who the day before couldn't have cared less about the red, white and blue, became instant patriots and started screaming, "You can't do that to my country!"

Determined to avenge this desecration on all blacks, gangs of white students touched off another extended racial brawl that landed more students in the hospital or Station 5.

The teacher who had beaten out the flames turned the ashes of the flag over to the FBI agents who came to investigate.

Two days later, a busload of 50 black Hyde Park High youngsters decided to go on a Valentine's Day joyride and forced the 50-year-old white driver to take them over to the McDonald's on American Legion Highway.

A rash of unseemly incidents like these led to the replacement of Best with Michael Donato, who was born and raised in Hyde Park. A star athlete at Boston College High and Boston University, he brought a more forceful presence to the Headmaster's office.

The same sorts of problems kept cropping up periodically under Donato's regime. He and Eddie would start the day with a strategy session around 6:30 or 7:00 to discuss any rumors either of them had heard. They would often end the day on the steps in front of the school, fielding questions from TV and press reporters from as far away as Italy and Spain.

When graduation time rolled around, the policemen and students had become so much a part of each other's daily school experience that the police officers bought ads in the school yearbook; Eddie Connolly took out one of his own to offer congratulations to those who had made it through the first stormy year.

At commencement, Eddie was given an honorary high school diploma and a "perfect attendance" award. But no student rejoiced more than Connolly when Hyde Park High closed. He had the whole summer off to work just his nighttime Drug Control shifts and to rest up for his second year of duty at racially troubled Hyde Park High.

23

A Lot of Baloney

Word had come down from the city fathers to Lieutenant Connolly to keep an eye on Deer Island. The minimum security House of Correction had been changing over the years. Situated at the tip of a peninsula at the north end of Boston Harbor was the plot of land that held the prison and the inefficient, foul-smelling sewage treatment plant that was polluting the waters of the bay.

At the top of a slight crest was the Hill Prison, a five-story red brick building that from a distance looked like a high school with its central steeple crowned with a cupola. Originally, it had been a women's prison, but later the space was needed to house male prisoners. In the 30's and 40's it was known as the Daddy-Owe Club, because it was full of harmless fellows, sentenced to months in prison for non-support or alcoholism. However, in the late 60's and early 70's, overcrowding of the Massachusetts prison system had forced Deer Island to accept some medium and maximum security offenders. The farming that used to keep the prisoners out in the fresh air was discontinued, and the Hill Prison, erected in 1901, began to really show its age.

Reginald Eaves, the Suffolk County Penal Commissioner, had a reputation for not being the most scrupulous caretaker of the place. It was rumored that drugs were showing up on the Island, but no one on the outside knew the extent of the crisis.

Connolly sent Boston policewomen in to pose as wives of prisoners and eavesdrop on female visitors in the waiting room of the prison. He hoped that the officers would overhear a conversation about a drug deal planned for the outside or perhaps even see contraband being passed from mouth to mouth during a farewell kiss. Unfortunately, this precaution did not yield any evidence.

One Memorial Day, Connolly got a tip that Buster, one of the Deer Island guards, was headed for work with decks of heroin on the frame of his car; he allegedly intended to sell the dope to addicts in the prison. In addition to being a guard, Buster was the Island's athletic director, a position that meant extra pay and prestige. Buster's good fortune excited the jealousy and dislike of his white co-workers, most of whom concluded that the black commissioner was playing favorites with one of the few black guards on the Island.

Because of the holiday, Eddie couldn't get a warrant nor could he get in touch with the regular judges who were on vacation or at some Memorial Day function. Even without the usual paperwork to back him up, Connolly knew that this was one of those emergency situations in which he was legally permitted to search without the warrant.

Connolly stopped Buster right on the Winthrop-Boston line, just before he approached the prison. When Eddie and his men went through the interior of the car, they found a dozen dime bags of marijuana under the seat.

"You got me!" Buster said.

"Not yet," Connolly countered, as he edged his way under the car. Using a flashlight and groping with his hand, the lieutenant found four magnetic keycases, clinging to the frame of the car and filled with decks of heroin.

"I want to tell you something, lieutenant. The marijuana is mine. The heroin is planted," Buster said. "I don't fuck around with that stuff. I make a few bucks selling grass, but the heroin's not mine. I swear on my kids."

They brought Buster to District 7 and had his car towed to a gas station where they put it up on a hydraulic lift in a fruitless search for more containers of heroin.

Buster was fired, but at the trial he had a strong defense put up for him by a public defender. Eaves testified that Buster was basically a

The Hill Prison on Deer Island
(Photo by R. Sennott, courtesy *Boston Herald*)

good guy and that he had a lot of enemies at the Island, any one of whom could have planted the decks and called the police to get revenge on him. Buster was convicted of the marijuana rap but not of the more serious charge of bringing heroin into a penal institution.

Either Eaves was covering up for a man he knew to be guilty, or one of Buster's fellow guards had planted dope in the athletic director's car to discredit him. No matter how one looked at the incident, it reflected very poorly on the prison administration and indicated that there was a drug problem on Deer Island.

When William Nickerson took over as Penal Commissioner for Suffolk County in September of 1975, Deer Island was in need of drastic reform. It seemed every month there was a stabbing, while inmates kept disappearing every few days. In fact, Deer Island was reputed to lead the nation in escapes. During a 12-month period, 112 out of some 200 prisoners managed to skip off. (Part of the problem was an unguarded gate that allowed prisoners to stroll out of the compound virtually whenever they pleased.)

After an initial tour of the facilities, Nickerson's assessment of the situation was "What the employees haven't stolen, the prisoners have destroyed.

"Because most guards got their jobs through patronage, the security has gone to hell. Most guards don't wear uniforms, but it's not hard to tell the keepers from the kept because, in fact, the prisoners are the keepers and the guards are the kept."

There hadn't been a comprehensive shakedown of the place in a long time. The smell of marijuana was so overpowering that it even managed to mask the odor of the adjacent sewage treatment plant.

About half of the prisoners were black and were kept segregated in the east wing. Roughly 40% of the inmates were white, and they were concentrated in the west wing. The remaining mixed-bloods and Hispanics were scattered between the two blocks.

Nickerson knew that the rampant thievery from the commissary and the free access to drugs meant that many of his own employees were involved in illegal activities. Hence, he had to look outside the prison staff for assistance in clearing up the drug problem.

Nickerson wanted to send a unmistakable message to the prisoners that he would not tolerate the current conditions, but he had little faith in his gurads, some of whom he knew must be involved in smuggling alcohol, drugs, contraband and even women into Deer Island. He wanted to show both the prisoners and the guards that if any emergency arose, he had a force behind him — the Boston Police.

At Commissioner di Grazia's suggestion, Commissioner Nickerson consulted with Ed Connolly, a man he had met briefly through his uncle, a Boston cop. Nickerson was not impressed by Eddie's stooped posture and general appearance, but Connolly had a reputation for being efficient and completely reliable.

Connolly had tried to place undercover police in the prison a couple of years earlier under the regime of Reginald Eaves, but within the first week the identities of the officers had been exposed. In fact, Eddie suspected that they allowed themselves to be unmasked because they were unhappy with their precarious position as spies.

This time, Connolly was determined to make the undercover operation work, but he needed faces that were unknown. He scouted out a number of prospects, but finally invited five young men to his office for the final winnowing. Prior to this interview, the prospective plants had been told only that the operation would not involve arresting other cops.

Among the men were Jack Parlon and Walter "Mitty" Robinson. As partners in District 5, they had posed successfully as hippies and bikies and made many drug arrests. They were able to blend into the drug subculture because of their unpoliceman-like appearance.

Parlon looked like an apostle with his neatly trimmed beard and shoulder-length hair and skinny frame. He wore a long GI overcoat with corporal's stripes as part of his dippy hippy costume.

Robinson was shorter and more muscular than his partner, but his beard was less well tended than Parlon's. Mitty wore a leather jacket and usually some sort of covering for his shiny bald pate. The day of the interview he was sporting a slouch hat with a feather in the band, one of the less outrageous items in his extensive collection of wild headgear.

Cautiously, Connolly began to sketch out the general nature of the assignment. After about twenty minutes, three of the officers excused themselves; they didn't like the sound of the operation.

Connolly then confronted the two remaining, "Are you two in?"

Jack and Mitty searched one another's eyes.

"You wanna?"

"Sure. Why not?"

Connolly began to reveal the details almost reluctantly. He wasn't sure that uncovering a few dope-dealing guards or the thieves who were raiding the prison pantry would be worth risking the lives of these fine young officers.

"What you're gonna do is work undercover at Deer Island . . . not as prisoners, but as guards. No one will know your identity as policemen except di Grazia, Penal Commissioner Nickerson, and myself.

"That means if you get into a situation at the prison, there will be no one to turn to; you'll be on your own.

"You're going to go down and apply for jobs as temporary guards. You'll take the tests and the physicals. You'll be photographed and fingerprinted just like anybody else. You'll sign the names we give you because, of course, you have to have new identities. You pick whatever names you feel at ease with. I'll take care of your security clearance and IDs with new addresses.

"This job is extremely dangerous. I'm thinking now that I want to back off on it. I don't feel right about it. Your lives would be in danger . . . I'm just going to lay this plan out for you. If you don't want to go, nothing will be held against you.

"I would be hesitant myself . . . I think that I would not accept the assignment. I don't know . . ."

Despite Connolly's reservations, both men indicated that they wanted the assignment. Eddie shook their hands.

"I'm going to try to make this as short-lived as possible," Connolly promised, "but I guarantee you one thing: if this thing turns out alright, you'll be made members of the Drug Unit."

Naturally, Robinson and Parlon wanted to know what they would have to contend with, but Eddie really didn't have much more information.

Jack Parlon, Jerry Dailey and Walter "Mitty" Robinson (left to right) in a rare photo showing them in uniform.

"I don't know exactly what's doing. I hear stories about how bad the drugs are down there, but I don't really know. But whatever happens, I put my trust in you. When you tell me there's a lot or you tell me there's none, I'll believe it.

"If at anytime that you think you're in jeopardy down there, anytime that you think you're going to have trouble, I want you to walk right out of the goddamned place, right through the gate, right out. Don't worry about anybody. Just walk right out and you give me a call. I'll come down and pick you up." Before the partners left Connolly's office, they made him a promise: "If someone's bad, he's going, even if it's the chaplain."

In establishing their undercover identities, the two officers decided to retain their first names, but to use their mothers' maiden names as surnames. Parlon became John Lombard; Robinson was known as Walter Ferris.

Connolly showed the officers photos of all the current inmate population. Any prisoners whom either of the men recognized were transferred to other facilities. Eddie took every precaution he could to ensure that these two were not "made" as quickly as the other men he had planted.

In a few weeks, "Lombard" and "Ferris" had passed all the required tests and found themselves scheduled for duty. Robinson and Parlon learned the harsh realities of prison life the hard way; both men had narrow escapes on their very first shifts on Deer Island.

Robinson strolled into a room where a group of inmates were playing cards. One prisoner looked up from his hand and remarked, "Hey, the new screw looks like an undercover cop from downtown."

"Shit," Robinson thought, "I can't be made on my first day!"

Despite the fact that he was cursing and sweating inside, he just chuckled at the suggestion.

Another poker player laughed, "If he was a cop, he'd have to be out of his fuckin' head to be in here with us."

The others, taking in his unimpressive appearance, agreed and returned to their game strategy. Robinson wandered off into another room where he could breathe a sigh of relief.

Parlon, on the night shift, had a real baptism of fire. As a prelude of things to come, he heard a great commotion being raised. Several prisoners were furious, swearing they would kill an inmate in an adjoining cell. His offense had been to spray cockroach repellent in his own cell, which sent the insects scurrying into the quarters of his neighbors.

No sooner had that incident started to simmer down than Parlon was instructed to accompany Dennis Fogg, a uniformed, permanent guard, to the Plant.

The Plant was the maximum security detention cellblock adjoining the administration building. When a prisoner was sent to the Plant for disciplinary reasons, he was forced to vacate his "house" in the Hill prison or one of the cottage dormitories. The cell and the prisoner were stripped down completely. The prisoner's belongings were put in storage until he was released from the Plant. At that point he could retrieve his property and set up in whatever new cell became available.

The Plant owed its name and unpleasant atmosphere to the steam plant in a nearby shed. Many leaky pipes that carried heat from the boilers to the other buildings ran through the Plant. Escaping jets of steam made the cellblock suffocatingly hot. The floors were always warm, and the dank, tropical quality of the air made it hard to breathe. The moisture also had the dingy paint curling and chipping off the thick stone walls.

To get a breath of fresh air, prisoners broke the panes of the high windows in the outer wall of the Plant. However, birds would fly in, attracted by the warmth, and then become trapped in the high-ceiling cellblock. Then the inmates had to listen to the frantic chirping of the birds, that like the prisoners themselves, were desperate to escape from the prison.

Only the two bottom tiers of the four-tiered Plant were used. There were no working toilets; inmates simply pissed or shat in a bucket. Their meagre food was just thrown in at them.

Parlon and Fogg passed through an unusually thick door with a fist-sized opening in it. Parlon found himself on a small platform elevated about three feet from the floor.

The platform was surrounded by a metal railing and held a desk and a stool. Once the guards were in, they locked the door from the inside and hung the key up on a little hook by the wall telephone.

The prisoners, about twelve of Deer Island's rowdiest malcontents, were taking advantage of a 20-minute release from their cells. Many of them were dressed just in their socks and shorts. They were sitting around with little milk cartons and the tiny cereal boxes that you slit and pour the milk into so you can eat right out of the container.

The release time had elapsed, and the inmates were ordered back into their six-by-eight stalls for the night. The men acted as if they hadn't heard a thing.

"Come on, you guys, back into your holes," Fogg said wearily.

Parlon just perched on his stool feeling like a dope, wondering, "What the fuck are we going to do if these guys don't want to go back into their cells? Fogg must have some kind of system. Maybe he just waits them out or something."

"Hey, I told you to get back in the cells. Now move."

Finally there was an acknowledgement. "Go fuck yourself. We're not going anywhere."

"The fuck you're not!" Fogg answered. "You fuckin' better move when I tell you."

The dozen cons began to get really ugly, but Parlon wasn't especially nervous yet. He kept telling himself, "Fogg must just press a button, and ten guys will come in, and we'll throw these bastards back where they belong . . ."

Then one of the inmates grabbed one of the brooms that were lying around, snapped off the straw end and used the stick to bang on the metal railing that protected the guard's platform.

"OK," thought Parlon. "This has to be it. Any second now, he's got to ring a bell or dong a gong or something . . . and then the troops are going to come."

The prisoners began pelting the guards with their empty cartons and half-eaten Rice Crispies packets.

Fogg calmly took the keys off the hook, slid open the slot in the door, and — much to Parlon's amazement — tossed the keys out, effectively locking himself and Parlon — alone and unarmed — in the Plant with 12 angry men.

Parlon's mind spun feverishly. "He must have made a mistake. Maybe he was supposed to throw something else out, and he tossed the keys out by accident."

"Wait," Parlon cried, "What are you doing? That's our only escape . . ."

Throwing the keys out was apparently a declaration of all-out war because the prisoners reacted by breaking the ends off five other brooms, and one guy snatched up a shovel. They were hollering and clattering their sticks against the railing. Others raced up to their cells, grabbed their buckets and began pitching the stinking excrement down on the guards trapped on the landing below.

As if on cue, the pipes started pumping out more steam, hissing symbols of the prisoners' overheated tempers.

Fogg calmly made a phone call, but what seemed like a month went by, and the cavalry still had not ridden to the rescue. One enraged inmate took a running leap and started clambering up onto the platform. Fogg promptly vaulted over the railing down on to the head of the prisoner who was climbing up.

"What the fuck did I ever do to deserve this?" Parlon thought, watching the ballsy, but rather small Fogg wrestle with an inmate. Parlon felt like strangling Fogg himself for getting him into this situation, but he knew he just couldn't let another guard get eaten alive. And so, cursing for all he was worth, Jack too forsook the relative security of the platform, hopped over the metal bars and threw himself into the fracas below.

Parlon was ready for the worst, but surprisingly the prisoners backed off once the guards got down on their level. Fogg kept the aggression on a verbal plane and limited the physical contact to shoving, rather than clobbering.

Finally, the reinforcements arrived at the door. Since the keys were on the floor on the outside, the back-up crew was able to enter swiftly. Once the prisoners saw five more guards, they lost all their bravado and returned to their cells, muttering threats.

"What an introduction to Deer Island night life!" Jack thought. "I haven't been in this stinking hole more than four hours, and already I'm covered with shit, piss and fucking cornflakes."

Thereafter Parlon and Mitty usually worked the same shift, but rarely in the same wing of the prison. Connolly didn't want it to look as though these two knew each other. The idea was for each man to find his own way of worming himself into the confidence of corrupt elements in the staff. Each officer chose a different tack.

Robinson developed a whole personality for his alter ego: Ferris was a bungler par excellence. He would purposely miscount the number of prisoners at lock-up time. By forcing recount, he would thus disrupt everyone's schedule and annoy the guards and inmates no end.

He made himself such a legend of incompetency that for a while a slang expression became popular: "to pull a Ferris" meant "to screw a job up royally." When anyone would ask him why he didn't make more of an effort to do a better job, he would shrug his shoulders and say, "I just don't give a fuck. I'm only here to collect a paycheck."

With this kind of attitude, he seemed like a person who might agree to any illegal scheme if there was a buck in it for him.

Parlon used a different approach. As Lombard, he chatted with the other guards about his love of hunting and fishing . . . and about how his growing family's needs made it impossible for him to enjoy these hobbies.

One day when he was moaning about his food bills, an inmate remarked, "Your kids like baloney?"

"Sure. But even baloney costs a goddam fortune these days."

"Not if you buy in quantity," the inmate responded. "Listen, for a very reasonable price I can arrange for a guard to get you some great baloney from the commissary."

That evening Parlon's wallet was a little lighter, and under his pea jacket was a huge, deli-sized baloney. Soon Robinson too heard about these cut-rate goodies, and both of them were buying stolen food and smuggling it out. Since Parlon was skinny, he could conceal a salami or a wheel of cheese under his coat. His stocky partner used an AWOL bag.

Whatever the technique, it was still a long, cold quarter of a mile walk down the hill to the parking lot after they got off duty. Each night after they got off at 11 they prayed that none of the honest guards would spot what they were doing and blow the whistle on them.

The two undercover men would turn over their booty to Connolly at their nightly rendezvous. After a few jokes along the lines of "This whole case is a lot of baloney," Connolly announced, "One of you guys is going to have to buy another fridgedaire or freezer and keep all this stuff in your home until we can present it as evidence in court against the guard that's pilfering from the commissary."

Neither man wanted to volunteer for this extra complication in his family's life.

"That's stealing from the City of Boston, all this food with the fancy labels is supposed to go to the prisoners," Connolly continued. "Now, who's it going to be?"

"At the rate we're going," sighed Parlon, "Mitty and I will both have to get meat lockers."

Though participating in the food theft was a major pain for officers bent on ferreting out narcotics traffickers, they knew that once word spread that Lombard and Ferris were involved in smaller crimes like this, it wouldn't be long before someone offered one of them a chance to participate in a drug deal.

The officers would meet Connolly in out-of-the-way places like the lot by Dolan's Funeral Home in Dorchester's Lower Mills because it was on their way home. Connolly would park in a dark area. Parlon and Robinson would pull up in their cars around midnight, get out and climb into the back seat of Connolly's vehicle to fill him in on what had happened that evening. Before heading home, they would agree on a different meeting place for the following night.

Sometimes on nights that Nickerson couldn't make it, Connolly would bring a trusted sergeant along. He wanted someone else to know about Parlon and Robinson's work just in case he happened to die before the project was completed.

Many a night the commissioner and Eddie sweated it out when the two undercover men didn't arrive at the designated time and place. Though it may have been a traffic jam in the Sumner Tunnel or on the Southeast Expressway that caused a delay, all Connolly and Nickerson could do was to wonder and to try not to worry.

"Stay calm and wait it out," they reminded each other. Nickerson always resisted the temptation to call the prison to inquire if Ferris and Lombard had left yet because that kind of concern would naturally have aroused suspicions.

The assignment began to take its toll on the undercover men's nerves. For one thing, they were constantly being taunted and insulted by inmates, particularly the black ones. One of their jobs was to monitor the use of the pay phone. At certain hours, inmates were allowed to use the public phone in each cellblock for no more than three minutes. Prisoners would line up, dimes in hand, waiting their turns with nothing better to do than verbally abuse the guard.

When the guards would try to hurry a talkative inmate up, he would laugh and say, "You honky mother-fucker, get off my ass."

The other men, impatient for their turn, would badger him, "Get that man off the phone. Can't you do anything right? I'm fucking your sister. I'm pimping your mother and your grandmother . . ."

Spying on the guards as well as the prisoners made Parlon and Robinson feel a little sheepish about what they were doing. Some of the guards involved in the drug sales were basically nice guys. A bunch of them collected money for flowers when Parlon's mother died. He didn't relish the thought of setting these guys up to be busted, but that was the job he came to the Island to do.

Once, after having set up a drug deal, Parlon felt bad and tried to call if off, saying, "Let's forget it. We'll get caught." But the other guard insisted on going ahead with the transaction.

A couple of inmates on furlough and two off-duty guards were eventually arrested by the Drug Unit, but after a month and a half, the two officers had not cracked any major dope-smuggling ring. Then their covers began eroding.

One day, Robinson was working out in the weight room with some inmates. He was lying on a bench and had just hoisted the bar up when he felt a blade bite into his neck.

"You sneaky, cock-sucking pig," a voice shrieked in his ear. "You thought nobody would recognize you, Officer Robinson, but I'll never forget your shiny bald skull."

Robinson tried to contract his throat to get his jugular away from the blade. At the same time he rolled his eyes back and studied the face of his assailant.

"You don't remember, do you?" the willowy young man railed. "If the Master would let me have my make-up and wig, I'll bet you'd recognize me. I'm Saundra."

In an instant, Robinson realized that here was one of the drag queens he had arrested several times in Boston's Bay Village clubs. Since he was used to seeing Saundra dressed like a woman, it was no wonder that he didn't recognize the face, wiped clean of rouge and mascara, in the book of mugshots that Connolly had shown him.

"You got me confused with somebody else, you crazy bitch," Robinson gasped, his arms quivering from holding the weights up so long.

Fortunately, Robinson was a convincing actor, good enough at least to shake Saundra's confidence.

"I'm 99% sure you're Robinson," the she-man said, pulling the blade away at last. "You're lucky there's this tiny little doubt in my mind."

Finally, Connolly decided they had gathered all the evidence they were going to get. He pulled Parlon and Robinson out as guards and planned a surprise raid, once again calling on the services of Captain Joseph Rowan and the Tactical Patrol Force, dressed in their paratrooper boots and riot helmets and wielding nightsticks.

Parlon and Mitty suited up in TPF jumpsuits, boots and helmets to join in the massive shakedown.

Unannounced, four busloads of men from the TPF and from Drug Control marched right into the Hill Prison. With Connolly leading the way, they assumed command of the facility and secured every exit before beginning the process of searching every inch of both cellblocks.

The two ex-guards enjoyed the looks of disbelief, and then of hatred that they saw in the eyes of their former colleagues and charges, who now realized that what they had thought were two incompetent screws were actually brilliant undercover cops.

The barking of the canines they had brought along, the blare of salsa music on radios, the clanging of metal doors and the protests of the inmates echoed through the cellblocks in a jarring jumble of noises.

Prisoners would be pulled out of their cells and ordered to strip down. The TPF searched their bodies and clothes and kept them handcuffed or leaning up against the wall while Connolly and his Drug Control Unit, armed with flashlights, combed the premises for contraband of any sort. The DCU unraveled rolls of toilet paper, riffled the pages of paperbacks, and pried apart the casing of TV rabbit ears.

Some inmates took the invasion good-naturedly and joked with the law enforcement men as they watched their cells being turned upside down. Other prisoners were outraged at this treatment; they had rarely been subject to strip-searches and regarded their cells as their private domain.

Many cells were decorated with centerfolds and graphic photos of nudes. Some of the more effeminate types had scented their cells with heavy perfume. They huffed and flailed as the DCU men ripped the gauzy canopy drapes from around their beds, thrust aside the frilly curtains that masked the bars or poked through their jewelry boxes with a penlight.

One man was busy at a drafting table, piled high with texts on engineering and structural steelwork. He was working on blueprints as homework for a course he was taking, preparing for the day when he was released.

"I got no drugs," he wailed as he was ordered to vacate the cell and to get naked. "Don't mess up my papers," he begged Connolly, "I've got to turn those plans in tomorrow."

The shakedown did not produce a hell of lot: some booze, drugs, chains, clubs and a razor. As a search for contraband, the raid was not successful, but psychologically, the appearance of the storm-troopers had a great impact.

Initially, the guards and the upper-level staff of the prison resented the fact that this undercover surveillance and raid had been executed without their knowledge. Eventually they realized how advantageous it was for prisoners and any corrections officers who were tempted to commit crimes to know that there was a quick-moving, hard-hitting police force, ready to pounce on them at any moment.

Eddie kept his promise and made Robinson and Parlon members of the Drug Unit. After their stint on Deer Island, they realized that prison life was a lot crueler and oppressive than they had imagined it or seen it depicted, even in the roughest movies. They felt that it was a healthy experience for them and thought it would be good if all police could see what prison is like. Day after day cops are nailing prisoners and judges are sending them away, but many law officers haven't any accurate idea of the conditions to which prisoners are being condemned.

When someone suggested that spying on guards smacked of disloyalty. Robinson defended himself and his partner by saying, "We saw a lot of good guards, gung-ho guys who like what they're doing. They're the ones who'll get hurt if an inmate gets high and things start to happen. That's the way it always is."

24

Redbird

It was damn frustrating for Connolly and the other men in the Drug Control Unit to think that they knew so much about Redbird, and yet he remained a man of mystery, someone on whom it was next to impossible to pin anything. They were sure that he was the biggest supplier of heroin and cocaine to the intown area, especially to the nightclubs and strip joints in the Combat Zone, but they could never prove a thing.

The Zone, where hungry-eyed sailors on liberty could find any number of cheap — and not so cheap — thrills, was an area in which Redbird could exercise his many talents as dope-dealer, thief and pimp. Though he looked and moved like a man of 40, Redbird claimed to have been born on Valentine's Day 60 years ago; no one knew his age for sure, but in any case his relatively youthful appearance was matched by a resiliency and ability to make successful transitions from one illegal means of making money to another.

In the 30's he had come to Boston from New York wearing a raccoon coat and riding in a big Bearcat sedan driven by a husky light-skinned black bodyguard known as "Heavy Cream." Redbird had left behind him a long criminal record for bootlegging and gambling. Some said that he had worked for Jack "Legs" Diamond in the Big Apple.

Anyhow, once he settled in Beantown, Redbird introduced the first large-scale numbers pool into the black sections of town. Soon white people began placing bets on the "nigger pool" as it was known. The gambling business soon became so lucrative that the Irish, Jewish and Italian mobsters forced Redbird out.

Ever resourceful, he turned to the after-hours speakeasy business and then expanded into the prostitution racket. In general, he was a good pimp, but it was not uncommon to see one of his girls walking around with a black eye, broken nose or other injury which Redbird felt she deserved for not behaving herself.

One evening Connolly sat in his office discussing Redbird with the two officers who knew him best: Detectives Arthur Linsky and Bill Currier. Together they tried to piece together what they knew about the dapper old fox and to devise a plan to get the goods on him, not just one of his flunkies.

"Maybe if we knock off some of his people, we might get them to talk about Redbird," Connolly suggested idly.

"You know better than that, Lieutenant," returned Linsky, dismissing the idea. "His people are so well trained they don't take a leak without his okay. His people won't talk. And the only way to get Redbird to sing is when we got him uptight."

Redbird was a master at dispensing information to the police. Only when the jail doors were opening for him or for one of his more valuable people, would he divulge something really useful . . . and then only in the presence of his attorney and "off the record." On those rare occasions, he proved himself one of the city's best informants because he knew the white and black organized crime bosses equally well.

"What if we pinch Belle?" Connolly mused. "Maybe she's on probation or a suspended."

Belle was Redbird's white wife, who worked nights in a downtown club selling her ass or cocaine while her devoted husband sipped Scotch and soda at the other end of the bar and collected her earnings and those of the younger girls in his stable.

"It might be worth a try," Linsky conceded. "I'll get my people in the joint checking her, but I still would like to get him personally."

"Maybe he'll give us his supplier if we get Belle," Currier interjected, "but then I'm probably just day-dreaming."

"We'll never know until we try," Connolly said. "So let's keep on top of this."

In between their court appearances and their work on other narcotics cases, Linsky, Currier, Eddie Simmons, Reni Kennedy, Frank Coleman and Peter O'Malley would always set aside a little time to ferret out scraps of information about Redbird. As months went by and they came up with nothing conclusive, Redbird put the word out on the street that he was bribing the Drug Unit so that he could operate freely.

One night in early November, 1973, the DCU's perseverance seemed to be paying off. Eddie Simmons had been watching Redbird's house for hours. Around 8 he noticed the little pimp hurrying out the door, followed by Belle, who was still half-in and half-out of her coat.

Simmons wondered where they were going in such a rush. "It's gotta be an unexpected delivery of a load."

He got on his walkie-talkie before Belle and Redbird reached to their gate.

"Call Coleman and the rest of the crew. Redbird's leaving 31 Glenhill in a real hurry. His car's moving down the driveway right now. I'm gonna tail him."

"Stay on the air so you can give us the latest location."

"Will do."

Simmons had no problem following Redbird's car through the streets of Roxbury. It was a brand-new, shiny red Eldorado with a white roof that he kept as brightly polished as the top apple on a fruit vendor's cart; the DCU men took it for granted that his partiality for fancy red vehicles had inspired the nickname "Redbird."

The Caddy hadn't gone far on Blue Hill Avenue when it came to a halt at the corner of Bradshaw Avenue. Simmons killed his headlights and coasted to a stop about 50 feet away from Redbird. He radioed Linsky and Kennedy who also happened to be on Blue Hill Avenue, and they arrived a few minutes later.

It soon became apparent why Redbird had stopped at this lonely spot. A tall, thin black man approached the car, accompanied by a white broad whose bleached hair reached halfway down her back. They got into the car. Redbird snapped on the inside light, affording the two police cars a clear view of the movements inside the Cadillac.

"That's a pickup," Linsky was voicing what was in all three men's thoughts. "We'll watch them and see where they're going."

Coleman, Currier and O'Malley were still about a mile away from the intersection of Blue Hill Avenue and Bradshaw.

"We'll move down in back of you," Coleman informed the other two units.

Suddenly, the inside of the Caddy went dark; a moment later the headlights flared into brightness.

"Watch it! He's coming at you, Arthur," Simmons breathed.

The tires of the Eldorado squealed as Redbird wheeled around in a U-turn and headed back home.

"The next traffic light he stops at, we'll box him in and take the old bastard," Coleman ordered as he passed the other two cars that were also reversing direction.

At the corner of Morton and Norfolk Streets, the three Drug Unit cars managed to surround the Cadillac. Within seconds, the DCU men were out of their vehicles and had yanked the doors of the Caddy open. With one muscular arm, Bill Currier lifted Redbird out of the driver's seat; his other mammoth paw clamped onto the bag of goodies that had been snuggled between Redbird's legs.

The other black passenger, Tom Tucker, fumbled for his small automatic revolver, but Kennedy and O'Malley knocked it from his fingers as they hauled him through the air and slammed him against the side of the car.

Belle and Blondie presented no problem for Simmons, Linsky and Coleman.

An examination of Belle's pocketbook revealed four tins of white powder; the DCU could nail her as a carrier.

"Redbird, we got you good," Linsky exulted, as he examined the packets of cocaine and heroin in a brown paper bag.

"Arthur, that's not my stuff," Redbird wailed. "It belongs to Mr. Tucker's lady friend."

"It's yours. You had it. We saw Tommy give it to you at the corner of Bradshaw."

Redbird composed his features into his most doleful, aged senior citizen look.

"Can't we straighten this out? If I could talk alone to you or to Lieutenant Connolly, I could give you something good."

Coleman was immune to Redbird's wheedling.

"Let's go," he ordered, as the DCU team hustled the two couples into their unmarked cars.

"Don't leave my car in this neighborhood!" Redbird bleated with a real anxiety in his voice this time. "They'll strip it!"

"Man, this is a black neighborhood, your neighborhood," O'Malley laughed. "We'll leave a big sign on the windshield saying 'Redbird the Dope Pusher's Car.' "

"Arthur, please drive my car out of this place. These people will steal it or torch it!"

The Drug Squad was enjoying Redbird's panic.

"Tell you what I'm gonna do," Linsky said slowly, "We're going to take your car to the police garage . . ."

A tiny sigh of relief escaped, a bit too early, from Redbird's lips.

". . . as evidence. We're confiscating it. That's the law. You were using it to transport drugs."

"Just think," O'Malley interjected. "Soon some Irish cop will be driving home in your big, beautiful Caddy. He may want to paint it Kelly green though."

Redbird choked on the thought.

Linsky had had enough ballbusting.

"Fuck his car. We're outta here."

At headquarters, Connolly greeted Redbird and his entourage with mock civility.

"Come in, my good friend. Take a load off your feet."

The DCU men pulled chairs from the various desks so that the four arrestees could sit opposite the lieutenant. Redbird, Belle and Tucker subsided into their seats, but the blonde, whose name was Karen, chose to lean against the wall.

"There's space for you here," Connolly said, gesturing towards a swivel chair.

"No, thanks. I'd rather stand," she replied rather sullenly. Like so many other hookers, she had once been pretty, but her profession and drug habits had coarsened her beauty.

Once the initial interview was over, the experienced narcotics officers booked and searched the two black men and two white women. They counted and weighed the seized drugs, then stored them in the evidence locker.

During these proceedings, Redbird kept whimpering about his old age and begging, not for the release of his wife or the sullen 18-year-old blonde, but for himself and his beloved Eldorado.

Coleman chuckled at the old pimp's entreaties.

"He'll do anything we want just to keep from losing that fire-engine of his!"

Linsky wasn't so sure. He had tangled with Redbird too many times before.

"Never trust this guy. Squeeze him too hard, and he'll double-cross you, me or anyone. He's real slippery."

Well after midnight, Redbird's attorney, Oscar Garrett, arrived with the bail commissioner. Tom Tucker had sat through the four hours of processing and waiting without saying anything. Karen paced about or slouched against the wall, talking in tense, low tones with Belle.

Soon all the arrangements for their bail had been completed, and as they walked out the door, the four of them glared disdainfully at the officers of the Drug Unit.

The next morning after the arraignment in Dorchester Court, Redbird's lawyer mentioned that he would appreciate an interview with Connolly, Coleman, and Linsky that night in their office.

That afternoon, Connolly went to get the permission of Assistant District Attorney Jim Hayes to bargain with Redbird. Though he was young, Hayes had a wealth of courtroom experience dealing with junkies, pushers and their lawyers. He was not likely to be conned by empty promises of a drug-dealer. But he had real respect for the judgment of the men of the DCU, with whom he worked on a daily basis. So he gave a tentative OK for Eddie to open negotiations.

At 8 pm Redbird, Karen and the lawyer Garrett trooped into the Drug Control Office along with two blacks who had not been present the night of the arrest.

Redbird was swaggering as if he were the vice-president of the First National Bank instead of a convicted felon who was in danger of being sent away for a long time. He made the introductions in what he considered an elegant manner.

"Mr. Connolly, I believe you already know these ladies," he smiled, nodding toward Karen and a striking-looking hooker, known simply as The Jet. Then Redbird, trying to sound casual, added, ". . . and this is my business associate, Jeff Waters."

Jeff was a nervous, wiry customer with a pitiless look in his eye.

"Won't you sit down with the rest of us?" Connolly said to Karen.

"She can't," laughed Jeff. "She's got a hot dose of the clap."

Gonorrhea, an occupational hazard of her profession, was thus revealed as the reason the young blonde was always on her feet.

After a half an hour of temporizing and irritatingly vague chatting, Redbird announced that he and his friends had to leave. Not a word had he breathed about the deal that he wanted to make with Connolly. The five of them sailed out of the office, leaving the DCU wondering why they stopped by in the first place. Particularly puzzling was the presence of The Jet and Jeff.

"Redbird's up to something," Connolly reasoned. "He said nothing. He never acted like this before. He didn't talk about giving us any information. He acted like all he did was go through a red light."

"He made sure we all met this Jeff character though," Coleman reflected.

"But he hasn't got anything to do with this case," Eddie said, "And where was Belle?"

"The hell with Redbird's information," said Linsky disgustedly. "We got enough on him for a conviction."

Two nights later, the mystery was resolved. When Connolly walked into the lobby at Headquarters, he spotted Redbird and The Jet, sitting on a stone bench, and Karen, leaning against the polished marble wall.

Redbird waved cheerily as Eddie walked towards the trio.

"We had no appointment tonight," Connolly said brusquely.

"I wanted to talk about that deal I mentioned earlier."

"You had your chance a couple of nights ago. Anyway, where's your trusty lawyer, Mr. Garrett?"

"I didn't think he wants to hear what I got to say to you," Redbird replied. "Let's go to your office."

"Not yet. You gotta wait here until Sergeant Coleman's squad comes in."

"Why can't we wait in your office? It's drafty here; Karen and The Jet are freezing their tails off."

"Tell them to wear more clothes."

"Besides," Redbird whined, "it's embarrassing for us to sit out here with so many cops — police officers — going in and out."

Connolly reflected that it didn't look right to have two whores and their pimp lounging around the Roll of Honor and the memorial to the deceased police officers, so he relented.

When Connolly and his three visitors got to the DCU office, Sergeant Burke's squad were in there, getting their walkie-talkies out of the charging units and picking up the rest of the gear they needed for a night on the streets. The banter quickly subsided when the squad members felt the presence of Redbird and his lady friends; the men left without saying another word.

Sergeant Coleman's squad were late getting in; they had had a long day at Superior Court.

"Redbird wants to make a deal in exchange for some information," Connolly announced. "I told him no promises. Any deal would have to be okayed by Assistant District Attorney Hayes and by you guys. You made the arrest. It's up to you to accept or reject the deal."

"Shoot," said Coleman to Redbird.

"First the deal," Redbird said, his eyes narrowing and his voice hardening. "Suspended sentence for me and Tucker. Dismissed for Karen and Belle."

"We want your supplier and you out of the dope business," Connolly retorted with equal firmness.

"I don't know who my supplier is. Jeff and Tom picks it up for me . . . ," Redbird began.

Connolly snorted.

"You can't jerk us off like that," Linsky snapped, "See you later and watch out for those rats at Walpole."

"Fuck you and fuck your information," O'Malley added.

Coleman's squad started getting their equipment together in preparation for a quick departure.

Redbird reeled back like a slapped cobra. He was angry at this rebuff and dismissal, but underneath he was scared. He didn't want to go to prison and saw that he was losing Connolly and the others fast.

"Listen," the little pusher said, adopting a much more conciliatory tone. "You got me. I admit it. But I got something much bigger than my supplier. More violent."

"Cut the crap."

"You remember Jeff that was in here the other night?" Redbird was desperate now. "He's been sleeping with The Jet. He told her all kinds of shit about the crimes he's done in the past. Tomorrow he and his gang are going to pull off another job with a machine gun."

Obviously, Redbird had brought Jeff by the other evening so that the DCU men could identify him easily when they saw him again. No wonder the pimp had made the last interview a social call. He didn't want the ruthless Jeff to suspect that he was being set up.

The Jet then recounted the details of her bedroom conversation with Jeff. Eddie took notes on the specifics of the robbery planned for the following day.

Connolly wanted to show Redbird he wasn't as clever as he imagined himself to be.

"When Jeff sees us putting the cuffs on him tomorrow," Eddie said slowly, "he's going to put two and two together from the other night. He's a smart boy. He's going to know you ratted on him to save your own hide."

"Jeff won't rest until you're dead meat," O'Malley sneered.

Redbird's jaw sagged, and his eyes widened.

"You better start using those sweet lips of yours to practice your prayers," Connolly said grimly.

"Lieutenant, you can't do this to me. . . ."

"No. You're right. I can't."

As reprehensible as a character as Redbird was, Connolly knew that he couldn't in good conscience jeopardize Redbird's life by allowing anyone connected with the DCU to be involved in the arrest. Making Redbird sweat had been a small recompense for their loss. They had to honor their deal by getting Hayes to have the sentences of Redbird and Tucker suspended and the hookers' charges dismissed in return for information that the DCU would have to turn over to another unit.

The next evening the Drug Control team had to sit back and read the headlines about the daring capture of Jeff and his machine-gun-wielding accomplices. All they could do was shake their heads as they watched the telecasts at 6 and 11 praising the other unit's "outstanding police work."

Though a dangerous criminal and his gang had been removed from the streets, Redbird, Belle, Karen and Tucker had gotten off scot-free — this time. Connolly's consolation was his certainty that sooner or later Redbird would be caught red-handed again.

During the ensuing months, Redbird was arrested three times for petty violations of the controlled substance laws. Though Connolly refused to make any more deals, the elusive Redbird managed to escape with minor penalties. Finally the tide turned against him. Someone close to him revealed to the DCU that Redbird stashed his heroin and cocaine underground in his backyard.

Around midnight, Lieutenant Connolly, Sergeant Coleman, Detectives Linsky, Currier, O'Malley, Simmons and Kennedy raided 31 Glenhill Road. A search of the house turned up only a small amount of cocaine. So the DCU men pulled the flashlights and shovels out of the trunks of their cars and ventured out into the backyard.

What little grass there had been in the 30 by 50 foot lot had been turned under by the paws of the four Doberman pinschers that Redbird kept. As some of the men tried to keep the lithe, snarling dogs at bay, the others did some exploratory digging. Before long everyone's shoes and pants cuffs were smeared with mud and excrement. It was frustrating work what with the poor light, the barking killer dogs and the slippery conditions underfoot.

Initially, the spadework just seemed to make the mess in the backyard worse. Then Linsky realized that he was instinctively avoiding the coils of Doberman feces when he was choosing a spot to dig. Perhaps Redbird was counting on that kind of natural aversion.

"Find the biggest pile of dogshit you can," he cried on a hunch.

Sure enough, under the most repulsive mound they found three large packages solidly wrapped in waterproof coverings. Inside were eight 3/8 ounce packages of heroin, along with over 100 hypodermic needles, dozens of glassine bags and vials filled with capsules of various colors.

There was plenty of evidence to arrest Redbird on. With the suspended sentence hanging over his head, the pimp was indicted by a Suffolk County Grand Jury and released on bail.

While awaiting trial, Redbird decided he had better raise some more money for Garrett's legal fees. Again on a tip, the DCU learned he was back to his old tricks. Late one night, big Bob Ryan smashed in the front door at 31 Glenhill. Connolly and Linsky raced into the kitchen. Redbird had the disposal going, feeding plastic bags of white powder into its maw.

Linsky elbowed the skinny old dealer aside and thrust his fingers into the mechanical jaws, chomping away in the drain. He triumphantly pulled one of the bags up, but it was stained with the blood that was dripping from his chewed-up flesh. He had retrieved the evidence, but had to be rushed to the hospital for an operation to save his hand.

Again Redbird was indicted, and true bill was returned by the Suffolk County Grand Jury.

At his trial, a plea of guilty was entered, but Attorney Garrett argued that Redbird was an old man with cancer who couldn't possibly survive in the unhealthful environment of prison. The judge didn't see it that way and sent Redbird off to Walpole on a five to seven year sentence with three years probation after that.

Years later, Eddie bumped into Redbird in the street.

"What are you doing these days?" Connolly asked.

"I'm into something clean," Redbird said jauntily. "I book numbers."

25

Copkiller

It happened all of a sudden a little before 5 pm on Friday, February 8, 1974. Angela Chung Sykes was telling her girlfriend Elaine Bailey about the unsatisfactory meeting that she had just had with her attorney as they strolled down Winter Street in the heart of Boston's shopping district.

Angela kept looking back over her shoulder at her brother Junior Chung, who was straggling along behind them. Junior's half-black, half-Chinese ancestry showed up in the sparseness of the goatee and mustache he sported. He liked to wear flashy clothes; that afternoon he was wearing a black three-quarter length fur coat over a sky-blue turtleneck and black wide-brimmed felt hat with a shiny ornament on it.

Though Junior was 23, a year older than Angela, she found herself having to watch him all the time and act like his big sister. Junior was not the brightest person in the world and had a tendency to get himself into trouble. He had lost his job at Morton's Bakery three months ago; he needed money but wasn't looking very hard for work. Even though Junior had a wife and child back home in Jamaica, Angela knew that he had been sleeping with Elaine.

Angela and Elaine passed 15 Winter Street, Baker Shoes. Earlier that afternoon, Angela and Junior had met their sister Sonia in the ladies' shoe shop. Now as Angela glanced back, she was startled to see her brother suddenly pull his gas pistol out of his pocket and duck into the store.

A feeling of panic swept over the two women. They raced back to the shoe store and saw that Junior had his gun jammed into the left side of the jaw of a clearly terrified cashier.

"This is a stick-up," he announced. "Everybody stand still. Don't nobody move."

Quickly all the chatter of the 40-odd customers examining footwear died away. Mothers drew their little daughters close into the folds of their winter coats.

Junior was becoming psychotic as he screamed at the cashier to hand over the contents of the register, but she was too frightened by the gun at her chin to do anything but tremble.

Angela hysterically pleaded, "Junior, don't do it! Don't do it!"

Impatient with the woman's delay, Junior brushed her aside and scooped $246.69 from the till and tried to put it all into his pockets. His sister kept interfering and begging him to stop.

She tried to tug his arm and pull him away. He shoved her aside. Just then Stephen Linton, a salesman in the store, stepped forward and demanded, "What are you doing?"

Junior spun around and pointed the pistol at Linton. Linton grabbed Angela and put her in between himself and Junior.

"Please don't shoot the gun," the salesman said, pulling his hostage tighter.

Angela started sobbing, "The gun, it is not a real gun!"

Junior then reached over his sister and began pounding Linton's neck and back with the butt of his pistol. The salesman tumbled backward into a rack of shoes and simultaneously propelled Angela forward into her brother.

Linton saw the murderous glare in Junior's eyes. As soon as he shrugged off the shoes and got back on his feet, Linton scrambled out the door onto Winter Street with Junior right behind him.

Junior fired one blast from his gas pistol, but then grabbed the gun by the barrel so he could use it to continue pommeling the man who had dared to interrupt the robbery.

In the middle of the street Linton tripped, fell and rolled over. As he tried to get up, he bumped into the pole of a "No Parking" sign and fell again. By that time, Junior had caught up with him and had resumed beating the black salesman's neck.

"Oh, God, he's going to shoot me," Linton cried.

Junior let up when he saw a policeman approaching. The Jamaican dashed toward the underground subway stop around the corner as he saw three Baker Shoe employees and his sister about to close in on him.

Linton, though somewhat stunned by the beating he had endured, recognized the familiar face under the white uniform hat. It was that of 50-year-old Patrolman John J. Murphy, the regular traffic officer at the busy shopping intersection.

"Are you alright?" Murphy asked, helping Linton to his feet.

Gasping for breath, Linton nodded and said, "The guy's got a gun. There he goes down the subway."

Murphy turned to catch a glimpse of the big black hat disappearing down the steps to the Washington station.

Pulling out his service revolver, Murphy ran to the top of the stairs, pausing only long enough to instruct a man standing there not to let anyone else go down the steps. Then he plunged down after Junior.

Junior couldn't decide whether to jump over the turnstile and go out onto the Orange Line platform or try to make his way back up the stairs.

Murphy charged toward Junior and grappled with him. The two struggled and banged into a display sign. Angela arrived and tried her best to pull the policeman away from her brother, but she got trampled in the struggle. Then Henry Delorey, an MBTA inspector, appeared on the scene and rushed to aid the traffic cop.

With a nightstick, Delorey whacked Junior on the head, opening a wide cut. Enraged, Junior struggled more violently and knocked Murphy's gun out of his hand. Delorey continued to strike with the nightstick, but Junior managed to get to the service revolver first. He sprayed the six bullets in the gun into the bodies of the Boston cop and the MBTA inspector as Angela screamed in horror.

In seconds, the men in uniform crumpled onto the filthy platform floor. Father of six, Hank Delorey lay dying from the chest wounds he had received. Murphy collapsed over a wooden workshed and then slid to the ground, slumped on his right side. Chung's bullet had pierced the officer's left temple and exited through the opposite side of the head. Some of the brain oozed through the openings made by the gunshot wound, and blood leaked over his eye and nose. He too looked dead, but was still breathing faintly.

John O'Driscoll, a sub-foreman for the MBTA, was on the opposite side of the tracks when he heard Junior pumping the bullets into the two officers. As a money man for the subway, O'Driscoll was licensed to carry a Smith and Wesson .38 police special.

As Junior hopped over the turnstiles, O'Driscoll pulled out his own weapon and lined the Jamaican up in his sights. He was just about to squeeze the trigger when a train started pulling in. O'Driscoll expressed the cars through the station without allowing the driver to stop or the passengers to disembark, but by the time the train passed, Junior had managed to escape down the stairs that led to the lower level where the Red Line system operated.

Collectors who sold tokens and changed money had witnessed the struggle, the shots and the escape; they were on the phone almost immediately summoning ambulances and alerting the police.

Lieutenant Connolly and Detective Vincent Logan had just filed a report on a narcotics arrest they had made that day. Earlier, they had had guns shoved into their stomachs, but they had managed to turned the tables on the dealers. Connolly and Logan thought the excitement was over for the day and had just climbed into an unmarked car, planning to head over to the Vic for a bite to eat, when the news blared over the radio.

"All cars on One . . . Shooting. MBTA station, Washington and Winter. Police officer shot. . . ."

Their vehicles streaked to and around Boston Common and arrived four minutes later at the Washington Street station. Two empty police cruisers with front doors flung wide open and lights still flashing indicated that they were not the first to arrive on the scene.

As they hurried down the stairs, they had to flatten themselves against the railings in order to let the firemen and EMTs pass with the stretchers. Within minutes, Delorey was being examined by the doctors at Massachusetts General Hospital, where he died about 90 minutes later. Murphy was rushed to Boston City Hospital, where an emergency craniotomy was performed to stop the bleeding from his head. He regained consciousness, but his name was kept on the danger list.

Lieutenant Connolly spotted Patrolman Marvin Emery grilling the two black women, whose hysteria had only partially subsided. When the police began interrogating them, the two wailed that "George Conley" had committed the crime.

As Connolly questioned Angela and Elaine (who initially tried to pass herself off as "Sadie Williams"), the women contradicted themselves with wildly inconsistent statements. They did let slip that this "George Conley" lived at either 86, 88 or 146 Worcester Street in the South End.

The lieutenant radioed District 4 that they needed extra man-power to conduct a search of these buildings. When Connolly and the other men who had gathered at the subway station got to Worcester Street, they hooked up with Detective Emmett F. McNamara and Patrolman Robert Vasselian.

Connolly broke the officers up into teams. He, McNamara and a couple of other men chose #88. They observed fresh footprints going up the steps. McNamara rang the doorbell, and a woman from the first floor answered.

"Do you know the other tenants in the building? Do you know a George Conley?"

"I don't know who lives here."

The policeman waved her aside and made their way up four flights knocking on every door. Connolly found a gossipy woman on the second floor who was more willing to talk.

"The Chinese guy? He's on the fourth floor."

On the top floor, a 55-year-old black man responded to their knock.

"Who lives in the room over there . . . the one that's open?"

"Name's Junior. That's all I know."

Connolly remembered something about a Junior in the welter of tearful evidence that the two women had given. He was practically sure that they had zeroed in on the murderer.

The policeman rushed through the open door. There appeared to be no one in the room. They checked in a large clothes closet and under the bed. When McNamara swung open the door of a smaller closet, there sat Junior cowering in a corner.

"Please, don't shoot. I give up."

Junior was pulled from his hiding spot, handcuffed and frisked. From his left pants pocket Emery produced a packet of money orders and bills tied with a shoelace, the money he had taken from the Baker cash register. Blood was still seeping from the gash that Delorey's sap had made on the back of his head.

Another detective lifted the blood-stained fur coat from a chair, and out of the pocket fell Murphy's .38 revolver with the BPD number 1053-M engraved on the butt.

Connolly marched the Jamaican into the bathroom and sat him on the toilet. One of the officers thrust a card with the Miranda warning printed on it under Junior's nose.

Connolly observed how Junior's forehead wrinkled as he tried to make out what was written there.

"This guy can't read. Logan, you read the warning out loud to him."

Eddie took this precaution because he knew that Junior and his sister spoke English poorly and with a decided West Indies accent. Connolly didn't want a wily lawyer to get Junior off on the grounds that he wasn't properly apprised of his rights because he had difficulty reading English.

Connolly raised the dispatcher on the walkie-talkie.

"Call off the search. We got the man. We got the gun. We got the money."

Commissioner di Grazia, who was at City Hospital with the brain-damaged Murphy, was told that the assailant had been captured. He just couldn't believe that Connolly and his men had arrested the person responsible less than an hour after the shooting.

Eddie was ordered to stand by until Deputy Superintendent Joe Jordan arrived to verify that the right person had been apprehended.

Finally Jordan climbed to the top of 88 Worcester Street, and Connolly greeted him by pointing to the skinny man seated on the toilet.

"Here he is, in the flesh! Now, can we take him to the station?"

By the time Connolly got Junior booked, his watch told him that he had been working 19 hours that day, but that amount of time was not unusual for Drug Squad men.

Boston cops showed up in droves for Delorey's wake; the heroic MBTA inspector was buried with full Boston Police Department honors.

Officer Murphy never really recovered from his head wounds. He lost his ability to speak and to control his bodily functions. A friend, Mary Martin, kept him clean and bathed. She even pushed him around in a wheelchair so he could make a few appearances at Headquarters and even at the Policeman's Ball.

He lasted only a couple of years, finally dying on a Sunday, March 14, 1976. Connolly and scores of other officers turned out for a special salute to one of few officers who had fallen in the line of duty in recent years.

At his trial Junior pleaded innocent to all charges: murder, assault and battery with intent to commit murder, assault and battery with a dangerous weapon on a police officer, larceny of a police officer's revolver, and armed robbery of the shoe store. Junior was able to get high-powered Walter Steele as his attorney because Angela had worked for Steele's mother, and he handled the case as a favor.

During the trial Connolly became friendly with Angela. She told him something of Junior's background, including the fact that he had never made it past third grade back in Jamaica.

There was little that Junior's attorney could do, however. The parade of witnesses from the shoe store, Washington and Winter Streets and the subway station incontrovertibly identified Junior as the man responsible for the string of crimes. Besides, Connolly had gotten a complete confession out of him.

Initially, police sympathizers feared that Junior would be sent to Bridgewater State Mental Hospital and pronounced not responsible for his actions because of his low intelligence. Though Junior did spend quite a bit of time there being tested, he ended up getting a life sentence for his subway shooting spree that ended the lives of two courageous men in uniform.

26

"Why Did You Do It, Billy?"

Maybe it was a wrong decision to pick a kid who was so young to work in the Drug Control Unit, but on the street there were so many young people buying and selling drugs. With his baby face, slim build and ringlets of brown hair, who would suspect Billy of being a cop?

Billy Galvin was willing; in fact, he had volunteered for the DCU. True, he hadn't been in uniform very long and had virtually no street experience as a policeman. On the other hand, he was a streetwise kid who had done some boxing locally and could take care of himself.

Lieutenant Connolly teamed Billy with Jerry Dailey, a cop from South Boston with all the answers. A few years older than Billy, Jerry was married and had kids. He had been in plenty of scrapes while acting as an undercover officer, but one situation he nearly didn't walk away from came when he was working a gay nightclub called Jacques in the Bay Village section of town.

Out in the parking lot behind the club, a drug dealer got wise to Jerry, disarmed him and was about to shoot him. Just then, one of the owners of the establishment, Carmen Vara, appeared, packing the pistol he was licensed to carry. Vara shot and wounded the junkie dealer, thus saving Jerry's life.

Vara was arrested and brought to Station 1 to be booked for assault and battery with a dangerous weapon. One lieutenant wanted Vara held on high bail, but Lieutenant Connolly ordered that he be released on personal recognizance. This mark of confidence was Connolly's way of showing that the safety of his men was of the utmost importance to him.

When Vara appeared in court, his case was dismissed in the light of the circumstances that he was aiding a policeman who was performing his duties.

Though Connolly did not find the man's business and transvestite clientele particularly appealing, he never forgot what Vara had done for Jerry that night. Years later, some of the command staff brass criticized Connolly for testifying at a licensing board hearing relative to another one of Vara's establishments.

In the hallway outside the licensing board hearing room, Vara caught up with Connolly.

"I hope you don't get into any trouble for testifying for me today, Eddie."

"Carmen, I wouldn't go into your joint to take a piss, but you do your thing to make a living, and I do mine," Connolly replied. "I owe you. You saved Jerry's life, even though you knew he was a cop. You did the right thing at the right time . . . and that's the reason I'm here."

"As for me and the top brass," he added, "fuck 'em."

The loyalty that Connolly felt for his men was a loyalty that everyone in the unit shared. When men work together under hazardous conditions, such as stopping drug trafficking, or simply spend a lot of time together cruising in a car, a special bond develops. Policemen don't talk about this kind of closeness. Psychologists may have a word to describe it; the cops don't. Oh, there may be a passing reference to "brotherhood," but just because there's not a whole lot of discussion on the subject, it doesn't mean that every officer doesn't feel it every time he goes out on a tour of duty.

Especially in dangerous situations, each man feels the sacred duty to take care of the other . . . regardless of personal differences or skin color. Black or white, yellow or brown, a cop knows only one color — blue, police blue.

Like the rest of the drug squad, Billy and Jerry worked hard day and night, but Connolly never saw an overtime slip in the Drug Unit. These men kept at it around the clock without making a big deal of the sacrifices and hardships they had to endure. They could be on a stake-out 36, 48, even 72 hours and sometimes come up empty-handed, but they were always ready to start all over again.

Lieutenant Connolly was proud of the men in his unit; he had hand-picked them all for their street experience, but mostly for their honesty. Real character was everything.

"All the arrests we make mean nothing," Connolly would remind the DCU men time and time again, "if we have no integrity."

Each man's integrity was sorely tested every day because drugs and money go hand and hand. There was always a temptation to pocket some of the money seized during a raid or accept a roll that the dealers were always proffering. Occasionally, a cop like Billy would succumb.

Billy's father had been suffering with cancer for a year or so. The heaviness in Billy's boyish face, the sad look in his eyes, reflected his knowledge that the end was near for his dad.

When old Mr. Galvin finally passed on, Connolly let Billy take extra days off to help his mother make the burial arrangements and straighten out the legal affairs. But when Billy finally came back to working the night shift with Jerry, all the men in the squad detected a change in him. Jerry would ask his partner over to his house for dinner, but Billy would always find some excuse to get out of the invitation.

One day Billy and Jerry were looking for heroin in Blackstone Park in the South End, where most of the dealers were Puerto Ricans. It wasn't long before they spotted a pusher; they agreed that Billy would try to make the buy and that Jerry would circle around behind for backup.

"Hey, Julio," Billy called to the dealer. "How about a couple of bags — okay?"

"I'm not Julio. My name is Hector," the little brown man answered, "and I don't know what the fuck you're talking to me about bags for."

"Wise prick," Billy muttered to himself as he closed in on Hector. Still two feet away from the Puerto Rican, Billy sensed that he was about to break for it. Sure enough, Hector started across the park towards Shawmut Avenue with Billy right on his heels. They raced up Pembroke Street to a playground with Billy inching closer to the little man, when all of a sudden, his foot caught in a hole in the ground and he tumbled to the earth, screaming in pain. Billy had broken his leg.

Lying where he had fallen, he kept hollering for Jerry who, he knew, was nearby with the walkie-talkie.

The locals started to gather to enjoy this spectacle of a man writhing in agony in a tot lot.

"What happened?" some inquired.

"Help me. I'm a police officer," he gasped. "Call the police and an ambulance."

The crowd was not sympathetic nor about to cooperate.

"Fuck the cop!"

"He was chasing Hector for nothing."

"Good for him. I hope he dies."

"Cops cause nothing but trouble."

Realizing that these people would show him no mercy, Billy redoubled his cries for his partner.

"Jerry, Jerry! I think I have a broken leg. The pain is bad. Get an ambulance. Jerry . . . JERRY!"

When Jerry finally heard, he had the walkie-talkie out of his jacket in a split second.

"Victor 223 to Control . . . Victor 223 to dispatcher. Get me an ambulance and a car to the playground on Pembroke Street . . . an officer is badly injured."

"Control to Victor 223," the response came crackling over the walkie-talkie, "I have that — an ambulance is on its way."

Before the dispatcher could alert a sector car, the 402 wagon and the Delta 104 car broke in.

"Wagon 402, we're on Tremont St., just around the corner from Pembroke. We'll take that call."

"Delta 104 on the way. We're close by."

In seconds, with sirens blasting and blue lights flashing, the wagon and the car converged at the playground. Instantly the pair of officers from each vehicle hit the pavement and began to make their way through the jeering crowd. Two minutes later, an ambulance arrived and nosed its way into the playground, stopping only a few feet away from the prone young policeman.

Other blue-and-white cruisers along with the cars of the sergeants and detectives were coming from all directions; a second ambulance was dispatched from City Hospital as a backup.

Observing the fleet of police vehicles on the scene, a sergeant alerted the dispatcher "We have enough help here. Call off the rest of the units coming in."

"OK, 911," the dispatcher responded, and then addressing those hurrying toward the location, "Anyone going to the Pembroke St. playground, back off. They have all the help they need."

While the sergeant had the area cleared of spectators, the EMTs slit Billy's pants leg. After carefully examining his ankle and leg, they put on temporary splints, bundled Billy into the ambulance and whisked him to Boston City Hospital.

After hours of X-rays and examination, a specialist diagnosed Billy as suffering from a double compound fracture of the right leg. So it was off to the operating room until the early hours of the morning.

That night, the DCU men gathered in the waiting room and nursed styrofoam cups of machine-dispensed coffee, determined to stay until they had some definite word about their buddy.

Lieutenant Connolly knew he had to call Billy's mother or ride over to Medford with Sergeant Jack Burke and break the bad news in person. The lieutenant decided to go on the visit. He didn't relish the prospect of facing Billy's mother, but he owed her that much. Breaking the bad news to a wife or, in this case, mother was always one of the toughest parts of being a boss; it is a job that never gets any easier.

Billy stayed in the hospital for the next two weeks. When he was released, he had pins through his leg, which remained in a cast for the next four months. His physical therapy lasted a year, then dragged on into a second year.

During that time, things had changed at the Drug Unit. Lieutenant Connolly had been transferred and reassigned as commanding officer of District 13 in Jamaica Plain.

It looked as if Billy Galvin would have to retire on a disability although he was still so young. Neither Jerry nor any of his former close friends had heard from or seen Billy in months, although he was still receiving full pay. The civilian personnel director ordered Galvin back to work. Billy refused on the grounds that his personal physician had warned him that he still wasn't fit for rough-and-tumble police work. His pay was promptly stopped. No one heard from him while his appeal was pending.

Meanwhile Connolly had been promoted again, this time to Deputy Superintendent of Area F. An old friend, Detective Lenny Weir of the Fugitive Unit, stuck his head into Deputy Connolly's office one afternoon.

"Why the long face, Lenny?"

Weir settled himself down in a chair and launched into his tale.

"About two weeks ago the state and county police from Richmond, Virginia, contacted me. They wanted me to check on a William Flaherty at an address on D Street in South Boston. They asked me to hold him for rendition back to Virginia for possession of marijuana with intent to sell.

"I went down there, D Street that is, and found that the address was a vacant lot. I checked back with the Virginia county police who stated that Flaherty was a cab driver in Boston, so I checked with the Hackney Carriage Bureau — no William Flaherty.

"But when Flaherty had been arrested by Amtrak police, he was photographed and fingerprinted. They flew the photograph up here within hours. Here it is, Eddie. Do you recognize him?"

Connolly studied the picture and then looked up at the ceiling.

"Yeah, Lenny," Connolly said after a while. "That's Billy. No doubt about it. What else happened? Give me the whole story."

"The Amtrak police boarded a train from Florida just as it crossed the North Carolina stateline into Virginia. Their marijuana dog sniffed out 60 pounds of grass in Billy's luggage. He was arrested in Virginia, photographed and printed. That's when he gave the phony name and address. He got bailed out in Virginia, and then he jumped bail."

Connolly shook his head and then said, "Of course, you'll check to see if the prints match, but there is no need to. That Billy. I wonder why he did it?"

Then after a moment a thought struck him. "Who else knows about this in the department?"

"Some of the boys in the Drug Unit."

"You'll be hearing from him, or at least somebody will be getting the word out to you," Connolly predicted.

"That's why I'm here," Weir said. "Billy trusts you, and the boys believe that he will try to contact you."

"If he does, he knows he will be turned in. He knows that damn well. All the drug men have been through things like this before."

Weir got up to go.

"Lenny, I'll be in touch with you if I hear anything. I still can't believe that the kid had such a bad time of it since his injury."

"See you later."

As Connolly had foreseen, it was not long — within three days of his conversation with Lenny Weir — before the phone rang on the Deputy Superintendent's desk; it was Billy.

"Hi, Lieutenant," he said. "I'm in trouble."

"I know, Billy. You're in bad trouble."

"What do you think I can do? I don't want my mother to know."

"Unless you tell her or the papers get a hold of it, that's the only way she'll find out. Look, Billy, you're going to have to surrender and go back to Virginia to stand trial."

"I can get up to five years down there. It's a felony in Virginia."

"You have to come in and see me, Billy . . . and get yourself a lawyer."

"I haven't got any money. I can't afford a lawyer and I am afraid to go with a public defender since I'm still a cop."

Connolly changed the subject for the moment. "By the way, Billy, how's your leg coming along since the injury?"

"Not too good. I have a lot of pain and trouble walking. I put my papers in, and I've been before the Medical Board. The Retirement Board is just waiting for word from the doctor to OK my retirement. I just hope this marijuana rap doesn't kill my pension. That's all I got to live on."

"Billy, how did you ever get into such a mess?"

"It's too long of a story, and you wouldn't believe it anyway."

"Maybe I would," Connolly said gently, "Try me sometime."

The next morning, Billy turned himself in to Detective Weir at District 1. He hadn't counted on the fact that Connolly, Jerry and some of the guys from the Drug Control Unit would be in the Detective's Room on the second floor. Nobody knew what to say to him.

Billy was visibly shaken when he was arraigned in Boston Municipal Court that morning. Attorney Walter Healey, a highly-regarded criminal lawyer and an old friend of Connolly's and Jerry's, took Billy's case without a fee. Healey was an experienced criminal lawyer who had a solid reputation for being on the level.

Healey agreed with the Assistant DA to have the case continued pending the arrival of the Virginia authorities. Healey was also able to get Billy released on personal bail.

If Billy had been sent to Charles Street Jail, his life would have been hell. Who knew how many inmates or persons awaiting trial had been arrested by him?

In a week the Virginia police officers arrived in Boston. Billy agreed to return to Virginia without a hearing. After Galvin signed the official rendition papers, Healey contacted a fellow attorney in Richmond to assist Billy in the Virginia courts.

All too soon Walter Healey brought the results of the trial to the concerned men in Drug Control: Billy had been given a stiff five years suspended sentence and five years probation. The court allowed him to return to Massachusetts and report to a Bay State probation officer.

For the time being he was being held in a county jail in Virginia.

"Thank God," Connolly thought, "that no one down there found out that he was a police officer or he would really have had a hard time down there — both in the court and the slammer."

While he was still being detained in Virginia, the Boston Police Retirement Board approved Billy's retirement since the incapacitating injury had taken place while he was on duty.

When Billy was released and got resettled in Boston, he called to thank Connolly for all the help he had received.

"Just one question, Billy. Why did you do it . . . why did you get mixed up in dope?"

"I told you," he sighed, "it's all too long to tell . . . ."

When Connolly hung up, he leaned back in his big leather chair and closed his eyes. He just couldn't stop wondering why a good policeman, a nice kid ended up in such a mess.

By asking a lot of people a lot of questions, he came up with an answer that he had suspected all along: gambling. Billy had lost heavily during the past year. Rumor had it that he was in debt to the tune of $60,000 to $80,000 to the wrong guys.

Everyone wondered if he had agreed to become a drug courier to pay off the people he had bet with or to repay the loan sharks who had lent him the money to settle the bets. The guys in the DCU all agreed that he must have been in heavy to the "wise guys" (racketeers), who really could put the pressure on someone like Billy if they wanted.

Every once in a while, Connolly would hear reports on Billy — that he had moved back in with his mother and was supporting her by doing odd jobs like running a canteen truck to supplement his pension check.

But whenever he heard about the man, Connolly found himself shaking his head and thinking something like, "Billy, Billy, you couldn't resist gambling and you lost. You lost everything . . . your promising career, your future, your good name . . . ."

Station 13 — The "Model Station"

27

From Dumping Ground to Model Station

It tore Connolly's heart out, but there was no bucking the Commissioner's order. di Grazia removed him from his position as head of the Drug Control Unit and put him in charge of District 13 in Jamaica Plain. The change had been necessitated by one of those domino-effect shuffles in the department, where a retirement in one unit meant transfers all over the place.

The move meant a demotion from Lieutenant Detective rating to Lieutenant and a cut in pay. More importantly, he thought glumly, the reassignment signaled a shift from the two-fisted excitement and closely knit teamwork with the men of the Drug Squad to the petty squabbles and easily flustered egos of a racially mixed neighborhood. His new schedule and responsibilities would literally be as different as night and day.

As he entered the 102-year-old red brick Station 13, Eddie scrutinized the clean, but dilapidated interior. District 13 had something of a reputation for being a dumping ground. Commissioner di Grazia had been besieged by complaints from the community about all the drunken, discourteous and disreputable cops that worked in District 13.

In an attempt to upgrade the personnel and turn 13 into what he termed Boston's first "model station," di Grazia transferred out the captain, all the lieutenants and most of the sergeants. He replaced them with a crew fresh out of the Academy and a few old officers from other stations, retaining the best of the old team.

Still, Connolly was succeeding the one man who seemed genuinely popular with the community, District Commander Lawrence Quinlan — a tough, experienced former Vice Squad cop well-liked by both his men and the community leaders.

The first week Connolly never left his office; his phone just wouldn't stop ringing. Everyone wanted him to deal with their complaints right off the bat. Businessmen were griping that the cops were tagging too many cars and driving away customers. Connolly promised to look into the matter. Other callers insisted that certain officers were being paid off to look the other way.

One anonymous male tipster phoned the lieutenant about an operation that had been condoned for a long time.

"Connolly, I hear you're on the level. If you are, listen to me. You got a drugstore on Centre Street. The cops have been letting him sell booze on Sundays for the past 20 years. There's always a police car, getting cigarettes for free or having his prescription filled for half price. In return, they close their eyes to the owner selling booze. Connolly, let's see what you're gong to do about this situation."

"I'm going to take care of it, that's what."

"Horseshit. I've heard that so many times before."

The man slammed the phone down. Connolly replaced his receiver more thoughtfully. He remembered hearing something about liquor being available at a J.P. drugstore on Sunday from some of the guys in the Drug Unit.

"Who can I get to knock this joint off?" he wondered. "I don't know any of the detectives around here well enough to know if I can really trust them. Maybe they're the ones getting free prescriptions at the drugstore."

Connolly knew he needed a stranger for the job. At first he considered calling one of the men from the DCU, but he stifled the impulse. As much as the thought hurt, he had to reconcile himself to the fact that the DCU was all behind him now. Anyway, he should be able to do this simple drugstore job without their assistance.

"Hell, I'm a stranger here," Eddie realized. "I may be criticized for doing it myself. Bosses aren't supposed to do these kinds of things. But what do I care? I'm in charge here. I've done this type of work a thousand times before. I can do it again."

Connolly needed a back-up, someone he could trust to keep his mouth shut. He tapped Eddie Giampolo, a former detective who had been reassigned to 13.

That Sunday afternoon Connolly ambled into the drugstore dressed in worn-out work clothes and sporting a plaid cap on his head. He headed to the back of the store toward the glass cases full of liquor. The clerk was openly bagging a couple of quarts of whiskey for another customer.

"Whaddaya want?" the man behind the counter demanded.

"Jug of Schenley's."

"Anything else?"

"Two six-packs."

"Of what?"

"Blue Ribbon."

Connolly held a $20 bill that he had inconspicuously marked with his initials. Before handing the money to the clerk, he asked, "How much?"

The clerk grunted, but didn't answer. He snatched the twenty from Connolly's fingers. Eddie carefully observed which part of the till the man placed the twenty in. At the same time, he lifted his cap off and wiped his forehead, a signal for Giampolo to move in slowly for the arrest.

The clerk had the six-packs in one bag and twisted the brown paper around the neck of the liquor in a second one. As soon as he handed the sacks to Connolly, Eddie said, "By the way, I'm Lieutenant Connolly of the Boston Police."

He pulled his badge out of his rear pants pocket.

"You're under arrest for liquor violation."

"You got to be shitting me."

"No, I'm not."

Giampolo had slipped up to Connolly's side.

"Here, Eddie. Hold these," Connolly said, passing the bags to Giampolo. "Now, you. Open that register."

The clerk complied sullenly.

"Carefully now, pick up that twenty dollar bill. Read that writing on the left hand margin on the back."

"E-F-C," The clerk overenunciated each letter.

"That's me!" Connolly smiled. Then the lieutenant had Giampolo verify that the serial number on the bill from the register was the same as the number Connolly had had him note on a slip of paper before they entered the drugstore.

Connolly let the clerk secure the rest of the money in the register, set the store alarm and call his boss to notify him that he was leaving the premises.

At the station, Connolly hauled the clerk before Lieutenant David Moran. When Eddie was a sergeant over at District 4, he had been impressed by Moran's work as a patrolman.

"David, book this fellow for violating the liquor laws. Make sure he's photoed and printed. Then let him call for bail."

"Somebody already called about his bail."

"Must be his boss."

Connolly went into his office to make out the report. Before long Moran let him know the boss had arrived.

"Send him in, but leave the door open. We don't need any privacy for this conversation."

A man in his fifties strode in and introduced himself.

"Your name is Connolly?" he asked.

"Lieutenant Connolly," Eddie replied. "Is there something I can do for you?"

"You arrested an employee of mine at my drugstore. Can you tell me why?"

"Yeah. He sold me some booze and beer."

Lowering his voice and glancing at the open door, the owner said, "Can't we straighten this out?"

"Why don't you try?" Connolly said darkly.

"No, thanks."

"Anything else on your mind?"

"No."

"I just want to give you a warning. Don't sell any booze on Sunday while I'm in charge of this station. Now, goodnight."

When the case came to court, the drugstore owner demonstrated that he had built up some pretty good connections during the past 20 years. The case was continued for six months without a finding.

A couple of days later, the same nameless informant called in to report that the druggist was boasting about how he got the case bagged.

"He did," Connolly admitted. "But we'll get him again."

"I got another tip for you. A friend of mine is running a bookie joint."

"Let me find something to write with, and then you can give me the details."

These leads proved to be solid. Connolly arrested the caller's buddy twice in the next six month for bookmaking.

Eddie began to find time to explore his new territory more closely. Before World War II, the Jamaica Plain area had been inhabited mainly by Germans and Irish who worked in the breweries and factories in the area. Many of the tenement areas had been taken over by blacks and Hispanics representing 17 or 18 Spanish-speaking countries.

Though many of the single and two family homes had deteriorated from urban blight, Jamaica Plain was graced with the most open green space in the city. There was Franklin Park, designed by Frederick Law Olmstead, encompassing the city zoo and golf course. Nearby was Harvard's Arnold Arboretum, where anyone could stroll through beautifully landscaped acreage featuring trees from around the world. Jamaica Pond was a lake skirted by jogging paths and wooded hills.

Richer folks lived in Moss Hill, an affluent section that bordered on the town of Brookline. Even along the busy Jamaicaway, there were many lovely Victorian homes.

Eddie enjoyed getting out into the streets to talk with the people from all parts of his little domain. Since people seemed to have so many grievances to air, Connolly actively promoted the monthly community-police meetings. Attendance at the meetings began to average 90 to 100, thanks to local leaders like Ruth Parker, a white woman who continues to live in the house she was born in despite the fact that most of her friends moved out when the neighborhood became predominantly black.

Eddie always made sure that some patrol officers, detectives or sergeants attended these gatherings with him, so that they too could get to know local residents over coffee and doughnuts and establish a rapport that was previously unknown in the area.

Connolly was the first district commander to hold community meetings in Spanish. Officers Al LaFontaine and Danny Ramirez interpreted for him. The interaction between the Anglo officers and the Hispanic community really strengthened the credibility of the police in the Spanish-speaking neighborhoods.

Black, white or Hispanic — the number one complaint was drugs. As Connolly and his men began to build the confidence of the community, the local people would feed them names and locations of pushers, so that the task of cleaning up the drug situation became a truly cooperative effort.

A night at home became a rarity for Connolly. Most evenings he was out attending a meeting, speaking at a dinner, or answering questions at a veterans' post. Whenever Connolly received an honorarium for a speaking engagement, whether from a local civic group or an out-of-state symposium on drug control, he always turned the check over to the Boston Police Relief Association.

Whether the issue was housebreaks, parking problems, kids drinking on the corner or removing an abandoned car, Connolly tried to be as straightforward and down to earth as possible with the people.

"If we can't do what you ask," he would tell them, "we won't lie to you. We can't promise you that we will always be able to help, but we can promise that we will always try."

Connolly was just as frank with his men. He would make it a point to say something significant each day at roll call. "My door is always open to any one of you that wants to talk and get a problem off your chest," he kept reminding them.

In a relatively short period what had formerly been known as a "dumping ground" was now actually living up to di Grazia's snazzy title of a "model station."

Two officers exemplified the ethnic diversity of District 13 as well as the Connolly's determination to put dealers on the run. This duo became known as "Chico and the Man," a reference to an old TV comedy.

This pair became a legend, partly because of their dedication and partly because they represented the best of the new and the old of Jamaica Plain itself. Born in Puerto Rico, Albert LaFontaine was assigned to his own neighborhood, JP, fresh out of the Police Academy.

John Ulrich, a rookie of German extraction, was raised in the Egleston Square section of District 13; he too was sent to work on his home turf as part of the "model station" plan.

Within the space of a year, "Chico and the Man" swiftly racked up over 900 drug arrests; Connolly rewarded them for this phenomenal achievement by giving them detective badges.

Whenever he could, Eddie tried to give LaFontaine and Ulrich the benefit of his experience, constantly hammering certain points home to them.

"Don't go off half-cocked; check all your informants' stories twice. Don't use dope to buy information. Never give a dealer a license to deal in return for information. Be extremely careful about handling money. Try not to touch it unless you're taking it as evidence, or you could wind up on the wrong side of the bars."

Eddie had seen too many guys ignore his fatherly advice and end up in serious trouble. In any case, these two made few mistakes, and when they did, Connolly was always ready to bail them out, reminding himself of his own days as a young officer, unhappy because of the lack of support from superiors.

Late one cold winter night, Connolly was home in bed when he received a call from LaFontaine.

"Lieutenant, sorry to disturb you at home . . ."

"No problem. What's up?"

"John and me just hit this house on Mozart Street. We got a shitload of stolen goods."

"Nice work."

"The problem is, Lieutenant, we don't have nowhere to put all the stuff — TVs, stereos, that kind of shit. Could we store all the loot in your office? That's the only place it would be really safe."

"If you want to come by my house. I can give you the key."

"We don't want to disturb your family."

"Never mind about them. They'll be alright. You know where the house is?"

"Yes, sir. We'll see you in about 20 minutes."

The next morning, Connolly retrieved the key from the desk sergeant and used it to unlock his office. Piled everywhere were 35 stolen televisions and stereo systems as well as bags of silverware and hangers with fur coats and other expensive garments.

Crawling all over these high-price items were thousands of cockroaches. The black-shelled insects were scurrying everywhere — on the floor, the walls, the ceiling, and all over Connolly's desk and swivel chair. Bugs were still creeping out of the holes in the backs of the TV sets and out of the speakers. They started heading for Eddie and the doorway.

Connolly slammed the door shut and hollered, "Quick, Henry, the Flit!"

Then he got on the phone to the exterminator and demanded that he report to Station 13 double quick. Next Eddie dialed the courthouse and instructed the sergeant in charge to send Chico and the Man back to his office instantly, regardless of whether or not they had given their testimony.

"Sir, they have an important case today," the sergeant demurred.

"You tell those two that they left a million little pieces of their important case in my office!" Eddie shouted. "I want their asses back here pronto!"

By the time Ulrich and LaFontaine appeared, the exterminator had come and gone. The reek of the fumes made Al and John cough as they stood, surveying the dead, dying and still frisky cockroaches that littered Connolly's office.

"They weren't here last night . . .," Ulrich began.

"Well, they're here now," Connolly retorted. "Get the evidence the hell out of my office tonight . . . before the whole station is carried off by these damned roaches. I don't care what you do with it . . . just take all of it, including every single one of these crawlers, with you."

"Don't worry, Lieutenant. We'll take care of everything."

The next morning Connolly ventured into his office to see if it were habitable. The stolen goods had been removed; he didn't inquire where LaFontaine and Ulrich had stored them.

John had decided to kill two birds with one stone. To ventilate the room and to kill the cockroaches that had survived the gasing of the exterminator, he had turned off the radiator in Eddie's office and left the windows open. Since the overnight temperature had dropped into the teens, many of the roaches did expire from the cold.

Eddie had a cadet sweep the stiff frozen corpses out of all the corners of the office while he spent the day in the Detectives' Room, wondering if the buggers had left eggs that would hatch when the heat was turned on or when spring came.

They had.

Chico and the Man also played a part in different kind of exterminating case. When the pride and honor of the police were at stake, all of Station 13 rallied to wreak revenge on those who dared to defy the men in blue.

The trouble started around 4 one spring morning. The patrol supervisor had only two cars out on the streets. One cruiser had been sent to Forest Hills to deal with a drunk driving accident. The other vehicle, the Sierra 101 car, was sent to tag the automobiles that lined both sides of Day Street, obstructing access to the fire hydrants.

The two men in the Sierra 101 car immediately saw what was causing all this early-hour parking congestion — a one-story brickfront club from which music with a salsa beat blared.

"Harry, you'd better call the PS," Joe said as he banged on the steel-covered door of 134 Day Street with his nightstick.

"Sierra 101 — would you have the PS meet us on Day Street?"

Before the dispatcher could put the message over the air, the patrol supervisor broke in.

"PS has that . . . will be there in a few minutes," Sergeant Leonard Marquardt answered.

The harder Harry and Joe pounded on the metal door, the louder the curses came from inside. In Spanish and broken English, the revelers shouted taunts and threats.

"Get out of here, you mother-fuckers. You cock-sucking pigs, we'll kick the shit out of you."

The officer tried to remain calm.

"Move your cars, or we'll have to tag them."

Sergeant Marquardt parked his car around the corner so as to avoid further blocking traffic.

After assessing the situation and conferring with the officers from the Sierra 101 car, he said in a voice loud enough for the gang inside to hear, "Fuck 'em. Tag every one of these shitboxes and call a tow truck."

A moment later the door burst open, and a horde of Hispanics rushed out onto the sidewalk. They began pelting the officers with both empty and half-full bottles of beer. As the crowd forced the officers to retreat, the angry contingent from the club began hurling rocks.

Jorge Sarmiento, a 6'2" Puerto Rican, was leading the charge. As the outnumbered policemen ducked behind the sergeant's cruiser to avoid the shower of bottles and stones, Jorge lobbed a piece of metal right through the windshield of the patrol car.

Harry pulled out his .38 service revolver and stood up, pointing it at the on-rushing mob. At the sight of the weapon, some of the Hispanics backed off, but not Jorge.

"*¡El no tiene los cojones para disparar! Vamos a cajerle encima,*" he cried to goad his followers. "He doesn't have the balls to shoot. We'll beat the shit out of him."

"Let's turn over their cars!" another man shouted.

Joe and Sergeant Marquardt whipped their guns out of their holsters and took aim, but all three were slowly backing down the street toward Hyde Square.

"Maybe we'd better call for help," Harry said hoarsely.

"What help?" snapped Marquardt. "The other car is off the air. Besides what good would two more cops do against 80 drunks?"

When the crowd saw that they had the trio of officers at bay, they began to laugh and make insulting gestures.

"If you come back, we'll burn your cars!" they jeered.

Jorge led his boisterous battalion back to their cantina, singing and shouting victoriously, "*Los tenemos corriendo.* We have them running!"

Later that morning, when Connolly arrived for work, Marquardt told him the story of how the officers had been forced to withdraw by the gang of Hispanics.

Eddie shared their feelings of humiliation, but he commended the patrol supervisor's decision to retreat.

"You did the right thing. Either that or you would have ended up killing somebody for parking on the sidewalk or drinking beer in a minority club. The *Globe* would have nailed your ass to the wall."

"Thanks. Lieutenant . . ."

"Your pride is hurt. Mine would be too, but you just wait." Connolly continued, "I know this Big George Sarmiento well, so well, in fact, that I know he's on a six-month suspended sentence from the House of Correction. Let's just lie low for a while. Don't let anyone go near the place. Then we'll see who's got the *cojones* around here."

Connolly was planning to obliterate the after-hours spot — not just because of the minor liquor and gaming violations, but more importantly because he was determined that this slight to the police's honor be avenged and that the confidence in his law enforcement team, which was doubtless the laughingstock of the whole community by this time, be swiftly reestablished.

That evening he summoned Ulrich and LaFontaine as well as another set of partners, Detectives Bob Bradley and Bob Kenny. Eddie explained that each of them had an important part to play in his plan. First they had to find out when the next big crap game would be running full tilt, when the beer and booze would be flowing, when the illegal club would be packed, and, of course, when Big George Sarmiento would be on the premises.

Finally, they settled on the upcoming Friday, payday, the night to unwind with a few pops of beers and a few turns at the dice-table.

Danny Ramirez, the Cuban-born officer who worked closely with Chico and the Man, developed an informant who had the key to the door of the club. That would give them access to the windowless brick building.

Detectives Bradley and Kenny spent a few evenings scouting out the club. They reported that there were always two "spotters" or look-outs watching the street. The one on the corner of Perkins and Day would have to be taken off first. The man at the other end of the block on Bynner and Day would have to be removed seconds afterwards.

Connolly needed an unusually large number of men to hit the club. Sergeant-Detective Russ Childers and his day detectives were all raring to join the nighttime mission. Eddie stripped District 13 of as many cars and foot patrolman as he could possible spare, but he still didn't have nearly enough manpower for this kind of assault.

A call to Captain Joe Rowan of the Tactical Patrol Force was all that was needed. The big aggressive men of the TPF had weathered school busing, jail riots, anti-war rallies and ugly racial conflicts; these guys were used to playing hardball.

Around 5 pm on Friday, LaFontaine and Ulrich parked on Day Street, then crawled into the back of the van to observe #134 through the one-way mirrored glass. Around 7 the patrons started arriving; by 9:30 about 85 of them had jammed themselves into the club.

Connolly and a good number of the men gathered on the grounds of Boston's major veterinary hospital, Angell Memorial. Though the backlot of Angell's property abutted Day Street, an eight-foot brick wall surrounding the grounds obstructed a direct view of the club.

Using a walkie-talkie, Eddie kept in touch with the men sneaking down the side streets. On Connolly's signal, two teams swiftly jumped the look-outs and dragged them away.

Seconds later, the police were climbing over the Angell wall and loping silently from the various side streets toward the club. The informant slid his key into the lock of the door; Ramirez drew his gun to make it look as if he had forced the informant to open the door.

Connolly nodded, the key turned, a burly shoulder forced the door wide open, and the police team surged into the already densely packed interior.

The detectives had been assigned to the room where the gambling was going on. Ulrich and LaFontaine took flying leaps and belly-flopped onto the gaming table, covering the money and dice that would be needed as evidence. Russ Childers and his detectives swiftly formed a ring around the dice-players, who were two or three rows deep around the table, cordoning off any chance of escape.

In no time the TPF, looking quite intimidating in their full riot gear, took over the bar area. Before the revelers knew what was happening, they found themselves lined up against the bar and walls of the room with their hands on their heads.

Crowded was not the word for the close quarters in the club; you couldn't move a step in any direction without rubbing up against somebody's belly or butt. Eddie's blue eyes flicked over all the sweating faces until he finally spotted Jorge Sarmiento, standing in the doorway between the gaming-room and the barroom.

"You, Big George, Big Mouth, you're under arrest for setting up this whole thing . . . you're responsible for all these gambling violations," Connolly said as he made his way over to the big man.

"I'm a visitor here," Jorge protested. "Besides, I'm nowhere near the table."

"Come here, baby," Connolly chuckled, dragging Sarmiento through the throng and thrusting him against the table. "Now you're right in the middle of the action."

Eddie went through Big George's pockets and quickly produced a large roll of bills and a bunch of keys.

"Over here," Eddie directed, as he had two officers push Jorge over to a large refrigerated chest. Using a small silver key, Eddie snapped the padlock, opened the door and revealed hundreds of cases of beer in bottles and cans.

"So you're just a visitor, huh? In here, next."

After trying several keys, Connolly unlocked the door to a little office, "How about that, Georgie-boy? You gonna try to tell me now that you don't have anything to do with this joint?"

The center drawer of the desk was open; inside were packs of bills and boxes of unused dice.

"You're a betting man, George. What are the odds that this last key is the one that opens the front door to this place?"

"*Hijo de la gran puta,*" Sarmiento spat the insult at him.

Connolly had Officer Billy Cantin read Sarmiento his rights. Meanwhile outside, the four wagons that Connolly had arranged to have there were beginning to fill up. Eddie made a decision to let go those who were just drinking. But first he had LaFontaine and Ramirez lecture them in Spanish. The two officers made it clear to them in their own language that the club was now closed for good and that nobody gets away with threatening police officers the way they had done earlier in the week.

Including Jorge Sarmiento, there were about 45 gamblers that had to be taken to 13 for booking. Connolly thanked the Tactical Patrol Force for their assistance, and as the troop of big-shouldered men pulled away from Day Street, Eddie remarked a bit wistfully, "I always wanted to be a member of that outfit."

Connolly confiscated over 125 cases of beer and $600 from the crap game. He also seized every stick of furniture, including the bar and freezer chest. Under the law he was allowed to — and did — take the front door as evidence. He wasn't about to worry about vandals wrecking the place; there was nothing left of the club but the walls and roof.

Some of those brought in had warrants outstanding against them for robbery and larceny in other courts and had to be held without bail. There was one "no-supper" guy wanted for non-support in Springfield. The booking officers kept rubbing it in that this crackdown was all George's fault for giving the police such a hard time.

The men with no records were let off with a $10 fine and a warning. Sarmiento was charged with allowing his premises to be used for gambling and as a liquor nuisance. He was hit with a $500 fine and was made to serve 30 days of his suspended sentence.

A week later, Eddie was telling a friend about the complaints he had received from the Internal Affairs Division.

"They wanted to know why I needed so many men and the whole TPF to knock off a little neighborhood club."

"Did you explain the reasons?"

"Most of the guys in Internal Affairs have never done any real police work; that's why they're in the IAD; anyway, they would never understand. But let them bellyache. I know we did the right thing. Our pride has been restored; the community has confidence in us again. Once in a while, we may have to back off, but we'll be back. Believe me, we'll be back. But don't take my word for it. Just ask Georgie.''

28

Field Services

Connolly didn't take his eyes off the report he was studying as he reached over to answer the phone that buzzed insistently for his attention. He immediately recognized the voice as that of Joe Jordan. The police commissioner never called to chitchat about sports or chuckle over a good story he'd heard. No, a call from Jordan meant someone somewhere was in trouble.

Connolly felt sure that the shit had hit the fan: he just didn't know what direction it was blowing in. Had someone from 13 been caught selling dope or screwing his partner's wife? Had his policeman son Billy been hurt?

"Eddie!" The voice on the other end was loud, and Jordan was characteristically rather soft-spoken. Another indication of disaster.

"Yes, sir . . ."

"Meet me in front of White Stadium in 15 minutes," the Commissioner said crisply.

"I'll be there in 10," Connolly promised and replaced the receiver.

As he wiggled into his uniform jacket, Connolly strode past Lieutenant Frank Kelly on the desk. Kelly looked up, expecting Connolly to announce when he would return.

"I don't know when I'll be back . . . ."

Out the door of the century-old stationhouse, down the steep flight of granite steps and into the marked cruiser he hurried. Connolly wasted no time heading down Seaverns Avenue toward Franklin Park where the stadium was located.

More possible scenarios crowded his mind. "Did I say something to the press or TV that they didn't like at City Hall? Or does the mayor think I'm getting too popular around here and want me out before I run against him next time he's up for reelection?"

Despite the fact that everything was going well in his district, Eddie was getting more concerned the closer he got to the park. He mentally reviewed all the other hard-working guys who had been broken by the brass for small shit — a careless remark or a frowned-upon political association.

"I knew this deputy superintendent job wouldn't last," he thought shaking his head as he entered the leafy environs of the park and headed towards the schoolboy stadium.

He was rehearsing defiant remarks and snappy comebacks he could use if Jordan lowered the boom.

"You can shove this deputy superintendent's job. . . .

"Better not, better be more respectful . . . if I want to go back to the Drug Squad."

In front of the gates to the stadium was parked a light-colored car with out-of-state plates, but there was no doubt that the tall, slim, well-groomed man behind the wheel was Jordan. Connolly recogniz- ed the vehicle as an undercover car of the Special Investigations Unit — also known as the Shoo-fly Squad.

The secluded rendezvous and the use of an undercover car made Connolly's stomach sink even lower. But he didn't let his concern show as he got out of his cruiser and came over to the Jordan's car.

"Hi, Commissioner."

"Get in," Jordan said flatly; there was no reading his impassive face.

Connolly crossed his fingers and bunched them into a fist as he walked around and got in next to his boss.

"Eddie, I want you to take over the Bureau of Field Services."

Jordan was dumping the top job in the city on his lap — the city- wide command of all uniformed police officers and detectives, and responsibility for all operations of the Department.

Connolly's first reaction was to think about Superintendent Daniel MacDonald, the man who currently headed the Bureau of Field Ser- vices.

"What about Dan?"

"He'll be moved to another job in the command staff."

"Why me? With all those college boys you got around . . ."

"I want someone on the streets, someone who will be seen and will respond to crimes anytime day or night, someone who will be around at all times. This is your thing. You know the city, the streets, and the people."

The implied compliments didn't make the job sound any more ap- pealing. Connolly knew the amount of paperwork that the position entailed.

"No, Commissioner. Thank you, but I'm happy where I am. I got good people, a good court . . . everything's in good shape. So I don't think I want the job."

"But I want you to take it. You'll be hearing from me soon."

The commissioner was determined to brook no opposition.

"See you later."

Connolly did not need any more hints that the interview was over. He climbed out of the car, and as he was closing the passenger door, Jor- dan added, "Keep your mouth shut about this."

The undercover car shot forward and out of Franklin Park, leaving Connolly to wrestle with his thoughts. He couldn't get over the fact that, in a department and a city so famous for political intrigue, he had been offered a position that so many others had been scheming and currying favor with the mayor to get.

"I never thought I was ever one of Joe Jordan's favorite people."

He considered that along with the promotion to superintendent went a pay raise, but neither of these factors really mattered that much. He'd had to leave jobs he'd loved before, especially that of head of the Drug Unit, but that was the way promotion roulette was played around in the Department.

Connolly began to think about how he would present the matter to his wife. She would, of course, be proud and impressed that Jordan had offered him the position. She had put up with so much already; she would go along with anything.

As Connolly pulled out of the White Stadium parking lot, he winced a bit, thinking of how he was going to feel the next time that he saw his immediate superior, Dan MacDonald, the man he was about to replace.

Though considerably younger than Connolly, MacDonald had already worked all over the city, first as mounted officer, then as a patrolman on the old Back Bay Station, a sergeant in Roxbury, a lieutenant in the North End, a captain in Internal Affairs, and finally Deputy Superintendent of the Bureau of Field Services. Eddie was especially conscious of the fact that MacDonald had been Captain of the Vice Squad when Connolly worked under him as head of the Drug Control Unit. There were no two ways about it; it was an embarrassing situation.

The secret of the imminent shake-up was a well-kept one, a rarity in the Boston Police Department, where hundreds of rumors are traded every day: who's going to be transferred, who's going to be the next commissioner, whatever else came out of the shithouse. Eddie often remarked that there was more intrigue at the Berkeley Street Headquarters than there was at the Kremlin.

Connolly knew he'd get his name in the papers the day the reassignments were announced, but before the shuffle was made public, he was shocked to see his picture staring at him from under some most unflattering headlines.

On Friday, April 20, 1979, the *Boston Herald-American* ran a front-page story asking, "Boston Cops . . . Why are there so many fatties?"

Someone had pulled a file photo of Connolly and used it as an example of Hub officers. Eddie had reached an all-time weight high, but the picture exaggerated his paunch and made him look ridiculously obese.

Boston Herald American

Telephone (617) 426-3000   ★★★   ®   20 Cents   Friday, April 20, 1979

Boston's cops . . . Why are there so many fatties?

Chicago

By ED CORSETTI
and HAROLD BANKS
Staff Writers

A rookie Boston cop comes out of a year at the Police Academy looking like an Olympic sprinter.

New York

He runs, he swims, he scales fences, he drags 125 pounds of dead weight 50 feet through an obstacle course.

But by the time he gets to be a long-time veteran he may no longer be svelte.

Atlanta

"The general appearance of Boston police officers," civilian personnel director Michael P. Gardner says, "is somewhat disappointing, but when you consider the average age, which is 47, they aren't really that bad."

Los Angeles

Few police departments in the country have mandatory physical fitness programs, but some do have mandatory weight standards.

Boston doesn't even have that. But neither do the New York, Chi-

cago and Atlanta Police Departments.

In Los Angeles, an overweight cop loses points in the semi-annual rating scale used to determine promotions, and if he doesn't get back into shape, he

Our Guy

can be dismissed.

Here, a chubby cop probably won't be promoted, but he can't be fired.

That's not the way things are

Continued on page 9

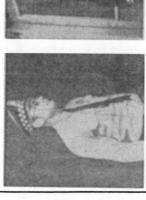

Letters protesting the publication of Eddie's photo in this context poured in to the *Herald* editors:

The person who chose to put this lightweight story on page one and the person who chose the photograph did a grave disservice to Deputy Superintendent Edward Connolly, labelled "our guy."

Deputy Connolly is one of the best, most selfless police officers in the City of Boston. I've had the pleasure to work with him as a community leader in Jamaica Plain for several years. He always has been courteous and responsive with my group and everyone else.

Richard Heath
Jamaica Plain

I agree we have many officers that aren't in good shape, but the picture in the paper was one of a man with more than 30 years on the force and who is still one of our best policemen . . . The pictures shown of other police departments are obviously of younger men . . . The writer should line up his staff of writers and bosses; what condition is the man in his late 50s and 60s in?

Detective Joseph Caggiano
District 6
South Boston

On Friday, April 20, yet another one-sided, misleading, incomplete and even cruel article appeared on the front page of the Boston Herald-American, in the area usually reserved for the most important news event of the day. The article . . . included the pictures of four obviously young policemen from various large city police departments. A fifth picture, of a white-haired police officer, obviously in his sixties, with a protruding stomach with the caption "Our Guy" was included.

The story that followed never identified this man as Eddy Connelly, a man who for well over thirty years has been known as a "Super Star" in the law enforcement field, as a nationally recognized expert in society's war on drugs and who for many years was the commanding officer of the narcotics unit of the Boston Police Department.

The pictures were presumably used as a humorous comparison of the physical difference between other city's policemen and our own; the comparison was, in fact, humorous, as each of the cities cited would gladly trade ten such untried young officers for one Eddy Connelly, even an old one in his sixties. If all four of these young policemen together were to attain just ten per cent of the record of success accomplished by Eddy Connelly, they will retire at the end

of their careers with the reputation of being "Good Cops." Few
policemen throughout the country will do that well....

Paul A. Conway and Walter E. O'Neil
Boston Superior Officers Federation

As heartening as it was to be defended and praised so vociferously
by both civilians and fellow officers, Eddie put himself on a strict diet
to lose 20 pounds.

The order finally came down in late July, 1979; Connolly's promotion to the rank of superintendent was announced as part of Jordan's
general reorganization of the Department.

The Commissioner's decision to reassign a dozen top-level officers
was not an easy one. He admitted to the press, "Some of these guys
were my personal friends. I've known some of them for more than 30
years. I'm sure they'll never forgive me."

Jordan said the changes were not intended to demean those that
had been demoted; it was rather that the switches had to be made
because his perception of increased demands on the Department.

"We're looking for different types of expertise these days. We try to
grab all strengths we can and utilize them. We're looking for a staff
that will really put forth that extra effort. We need people who will accept the fact that they're part of the command staff and will not pass
everything along the line."

The Commissioner went out of his way to cite Eddie Connolly as "a
rare individual who has the ability to instill leadership. He works 15
hours a day. He's concerned. He relates to the community much more
effectively than you would expect."

Jordan's tribute took some of the sting out of the embarrassing
newspaper photo incident.

The day arrived at last for Connolly to walk through the doors of
the Bureau of Field Services into the office that MacDonald would
soon have to surrender to him.

"I'm sorry that I'm replacing you, Dan," Connolly was fumbling
for words. "I don't know what I can say."

"Eddie, don't worry about it," he laughed gently. "Nobody lasts
too long in this job. Everybody gets to take a shot at you when you're
sitting at this desk. Frankly, I'm glad to get the hell outta here."

Dan MacDonald gave his successor some friendly, much-needed
advice on the pitfalls to avoid, the enemies to sidestep, and the way
to bow out gracefully when it was his turn to go. About the only thing
that MacDonald didn't cover, a bit of information that Eddie would
soon need, was what to do when someone you trust puts a bullet
in you.

29

Taking Sundstrom's Bullet

Ed Connolly and his family always knew that someday he'd be shot. It was not something they dwelt on, but simply accepted. After all, a man who had been injured 32 times in the course of his career was bound to run into a bullet somewhere along the line. However, on the morning of July 25, 1979, Connolly had no inkling that that someday had finally arrived.

The afternoon began on a rather humdrum note. At 1:00 he attended a retirement ceremony for some colleagues. Commissioner Joseph Jordan presented them with their old badges encased in lucite. After all the reminiscing and chatting with wives was over, Connolly was heading back to the Bureau of Field Services when a cameraman gave him some photographs he had taken of Eddie posing with his grandson Anthony.

When Connolly was slipping the pictures into his center desk drawer, he noticed a note with an urgent message to call Detective Sergeant Russell Childers, his old buddy from Area E.

"Eddie, we've got a hostage situation on our hands."

"Oh, yeah?"

"It's a friend of yours. . . ."

"Who?"

"David Sundstrom. He's got his wife, his kids and his mother in there."

As Childers filled him in on the details, Connolly shook his head, thinking about his "friend" Sundstrom. Though he had only met the man twice in person, they had talked on the phone almost daily for the past three or four years . . . a thousand times at least.

Their initial encounter had come in January, 1976. David Sundstrom, a nervous-looking but solidly built man about 5'11", had burst into Connolly's office at District 13, hurling accusations about the blacks and Hispanics that had moved into the Egleston Square neighborhood. His demeanor was respectful, yet very demanding.

"You've got to protect me! The niggers and spics are after me. They're trying to kill me!"

"Now don't worry. I'll see that nothing happens to you."

"You gotta give me 24-hour protection."

"Who's after you? Gimme their names and we'll look into it."

Even though Sundstrom could not come up with any names, he poured out the story about an elaborate plot against his life. Apparently, he had been calling the police and the FBI for months with information about all the illegal activities that he believed his Hispanic neighbors were engaged in.

Sundstrom had become convinced that his calls had led to a recent bust of a local Hispanic drug ring and that, in revenge, members of the gang had put out a $5,000 contract on his life. Fearing that many people were after him hoping to collect the money, Sundstrom "went underground" and stayed indoors for three months. In reality, Sundstrom's tips always proved to be completely groundless.

However, the superintendent was not about to laugh him off and hustle him out the door.

"Look, take this number. It's my private line." Connolly said, handing the man a piece of paper on which he'd scribbled the digits. "You keep in touch."

From then on, Sundstrom would call virtually every day, and as with the other poor souls to whom Connolly had given his private number, Eddie would talk with him when he didn't have more pressing business.

During the years, Sundstrom's life story came out in bits and pieces. At age 16 he dropped out of school, having only made it to the seventh grade. Shortly afterwards, he was caught in a stolen car and was given the option of going to jail or joining the military.

After nine months in the service, he was discharged when it came out that he was a hemophiliac. At that time, he was examined by a psychiatrist who characterized him as "a schizoid personality of a severe nature manifested by eccentricity, unsociability, marked suspiciousness and stubbornness."

Sundstrom was tormented with remorse at having sold his brother a bottle of whiskey on the very day that his brother was murdered for the check he was about to cash. David's use of alcohol, marijuana and occasionally cocaine further undermined his mental stability and contributed to his paranoia. He felt so guilty about his use of pot that he took the precaution of driving to the neighboring city of Quincy and stood on the shore watching the waves as he puffed furtively on a joint.

Even there he felt he could not escape the scrutiny of the FBI or their agents, who observed him through one-way glass from a beach house. These agents, he was convinced, had also implanted a tiny transmitter in his wristwatch which enabled them to monitor and tape-record his innermost thoughts.

So he alternated between calling the FBI to tip them off to deals that he imagined his black and Hispanic neighbors were plotting and taking elaborate precautions to avoid the FBI's surveillance of his own activities.

Sundstrom's complaints about FBI harassment and about contracts being put out on his life by Hispanic neighbors all proved unfounded. One summer day, about eight months after their initial meeting, Sundstrom called in with a story that had a different ring to it than his usual persecution fantasies.

"Eddie, I know somebody that's got some hand grenades and dynamite in a box and wants to get rid of it."

"I tell you what, David. Why don't you just turn that stuff over to me . . ."

"It's not me, Eddie. Honest."

"If you ever had a fire in there, you could blow everything up. So why don't you give me your grenades?"

"It's not my stuff. I'm doing a favor for a friend."

"I tell you what's going to happen, David. If you've got them in your closet, when that MBTA goes by over your house, the vibrations could set off your blasting caps, if you've got any blasting caps. You've got your four children in the house, and your mother downstairs is elderly . . . they'd all be dead. You don't want to take that kind of risk."

"And if I give them to you, what will happen to me?"

"Nothing. You have my word on that."

Eventually, David agreed to meet Connolly on Chilcott Place, a sidestreet near his home on Washington Street, around 7:00 that evening.

Connolly told Patrolman Bill Kelley, "Go get an unmarked car. We got something to do."

Kelley called around, but no unmarked cars were to be had on such short notice.

"We'll take my Caddy," he suggested.

So Kelley drove Connolly to Chilcott Place in his brand-new, silver-gray Fleetwood. The Cadillac still smelled new, and as they drove along, Connolly fiddled with all the doodads. When they got to Washington Street, Kelley parked around the corner from Chilcott Place. Both men turned off their walkie-talkies for fear the radio signals might set off some of the explosives.

"Cover me," Eddie said as he got out of the car. "I don't know what this guy is going to do."

Connolly waited on Chilcott Place, half hidden in an alley. Soon Sundstrom appeared with a blue knit watch cap drawn down over his ears and forehead; the upturned collar of his dark coat concealed most of the rest of his face.

Putting the cardboard box he was carrying on the ground in the alley, Sundstrom stepped back and gestured to Eddie.

"Be careful," he whispered.

Connolly bent down and picked up the box, saying quietly, "I'll get rid of this."

"I won't get into trouble?" Sundstrom said apprehensively.

"I gave you my word."

Connolly directed Kelley to drive him to a deserted area in Franklin Park.

"What'll we do if this stuff blows up in your car? It'll ruin your nice new Caddy."

"If that shit goes off," Kelley laughed, "you ain't going to worry about the car, I ain't going to worry about the car and fuck the insurance company."

They reached a secluded spot in the woods near White Stadium, and there they carefully inspected the contents of the carton. Inside they found a grenade, several sticks of dynamite, one of which had been dipped in glue and then rolled in buckshot, forming a homemade bomb that would scatter fragments in all directions. Sundstrom also had several blasting caps and detonators in the collection that he had handed over.

They left the box there and immediately contacted the Bomb Squad to come to examine and dispose of the explosives.

Having managed to convince Sundstrom to surrender the explosives three years earlier, Eddie felt confident that he could talk him out of the hostage situation. But before venturing out to respond to Childers' request for assistance, he stopped by the commissioner's office to apprise Jordan of the situation.

"This guy I know has barricaded himself and his family on the second floor of his house down on Washington Street in Egleston Square. I'm going to see if I can talk him out of it."

Chuck Wexler, a 28-year-old civilian working as assistant to the commissioner for operations, overheard Connolly's story.

As coordinator for the Hostage Negotiation Program for the Department, Wexler itched to go along.

Noting the eagerness in the young man's eye, Connolly asked casually, "You want to go for a ride, Chuck? We'll be back in five minutes."

They hopped into Connolly's squad car and, as they sped toward Egleston Square, Connolly repeated to Wexler the outline Childers had given him of the recent events which had led to the stand-off at 3149 Washington Street.

Until a couple of days earlier, Sundstrom had had a CETA job as a custodian at Curtis Hall, a municipal center in Jamaica Plain. His performance had become increasingly dissatisfactory. He was showing up late, leaving early, sometimes failing to lock up. The last straw had been his kicking the kids out of the swimming pool and closing the building early on a sweltering night.

On Tuesday, July 24, he was summoned to City Hall by the Superintendent of Custodians, David Hurley, to be reprimanded for his irregular performance. Sundstrom did not show up at 9 am as ordered; around 11:30 Hurley went upstairs to the coffee shop.

Shortly afterwards Sundstrom finally appeared at Hurley's office wearing mirrored sunglasses and a windbreaker zipped up to his neck. He was told that the superintendent had gone up to the eighth floor for a cup of coffee.

Once the irate custodian found the coffee shop, he buttonholed Hurley, demanded the checks that had been withheld and screamed, "I'm gonna get fired! I'm gonna get fired!"

Sundstrom's ravings got Hurley angry too, but he still was willing to give the man one more chance. "I told you to be here at 9 this morning. Now go back down to my office and make another appointment."

Sundstrom took this order as a refusal to hand over his back pay, so he punched Hurley on the left side of the face and dashed out of the coffee shop. One of the other patrons alerted Hurley to the fact that there was a bulge in Sundstrom's windbreaker that looked suspiciously like a weapon.

Hurley notified security and the police that there was a nut running around who might be carrying a gun. The whole incident upset him so much that he went down to the first floor to have the nurse check his blood pressure.

A few minutes after he had left the nurse's office, he passed by an unmanned security desk and heard the phone ring. It was Pam DeVellis, the woman who had just taken his blood pressure, and she sounded frantic.

"Dave, that guy was just in my office! He had a gun and he was looking for you. He told me, 'You better run upstairs,' so I did."

Pam had left Sundstrom standing behind the open door of her office with his gun drawn. Sundstrom kept a transistor radio pressed to his ear, believing that it was broadcasting special instructions to him on how he should proceed.

Once he was sure Pam was safe, Hurley immediately contacted Richie Bennett, a husky, plainclothes security officer. Even though he was unarmed, Bennett charged down to the nurse's office and chased Sundstrom out and into a stairwell. As they scrambled up the steps, Sundstrom started throwing down cinder blocks that were used to keep the firedoors ajar. Sundstrom managed to elude Bennett and the guards posted at the exits and got home safely.

The next morning, Wednesday, the day of the shooting, Sergeant Childers had called Sundstrom's residence to see if he were in. His 75-year-old mother Catherine answered and reported that David was not at home, having used the family's brown-and-black van to drive his brother Carl to work.

Childers and two other officers from District 13 maintained surveillance of the ramshackle three-story wooden structure all morning and into the afternoon. As soon as David returned they intended to make service on a Boston Municipal Court warrant of arrest charging him with assault and possession of a deadly weapon.

At 1:30 pm, the surveillance team had to leave the stake-out on Washington Street to investigate a drowning of a girl at Jamaica Pond — a possible homicide.

When David returned home after stopping at the beach in Quincy for a few puffs, his mother informed him that the police had been asking for him. He immediately Dutch-locked the entrance to the staircase to the second floor, a practice he had adopted after the house had been broken into a week earlier.

At around 3 pm, Sundstrom called Childers, but hung up before it could be determined where he was calling from. Ten minutes later he called again, and Childers dispatched a car to #3149 Washington Street where Officers Martin and Quinlan observed the parked van. They tried to gain entrance, but the plank that David had barricaded the door with wouldn't budge.

Meanwhile Childers got a call from David's mother. She blurted out that every time she went to answer the phone, David pulled her away and slammed down the receiver. Finally he confined his mother to the bathroom and told her to stay there. But she had escaped and managed to call the police to warn them that her son was armed with all kinds of weapons.

"He'll shoot anyone that comes into the house."

When Sundstrom got on the line, Sergeant Childers almost tricked him into admitting the officers into the building.

"They're knocking on the door now," Sundstrom cried. "They're going to kill me."

"Look, I got an important message for the officers. Would you let them in and put them on the telephone?"

Just as Sundstrom was considering this request, Martin and Quinlan tried to kick the door down. This action put David right back on the defensive.

"I'm not letting anyone in here. I'll shoot anybody that comes in here."

Using the walkie-talkie, Childers ordered Quinlan and Martin to back off for a while. It was at this point, shortly after 3:00, that he had called Ed Connolly, recalling that the Superintendent had frequent phone conversations with Sundstrom.

Connolly and Wexler sped from the Berkeley Street Headquarters to Columbus Avenue and then to Washington Street. They raced along underneath the Orange Line elevated, which straddles much of Washington Street, for about three-quarters of a mile until they reached the vicinity of the Sundstrom home.

Most three-deckers in the city of Boston have a small front lawn and a wide front porch that is reached by climbing five or six steps. Even this modest distance from the street lends these homes a little privacy and dignity. However, the dilapidated three-and-a-half story structure at #3149 Washington directly abutted the sidewalk. The El was constantly clattering almost immediately overhead, shaking soot down making the peeling gray paint look even shabbier.

Even before they left the air-conditioned comfort of the squad car for the sultry air outside, they could feel that there was a *Dog Day Afternoon* situation developing. When word spread through the neighborhood that gun freak David Sundstrom was holding his family hostage and that police sharpshooters were assembling outside, a crowd of a couple of hundred gathered to watch.

Connolly recognized many familiar faces from his days as deputy superintendent in District 13 as he shouldered his way through the throng, saying, "Stand back and let me see if I can talk to this guy."

On the ground floor porch of the Benirowski house, which was next door to the Sundstroms', he caught sight of Mrs. Ruth Parker, a long-time resident of the neighborhood and a friend of Connolly's. He stopped for a moment to hear what she had to say.

"I've known David since he was a little boy," she reminded the superintendent. "Let me go up and straighten him out. All he needs is to hear is a familiar voice and he'll stop his nonsense."

Connolly raised his hand and said, "Thanks, Ruth, but I'll handle this. You stay right here."

The Superintendent knew that the second floor, where Catherine resided, and the third floor, where David and his wife and children lived, were both barricaded. Since others had been unsuccessful in communicating with David from the front entrance, Connolly took a bullhorn, went around behind the house and climbed up to the back porch on the second floor.

"David. It's me, Eddie Connolly," he called through the boarded windows. "You know me. We can talk."

Sundstrom gave no sign that he heard Connolly's call. Meanwhile on the front porch, Chuck Wexler kept insisting that the lieutenant summon an ambulance just in case anything happened.

Ted O'Brien, a reporter from Channel 7, arrived with a camera crew. They had been heading to the Faulkner Hospital to cover the story of a blind concessionaire who was being evicted when they heard a man with an arsenal was holding the police at bay. It was hot and sticky, and they figured the incident probably wouldn't amount to anything, but they decided to check out the situation anyhow.

Shortly after the Channel 7 crew arrived and began taping the scene, Connolly decided to try to gain access through the front door. The sharpshooters and other police officers stayed on the porch; O'Brien slouched against a post, leisurely scribbling notes.

In the dimly lit, five-foot square foyer, Connolly could barely make out the plexiglas and heavy crisscross metal grating set in the upper half of the door leading to the second story. He crouched down out of the line of fire and kept rapping on the door, calling David's name and identifying himself as Eddie Connolly. After about five minutes, he still got no response.

The noise drew David to the landing where the stairs to the second floor turned. Though he too couldn't see anything in the pitch dark, he did detect a rattling metallic sound and concluded that hostile forces were trying to pry loose the door bolts.

He raised his Colt .45 semi-automatic pistol, ready to blast the first intruder. On the other side of the door, Connolly decided to shift his position and started to stand up.

There was a loud blast. Sundstrom watched the plexiglas shatter as if in slow motion and a wisp of smoke drift lazily out into the hall.

The single bullet that had burst through the plexiglas plowed through Connolly's body, traveling diagonally downward. It struck the right breastbone and was deflected down to the left.

In a split second it caused major damage to the chest, stomach, liver, and the small and large intestines, before coming to rest in his left flank.

The immense force of the copper-jacketed .45 slug carried Connolly across the little foyer and slammed him against the opposite wall. The impact caused a severe ￼ow to his back and threw him to the floor, knocking his gold-braidel cap off his head.

Since an officer, even a wou￼ led one, does not go out without his hat, Connolly struggled to his feet, retrieved his cap with one hand and covered the hole in his chest with the other.

As the intense pain in the middle of his chest started spreading down to his left hip and burned to the core of his body, Connolly gasped, "I'm hit."

He reappeared at the door, clutching his chest saying, "He shot me. That son of a bitch shot me."

Immediately, the officers and crowd became electrified; the wounding of the third highest-ranking policeman on the force and perhaps the best-loved officer in the city changed things completely. As Connolly staggered over the threshold, Wexler caught him on the right side, and Patrolman Frank Delaney rushed over and grabbed his left shoulder, crying, "Oh, my God!" Together they trudged across the porch and down the few steps on to the street.

Upstairs, David listened for a moment to the shuffling of feet and the cry, "I'm hit." He then went to his mother and told her "Everything is alright now. The FBI filmed the whole thing, and they have a record of what happened."

Connolly's face was twisted in a grimace; his sharp, labored inhalations sounded like the cries of a hurt bird. He continued clutching his chest; the pressure of his hand seemed to lessen the burning sensation a little, and he hoped to staunch the flow of blood that was seeping out from between his fingers and staining his white shirt with a ragged, deep red patch.

The ambulance that had been called to stand by still had not arrived, and standard police procedure required that they wait for its arrival. But precious seconds were slipping away, and Connolly gestured toward a nearby patrol car and gasped, "Let's go."

Wexler got into the backseat first so as to be able to help the wounded superintendent in. Delaney jumped into the driver's seat and took off. Because the car was a police vehicle, the windows had been fixed so they couldn't be rolled down, but Connolly's lungs were screaming for air. So as the cruiser leaped foward and the siren started its wail, he used his left arm to keep the door open for the first couple of hundred yards, gulping down as much as he could of the steamy, but fresh air.

Chuck Wexler was murmuring words of encouragement, "Come on, Super, hang in there," not only to comfort him, but to help him retain consciousness.

In the throes of what felt like a heart attack, Connolly took his hands away to inspect his wound.

"I don't think I'm gonna make it. I think he got me this time."

"Eddie, don't let me down. Stay with us — don't let me down."

But Connolly was not optimistic; he kept repeating to himself, "Well, I'm going to die, but that's the way God wants it . . . I was born on November 23, and I'm going to die on July 25. At least Irene will get a good pension after I'm gone . . ."

The Shooting
And Its
Aftermath

Outside 3149 Washington Street, police watch for any movement inside the building where David Sundstrom holds his family hostage.

(Courtesy of the *Globe*)

Sgt. Frank Delaney and Chuck Wexler help Connolly to a cruiser after he had been shot by David Sundstrom.

(Bill Curtis, *Globe*)

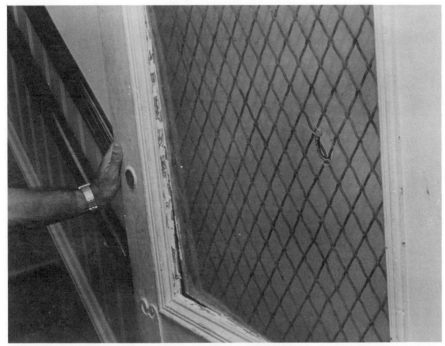

The door through which Connolly was shot.   (Courtesy of the *Globe*)

Part of Sundstrom's arsenal, confiscated after the shooting.

Irene Connolly is rushed into the Faulkner Hospital, escorted by two officers dispatched to pick her up at the Connolly's Milton home. Son Billy
arrives at the same moment.
(Thomas Tajima, *Herald*)

Connolly's daughter, wife and son anxiously
await news of Eddie's condition.

(Stan Grossfeld, *Globe*)

Without his shoes, David Sundstrom is led
from the West Roxbury District Courthouse
following his arraignment.

(Jack O'Connell, *Globe*)

David Sundstrom (Courtesy of the *Globe*)

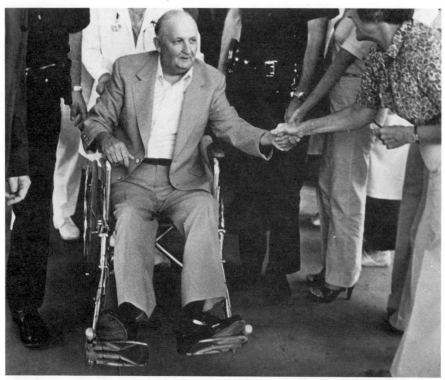

Upon his release from the Faulkner, Eddie shakes hands with well-wishers.

(Stanley Forman, *Herald*)

Son Billy drives Eddie home from the hospital.

(Stanley Forman, *Herald*)

Grandson Anthony Landry greets Eddie upon his return home after spending only 13 days in the hospital.

(Stanley Forman, *Herald*)

Commissioner Joseph Jordan awards Superintendent Connolly the Schroeder Brothers Medal for Courageous Police Service as well as five other citations for heroism at the 109th Policeman's Ball.

(Wendy Maeda, *Globe*)

30

Surgeons and Sharpshooters

Sergeant Delaney flew the cruiser to Faulkner Hospital in an amazing five minutes. The hospital was only two miles away, but he had to charge down the wrong lane through rush-hour traffic at breakneck speed to get there.

While dodging the oncoming cars, Delaney managed to contact the Faulkner Hospital via the Police Communications Bureau to alert them to the fact that a wounded police officer would be on their doorstep momentarily. A team of eight doctors, nurses and technicians was ready to receive Connolly at the entrance to the emergency room. They took him out of the arms of Delaney and Wexler and had him on a gurney in a matter of seconds. Immediately, they put tubes in him to replace the blood he had lost.

Somehow the crack medical team got him under an X-ray machine even before they got him out of his uniform. As the doctors studied the X-rays before they began the delicate exploratory surgery, one of them squinted at some unusual markings on the cloudy skeletal image. He then recognized the shapes as four five-pointed stars on each of the shoulders — the symbols of Connolly's rank.

"We better do everything we can to save this guy. He's some sort of big shot with the police."

Dr. Christos Hasiotis replied quietly, "We'd put the same effort in, even if he were the lowest man in the Department."

Connolly's vision was blurred, and all he could see were the bright patches of light overhead as he was wheeled around. The soft hand of a nurse provided some comfort, but he could barely respond to the doctors' questions. Still, in the emergency room Connolly asked a police aide to make sure that his wife Irene was given the two manila envelopes that were in his desk back at Headquarters; they contained the pictures of him holding his grandson Anthony that the thoughtful newspaper photographer had given him that morning at the retirement ceremony. Eddie thought that he would miss the little fellow as much as he'd miss anyone else and felt a pang at the thought of not being at Anthony's first birthday party, which was still a month away.

The pain was becoming unbearable. "Jesus, this is it," he said and whispered a short prayer. Then he heard the familiar voice of Father William Francis, the Department Chaplain, asking him if he were sorry for all his past sins and whispering the last rites of the Church over him.

Connolly was convinced he was going to die. The thought of death didn't scare him; he was ready for it. He had always accepted the fact that he would probably die on the job.

"That's why policemen are here," he reflected. "Some of us are going to live, but some of us have to pay the penalty to keep the place safe."

More lights flickered by overhead as he was taken down a hall, then transferred from the gurney to a table. He figured he must be in the operating room.

"Do what you have to do," he murmured to the surgical staff he couldn't even see. "I'm in your hands."

Then he heard a new voice — one with a distinct British accent. The voice, which he later learned belonged to Dr. David Campbell, reassured him, "You're going to make it . . . ."

Tears began to roll down Eddie's cheeks — not from the pain, but from the joy he experienced once he began to believe that he was going to live after all. He let himself relax and slip into unconsciousness . . . .

When Commissioner Jordan got the message "The Deputy's been shot. They're taking him to the Faulkner," he immediately set out for the hospital, thinking that the deputy referred to was Stanley Dirsa, who had just been promoted to that rank. Actually, the officer who called in the report was so used to thinking of Connolly as a deputy superintendent that he didn't remember that Eddie had been recently promoted.

So when Jordan arrived, he asked, "How's Dirsa?"

"Not Dirsa. Connolly's the one who got shot."

"Not Ed Connolly?"

"I'm afraid so . . . ."

Whatever disagreements they had had in the past, Jordan put them aside at an impromptu press conference held outside the Faulkner. When asked if he disapproved of Connolly's practice of continuing to work the streets, Jordan had only praise for the superintendent's actions.

"At no time have I ever tried nor would I ever attempt to discourage Ed Connolly from doing what he thought best. He's simply not the kind of a guy to remain behind a desk. Everyone who knows Ed Connolly knows he's the type of a person who gives 150 percent of himself to his job. He has taken many chances and risks in the past, and I'm sure he will continue to do so.

"He's a phenomenal kind of a man. He was injured during the Hyde Park school integration problem. He was hit that time with a two-by-four during a demonstration. Another time he was shot at. He's a cop's cop."

Mayor Kevin White, who was driven to the Faulkner within minutes of hearing about the incident, was equally effusive.

"Any officer shot in the line of duty is a hero, but Eddie's something special. It was typical of him to walk up there the way he did. He's the best cop in the city . . . the best."

As word of the superintendent's getting shot spread throughout the police community, virtually every cop in Boston converged on one of two places. Some came to the waiting room at the Faulkner to keep a vigil, to pray and to be on hand in case more blood was needed.

Others in or out of uniform raced to Egleston Square. Some off-duty officers came in their civies, packing only their pistols. Sharp-shooters clad in flak-jackets sought vantage points in or atop neighboring three-deckers, training their telescopic sights on the second-floor windows of the Sundstrom home, straining for a glimpse of the slightest movement behind the venetian blinds.

The crowd of spectators which had swelled to about a thousand edged closer and closer to the cordoned-off house, increasing security headaches. People were hooting and jeering; some munched on snacks, others drank beer or sucked on bottles in brown bags as they would on an afternoon at Fenway Park. Some reckless individuals climbed on top of a billboard to get a better view.

Shortly after 5 pm, Sundstrom fired off three random shots, sending reporters, photographers and spectators scurrying for cover. Instead of returning fire, the police just stepped up their attempts to negotiate.

"Pick up the telephone, Dave. We just want to talk with you. Please let your family go, Dave. We don't want anything to happen to them."

At this point police suggested to the MBTA that Orange Line service between Egleston Square and Forest Hills be suspended for fear that Sundstrom might decide to take potshots at passengers as the cars went by overhead.

Trained hostage negotiators were getting nowhere, so efforts were redoubled to find Sundstrom's family. Mrs. Parker told them how to reach his father Gunnar at a friend's home in Jamaica Plain; Mrs. Benirowski said her son-in-law worked at the same place as Sundstrom's brother Carl. But neither of these men nor Sundstrom's brother-in-law Robert Boudrot was able to persuade him to release his family from the shifling heat of the barricaded house or to surrender himself to the police.

At 7:10, Sundstrom announced that he wanted cruisers from Quincy, the state police and the MDC to line up in front of his house. Apparently, if he intended to surrender, it would not be to a Boston police officer since he had just shot one of their own.

In the Quincy car was Sergeant Robert Quintiliani, a hostage negotiator for the Quincy Police who had recently resolved a crisis involving a Vietnam vet who started spraying bullets around the Mt. Wollaston Cemetery.

The cruisers filed up to the house with their doors open. Quintiliani stepped out of the car and into the line of fire. He picked up the bullhorn and talked with Sundstrom for about 15 minutes.

Finally, State Police Colonel Jack O'Donovan got back on the horn, standing about 20 feet in front of the building.

"David, please come out. Keep your hands up in the air, and we'll all go home."

At 8:06, almost four hours to the minute after he had put the bullet in his friend Connolly, Sundstrom walked out of the building, his hands up in the air, his wife and mother trailing along behind him.

The instant he stepped out of the darkened doorway and into the greenish glare of the spotlights, Sundstrom was rushed by police from all sides; the frightened women were roughly thrust aside.

The cops slapped the cuffs on him behind his back, then attached the cuffs to the seat belts in the front seat of the Quincy patrol car. Sandwiched in between Quintiliani in the driver's seat and a Boston officer riding shotgun, Sundstrom was sweaty and flustered and nearly incoherent as he pleaded, "Please don't hurt me. Please don't hurt me. Is my family alright?"

The crowd crashed like waves around the car and broke into cheers and applause. One cop asked, "Are those cheers for him, or for us for getting him out alive?"

Clearly, the tribute was for the officers who had showed such restraint in not firing a single shot or endangering another life, even though a certain thirst for revenge was evident in the ranks.

Around 8:20, while being booked at District 13, Sundstrom inquired, "How is the man that got shot through the door?"

After advising Sundstrom of his rights, Colonel O'Donovan asked, "You mean, you don't know who you shot?"

"No."

"You shot Superintendent Edward Connolly."

"Oh, no . . . I've known him for about five years."

Meanwhile a team of officers had searched Sundstrom's apartment. They made sure that no injury had come to the children: Diane, age 13; David, Jr., age 12; Thomas, age 10; and Robert, age 9. All of them were dazed and exhausted after the nerve-jangling ordeal. Sundstrom had been very persuasive in convincing his family that vicious people were after him with guns, and the events of that afternoon and evening certainly had seemed to prove him right.

Among the officers who seized and catalogued David's cache of weapons was Al LaFontaine. That day "Chico" was wearing his "Kiss Me, I'm Puerto Rican" T-shirt. It would have rankled Sundstrom to think that a member of the racial group he most feared and suspected would end up taking possession of his private arsenal:

US Army .45 caliber Colt pistol
Smith & Wesson single shot .22 caliber hand gun
Smith & Wesson .38 caliber pistol
Colt cap and ball .41 caliber revolver
Mossberg .22 caliber bolt action rifle
12-gauge sawed-off shotgun
Marlin M-75 Olenfield .22 caliber rifle with scope
X-L shotgun (30 or 38)
Tasco zoom rifle scope
Machete

These weapons, along with boxes of ammunition and casings found in the apartment and in the hallway, were remanded to the Department Ballistician for examination and comparison. After the police had finished searching and videotaping the premises, they allowed a small delegation of friends to visit with Jeanne and let her know that she and the children had their sympathy.

Representatives of the media were everywhere badgering neighbors for background information on Sundstrom. They were literally crawling over garage roofs and fences to get into people's backyards. Most neighbors refused to talk; they were in shock, but more importantly they felt that there had been enough of a tragedy without more outside interference. Two families were shattered that afternoon — the Sundstroms and the Connollys...

A cruiser had brought the two Irenes and the baby to the hospital. They arrived at the front steps at the same time as Billy got there, and they all hurried in together.

During the four-hour operation and through the night, Connolly's family and friends prayed and reflected on the things that they had to be thankful for. The superintendent had been lucky in several ways. The bullet had lost some of its momentum as it went through the plexiglas and first struck the 59-year-old man's breastbone.

It was fortunate too that the incident did not take place even 20 minutes later, for by that time Dr. Hasiotis and Dr. Campbell would have left the hospital for the day, and more precious time would have been lost trying to locate them or other expert surgeons. In fact, when Wexler and Delaney delivered Connolly to the hospital, the emergency staff estimated that he would probably only have been able to survive another minute without receiving medical care.

When Connolly slowly regained consciousness, it took him a while
to realize where he was: in the intensive care unit. His room was
guarded around the clock both by the police and the Faulkner security staff. Slowly Connolly became more and more aware of sensations
in various parts of his body — none of them pleasant. His whole back
was sore, and there was some sort of bandage on his buttocks.
Though too groggy and weak at this point to lift his covers to inspect
the sutures extending from his chest to his crotch, he nevertheless
imagined that this was the way a corpse felt after an autopsy had
been performed on it.

When his eyes at last began to focus properly, he was able to make
out the faces of his wife, daughter and son, sitting and standing
around his bed.

The tubes in his nose and throat and other parts of the body made
it difficult to respond to his family's questions with anything more
than grunts.

"I still got some pain," he croaked, "but if I got this far, I guess I'm
on the road to recovery."

Though Irene was overjoyed at Ed's improved state, she didn't
allow a single tear to escape. Long ago, she had learned the first rule
of being a good wife of a policeman: "No matter what happens, never
cry." Throughout the whole ordeal, she never permitted herself this
release.

Later that day, Commissioner Jordan and Mayor White looked in
on him. The mayor seemed particularly curious about the pain Connolly was experiencing.

"A lot" was all Eddie could get out; Connolly suspected that part of
White's interest stemmed from the fact that the mayor, who had
more than his fair share of enemies, could very easily imagine
himself in Connolly's condition.

31

Scapulars, Emmys, and a License Plate

Sundstrom's contrition for having shot his confidant Connolly was no longer in evidence when he was arraigned the next day at West Roxbury District Court. He tapped his heels loudly on a wooden bench, creating a stir, and ignored the judge's orders to be quiet. It took ten officers to subdue him as the court waited for his psychiatrist, Dr. Stuart Grassian, to appear.

Grassian testified that David was not criminally responsible for his actions of the day before. Judge Paul Murphy accepted an innocent plea from Sundstrom's attorney, Samuel Silverman, and ordered that David be sent to Bridgewater State Mental Hospital for further observation.

Just 24 hours after being shot, Eddie was talking about getting back to work. Since he hadn't taken any vacation in five years and had accumulated 400 sick days during his career as a police officer, he could afford to take it easy, but he wanted to get back into uniform as soon as possible.

Connolly became the Faulkner's star patient. Doctors, nurses, and friends were in and out all day and night long. The Faulkner's Chief of Cardiology, Alberto Ramirez, came in personally to monitor his blood pressure and heartbeat. Doctors Hasiotis and Campbell checked him three or four times a day.

Clergy from all over the world stopped by with their blessings. In addition to the procession of Catholic priests and nuns, there were ministers from all over Massachusetts. Russian Orthodox, Syrian and Lebanese men of the cloth invoked the Lord's special care for the wounded superintendent.

Finally, the crush of clergy and well-wishers began to get out of hand, so guards at his door in the Progressive Care were instructed not to let in anyone but family. Jordan asked Bill Murphy, a Deputy Commissioner in the Penal Department and friend of Eddie's, to stay with the family around the clock and tend to their needs; he also helped screen the mail.

One afternoon, however, Connolly awoke from a nap to see the forms of two tall, burly men in front of him. One was Colonel Jack

O'Donovan, who had been so instrumental in talking Sundstrom into surrendering; the other giant was ex-Boston College football player, Edward King, the Governor of Massachusetts.

Asked if there was anything they could get him, Connolly thought, "This is my chance."

"There is one thing I've always wanted, Governor . . ."

"Anything the Commonwealth owns is yours."

"I've always wanted a four-number plate. I like 1919; that's the year that I was born."

"You got it."

The Governor proved almost as good as his word. Sometime after Connolly was released from the hospital, he received a call from Registrar of Motor Vehicles Richard McLaughlin to come in and pick up his license plates.

"We tried, but we couldn't get 1919. 1917 was as close as we could get."

The promise of a prestigious four-number plate for his personal car was not the only present that Connolly received. Eddie was showered with all kinds of religious gifts: scapulars, St. Christopher key chains, spiritual bouquets, and a cloth blessed by healer Father Di Orio. Three different people enrolled him as a perpetual member of the Glastonbury Mass Guild.

Then too the scores of floral arrangements and fruit baskets threatened to crowd him out of his own room. Daughter Irene took Polaroid snapshots of each arrangement and basket, carefully noted the name of the sender, and filled a photo album with the pictures.

Since there were far too many flowers and plants and too much food for the family to use, most of these thoughtful tokens were passed on to orphanages like the New England Home for Little Wanderers and the Italian Home for Children as well as convents like the Poor Clares.

During his stay in the hospital, mail flooded in from around the world. Connolly read every one of the approximately 8000 letters and cards he received, but lacking secretarial help he was able to respond to only a fraction of them. People from all walks of life and distant countries wrote him. Some cards, like the one from the Centre-Knoll Street Neighborhood Association, contained over 100 signatures.

The letters and cards brought home to Eddie how wide a cross-section of humanity he had touched in his years as a policeman. Some messages were sweet and sentimental; others were terse and sharp, but they all made him feel that he had made a real difference in the writers' lives:

. . . News of your heroic actions in the attempted rescue of a family being held hostage on July 25 has reached the West Coast. It is only a true police professional such as yourself who would take charge of matters rather than delegate the dangerous aspects of the operations to lower echelon personnel.

All of California's law enforcement is praying for your speedy recovery. You are truly a leader in an often leaderless society.

> *John Norton*
> *Chief of Police*
> *Foster City, CA*

. . . You may not remember me, but you gave my father and me permission to go up to the police Stable on Allandale Rd. to ride "Prescott." You made that day very special. I thank you very much!! God bless you and keep you always. . . .

Hi, next time I'll have to teach you to duck!

I was in New York City when I saw your picture in the New York Post on Page 3 as you were being helped away from the shooting. In a way it is opportunity for you to see how highly regarded and loved a man you are — probably something you could not have known without this kind of event in your life . . . I am proud to know you and grateful that the Lord has spared you to continue to do good in this world, hopefully out of target range . . .

Hang tough!

> *Sgt Victor Smith*
> *Training Range*

State Representatives Michael Flaherty from South Boston and James Craven from Hyde Park and Jamaica Plain offered to arrange for Connolly to retire on 100% disability.

Connolly thanked them very sincerely for their suggestion, but eventually told them that he preferred to earn his pay by continuing to work for the Boston Police Department.

Connolly was released from the Faulkner 13 days after being shot. In the Faulkner lobby, a cheering crowd of about 60 reporters, hospital personnel and fellow officers, including Commissioner Joe Jordan, gathered for a farewell to the hospital and a brief press conference.

Emceeing the event was Mayor White, who pointing to the pale, but undaunted man in the wheelchair, said, "Here he is, gentlemen, alive and breathing and well and expected back on the job . . . tomorrow?"

"Tomorrow night." Connolly wryly replied, though he knew that it would be many weeks before he could realistically expect to resume his duties.

When the inevitable question as to how he felt was posed, Connolly was frankly emotional.

"I feel good. I'm weak and tired, but I feel good. Not good — wonderful. Wonderful because of so many people, so many cards, so many flowers, so many prayers.

"Joe Jordan — God bless him — I could cry. He and Mayor White had such confidence in me to promote me to superintendent . . . .

"When I arrived at this hospital I thought I was going to die, but there was wonderful nursing care; it's a wonderful hospital.

"I have heard from my Hispanic friends, my black friends, whites, Protestants, Catholics and Jews. I have received cards from Paris and Puerto Rico and other places."

His voice trailed off as he reflected, "Policemen will get shot and policemen will get killed, but it's still the greatest job in the world."

Without assistance, he got out of the wheelchair and climbed into the front seat of his son Billy's black T-bird. Connolly turned to wave goodbye as Billy headed for his dad's home in Milton, followed by a police escort.

When the car pulled up in front of the gray-shingled two-family residence on Randolph Avenue, there was a small, but enthusiastic reception committee. One of the half dozen kids waiting at the curb sang out, "Hi, Mr. Connolly. I hope you feel better."

Three adult neighbors applauded as a pair of Boston policemen helped Connolly out of the Thunderbird and up the steep lawn to the picnic table at the side of the house. Connolly smiled when he saw the sign that his daughter and son had drawn and hung on the back of the house:

Welcome Home
Number 1

A friend advised him to take it easy. "Eddie, you'd better get inside and rest."

But Connolly was looking for one more welcome. "Where's my boy? Where's Anthony?"

When Irene brought the 11-month-old tyke out, the doting grandfather took him into his arms. "What do you think?" he said displaying Anthony to reporters, "He's quite a guy, isn't he?"

Though weary, Connolly was finally back home with a rambunctious little fellow who would make the next nine weeks of recuperation less irksome.

On October 1, Pope John Paul II was scheduled to visit Boston, the first stop on a historic journey across the nation. Though President Carter had assigned the Secret Service to protect the Pontiff, the Boston Police had a tremendous responsibility to shoulder. The deployment of police personnel was Connolly's job, and he was invited to lead the papal procession.

But Connolly declined. He felt that returning just in time to head a parade would be grandstanding. "I don't want to take away from the people who really did the planning for this event."

Still not fully recovered, Connolly did address the entire Boston police force via closed circuit television and underscored the importance of their mission.

"Over the next several days, the Boston Police Department will be asked to display an extraordinary effort for the visit of Pope John Paul II. No matter what the Department has been asked to do in the past, we have met any challenge with patience, pride and professionalism, whether it be in a blizzard, school busing or riots.

"Although this visit is going to last only 24 hours, the attention of the public and the news media will last forever. All officers assigned to the papal visit will encounter a variety of situations—whether traffic, crowd control or security. Needless to say, I expect you to act, as you always have, in a professional manner.

"I am very sorry that I can't be with you for the visit of the Pope, but I will be watching on television.

"Many people will be in Boston from other cities and other countries. The surroundings will be unfamiliar to them. Be patient; be helpful in all situations. Be courteous. Look your best. Be effective; be efficient.

"Our demeanor will be closely scrutinized not only by our own citizens here in Boston, but those of other states, other countries. Our effort and your behavior will reflect upon yourselves and the Department.

"In the past I have worked with many of you and know that you are the finest of the finest. Now the whole world will be watching you. This will be the first city that the Pope will visit, and we want it to be remembered as the best one he visits . . . ."

The morning of the Pope's visit the weather was threatening, and torrential rains doused the faithful that gathered in Boston Common for the outdoor Mass. Watching the ceremony at home on TV, Connolly was doubly sure that he had made the right decision; he might have suffered a severe relapse with all the strain and the raw weather. On rainy days, his hip felt a little sore at the point where Sundstrom's bullet came to rest.

On October 9, Connolly finally got the go-ahead from his physicians to return to his duties as head of the Bureau of Field Services. Once again the mayor and the commissioner were on hand to officiate at the media event. White proclaimed, "No one deserves a better homecoming."

His Honor also joked with the cameramen, "This is probably the most unusual scene you'll ever witness — Eddie Connolly behind a desk. You watch, he'll be back on the street sometime today."

White also praised Superintendent Earl Bolt, who had stepped in for Connolly. Bolt, a classmate of Connolly's in the Academy, was the Chief of Investigative Services and the city's highest-ranking black officer.

"Earl did a great job filling in. He had some tough assignments — the Pope's visit and the Williams shooting, and he handled them superbly."

Connolly too focused on the recent tragedy of Darryl Williams, a black Jamaica Plain High School football player who was shot during a game in Charlestown, an all-white section of the city. The reserve wide receiver became permanently paralyzed from the waist down.

"My message to the city is 'Stop the violence, stop the hatred.' I ask all of you who prayed for me to pray for him."

But Connolly didn't want to spend too much time talking to the media; his immediate task was to work with Secret Security for the visit of another important visitor to Boston. President Carter along with most of the Kennedy clan was going to be at Columbia Point in Dorchester to celebrate the opening of the John F. Kennedy Library and Presidential Museum.

By getting right back into the thick of things so soon after suffering such extensive injuries, Connolly had hoped to set an example for less conscientious officers in the department who stay out for years with a minor problem.

"I wanted to show that you've got to come back and perform in some way," the superintendent confided to a friend, "But it didn't work. It didn't impress anybody, me coming back early."

In early December, Connolly received a letter from Sundstrom's wife:

Dear Superintendent Connelly,

I really don't know how or what to say to you after the hell David put you and your family through. I have waited this long to write to you because I don't know what to say to you. I thank God you made it through.

I really and honestly don't think David knew what he was doing in spite of the competencing hearing out come, I am writing you from the hospital at this time. I don't even know what or why it all happened including what went on 2 days before David reached his breaking point. I can't put down in words how sorry I am that this whole mess happened. I have know right to ask you this but I will anyway. God forbid anything like what happened in July should happen again. I wish your officers wouldn't be so rough when making there arrests, especially if someone is in front of your suspect. I ended up with bruised ribs on the right side and a slight concusion due to they're roughness. Mind you I'm not complaining about it. I know they were only doing there job. But they shouldn't have been so rough when they pushed me out of the way. So I will close this letter now. i am truley very sorry that you got shot (or anyone else). Please except my personal regrets over this whole matter. My children are even paying now for what they're father did. You know how cruel kids are to each other without meaning to be. So once again except my apologies for what happened.

Sincerely Yours,
Jeanne Sundstrom

Just before his trial, Sundstrom was moved from Bridgewater State Hospital, where he had been kept under observation, to the Charles Street Jail in downtown Boston. Three times David's minister came to Connolly with a request that the Superintendent visit the prisoner and assure him in person that he was forgiven.

"I bear David no animosity. I understand his condition. From the day I met him, I knew that he wasn't well. You tell him that I forgive him completely," Connolly would say, but he couldn't bring himself to visit the man's cell.

When the case finally came to trial, three psychiatrists testified that Sundstrom was not criminally responsible for his actions.

Assistant District Attorney Timothy P. O'Neill put into evidence before Judge James McGuire all of David's arsenal — the collection of rifles, the sawed-off shotgun, the handguns, the blasting caps, and 800 rounds of ammunition.

On March 31, 1980, David Sundstrom was found innocent by reason of insanity of the charge of assault with intent to murder. However, Judge McGuire committed him to the Bridgewater State Hospital for an indefinite period. His condition is evaluated each year, but he remains there to the present day, partially because he refuses to take the prescribed medications.

Finally, that spring, the National Academy of Television Arts and Sciences invited Eddie and Irene to be their special guests at the awards ceremonies for the New England Emmys. News stories about Connolly were up for awards in three different categories.

Channel 7's on-the-spot coverage of the hostage and shooting drama netted the station two Emmys: one for best team coverage of a breaking news story, the other a personal Emmy to Ted O'Brien for individual coverage of a breaking news story.

Unfortunately, the Connolly luck didn't quite stretch to make it a hat trick. Mike Taibbi's profile of Connolly couldn't edge out a Channel 5 salute to the visit of the Tall Ships to Boston Harbor. But the Connollys got an unexpected close-up look at the glittery TV gala and were glad that at least the Channel 7 reporters and camera crew got something good out of the Sundstrom tragedy.

32

A Question of Loyalty

Returning to the Bureau of Field Services, Connolly reassumed his post as the third-highest ranking policeman in the city. The position allowed him a quite a bit of power, but there was one aspect of the job that he didn't like: interference from the Executive Officer and, mostly, from City Hall.

Connolly would get a call from one of these power centers to transfer a particular officer who was politically well-connected to a good berth. If a hard-working guy on the street, on the other hand, wanted any sort of transfer, he had to fill out a lot of forms, and his petition was likely to get strangled somewhere along the convoluted chain of command.

On one point Connolly and the commissioner saw eye to eye. Jordan wanted the Chief of the Bureau of Field Services out on the street. Since Connolly preferred responding to calls rather than fiddling with paper clips, he welcomed the commissioner's directive.

So Eddie spent most of the day shooting from one part of the city to the other. Many a time he arrived on the scene of an incident before the local sector car got there. Connolly didn't hesitate to make the arrest himself if the situation warranted it.

Over and over, he would remind his men, "I may wear gold on my cap and shoulders, but I'm still a patrolman at heart."

Most of the rest of the brass thought Eddie was lowering himself by answering calls with the patrolmen. But he would always answer his critics by retorting, "If you ever got into this police business, you would find it very interesting."

Connolly instituted a program that he hoped would insure that other superintendents would get the street experience so many of them sorely lacked. He set up a system by which the superintendents would take turns pulling weekend duty. That way they would have to patrol the city on Friday and Saturday nights, and thus would get to know the crime situation in Boston first-hand.

For a short time, Connolly was able to maneuver the desk jockeys out into patrol cars, but soon the superintendents worked out a deal with the duty officer in Communications. Whosever turn it was to "patrol" simply left his home phone number with Communications.

If anything truly extraordinary happened, the duty officer would alert the superintendent to get out to the scene.

Connolly, on the other hand, didn't need any hotlines to alert him to what was going on in the city. Whenever he was at home and off-duty, he would keep his private scanner going. Since the early 60's, he had gotten into the habit of hitting the sack around 1 or 2 am; his private scanner would be blinking and babbling till then.

If anything important came over the air on a city-wide radio call, Eddie could hop into uniform and respond in his cruiser. He believed that the patrolmen liked to see a representative of the brass at the scene of a riot or other dangerous event. He felt it was the duty of the superior officers to be at the hospital to comfort the wife of an officer injured or killed in the line of duty.

Furthermore, Connolly enjoyed being out there where the real police work was being done. He truly respected the hard-working officer, and he showed his regard by shaking hands with his men when they met on the scene.

Connolly never doublecrossed any of the streetmen, whether he was a patrolman, a detective or a sergeant. As much as he liked his men, he didn't waste any time disciplining them in his own way if the situation demanded he do so. He sent more than one policeman to prison, an aspect of his career that he was never proud of, but he always warned his men that if they violated the laws they had sworn to uphold he wouldn't hesitate to throw them to the wolves.

His tenure as Chief of Bureau of Field Services lasted only 18 months. His fall from grace was precipitated by a misunderstanding with Commissioner Jordan over the discontent that had been brewing among some of the captains on the force.

"Mr. Commissioner," said Connolly, using the respectful form of address for his old friend in order to signal Jordan that this was not a social call. "I have all the captains in my office. They wish to see you as a group."

Jordan straightened up in the big black leather chair at his desk and said calmly, "No."

"That article in Wednesday's *Herald* has them shaken up pretty bad."

Connolly was referring to a June 12, 1980 piece with unattributed sources that quoted Mayor White as having said that the captains should be replaced because, as men in their 50's, they had lost touch with both younger officers and the civilians.

"I believe that they're going to press hard to see you whether it's today or some other time. I think you should talk to them."

Jordan considered for a long minute, and then said reluctantly, "Okay, I'll talk with one captain . . . whomever they pick."

After conferring, the group made a choice, which to Connolly's mind was an excellent one. The senior captain, Arthur Cadegan was a calm, extremely well-spoken man, a graduate of both Boston College and Boston College Law School. He had reached the rank of deputy superintendent, but had been broken by Commissioner di Grazia because of personality differences.

Carefully and concisely, Cadegan laid the captains' request before Jordan; they wanted him to go on the 6:00 news and refute the accusations that the captains were do-nothings and make it clear that he stood behind his men.

"I'll think about it. I'll give you your answer on Monday."

Cadegan returned with this news to the monthly Bureau of Field Services staff meeting on the fourth floor of Headquarters. After the last bit of official business had been transacted, Captain Earl Crocker asked Connolly for use of the room for a meeting of captains only. Eddie agreed and ushered the last of the non-captains out himself.

"Monday's not good enough."

"Either he's behind us or he's not."

Connolly became more and more convinced that only a face-to-face meeting would resolve the mounting tensions.

While Cadegan was relaying the commissioner's response, Connolly returned to Jordan's office and found that he had called a summit. Superintendent John Kreckler, Labor Officer, and Superintendent Paul Russell, head of the Bureau of Administrative Services, encouraged Jordan to go through with the meeting. But Superintendent John Doyle, Executive Officer, and Chuck Wexler, Jordan's administrative assistant, were urging him to reconsider.

Kreckler suggested that Connolly and Russell return to the fourth-floor powwow. Connolly knew that Kreckler was hoping that these two could prevent the captains from handing Jordan the "no confidence" vote they were threatening.

Kreckler and Russell were respected by their peers, and Connolly thought there was a chance that they might defuse the growing tension. But then Doyle, who was not popular among the captains, invited himself along for the talk with the captains.

The foursome reasoned with the captains to no avail. They were adamant in their demand that Jordan appear on television and state unequivocally that he backed all his captains.

Finally, Jordan agreed to speak with all the captains. Connolly could tell from the tight expression on the commissioner's face that he was most displeased at being backed into this corner.

Jordan's response was short and to the point, "I feel and know that some captains are outstanding, others are not as good, and some are just paper-shufflers."

When the commissioner refused to make a public defense of all the captains, a "no confidence" motion was unanimously carried.

Though Connolly's part in the controversy had only been to shepherd people back and forth and to play peacemaker, he sensed that Jordan blamed him in part for the humiliation he had suffered at being handed this public rebuke. Eddie knew that his job, as well as Russell's and Kreckler's, was in jeopardy.

The extent of the Commissioner's wrath at those that he perceived to be disloyal to him became apparent on September 15. A major reshuffling of the department took place. All captains were removed from command of the individual districts, and newly appointed deputy superintendents were put in charge. The captains were reassigned to positions such as executive officers or night inspection officers.

Superintendent Kreckler was banished from the Labor Unit and sent up to "The Turret," the Department's communications center on the top floor of the Berkeley Street Headquarters. Superintendent Russell lingered on a year or so as head of Administrative Services, but then was reduced to the rank of a captain and assigned to Suffolk Superior Court as Supervisor of Cases, a job usually left to a sergeant or a lieutenant.

As part of the reorganization, the city was divided into a North and a South Zone. Connolly was put in charge of the South Zone, so he was considerably reduced in rank and now oversaw only half the men in the city. Doyle was given command of the North Zone.

Though Doyle professed to find the new assignment a "challenge," Eddie saw it as "unquestionably a demotion." Connolly wanted no part of this figurehead "South Zone" position because he would not have direct command of the men in his zone, since all uniformed personnel were under the jurisdiction of Frank Coleman, the current Chief of Field Services. Eddie asked to be demoted to the rank of lieutenant, but Jordan insisted on his taking the job.

So Connolly gritted his teeth and tried to put up a cheery front, "I was getting a little tired of shaving in the bathroom on the sixth floor of Headquarters anyway. Now I'll have my own toilet and shower at my new headquarters at District 13."

One would have thought that Connolly would have been more careful how he spoke and acted as a result of this demotion, but Eddie was determined to speak his mind whatever the cost. He soon unintentionally riled the commissioner even further.

The Mayor's Office sent word that Connolly was to take a camera crew from Channel 7 on a ride-along through the South Zone. Brash, blonde reporter Susan Burke was assigned to interview Connolly as they went through the streets of Dorchester, Roxbury, Hyde Park and West Roxbury.

City Hall had designated Connolly as the interviewee because he was comfortable with the press. Since Eddie had been the subject of much favorable publicity over the years, the mayor's public relations people felt he would be able to conduct himself properly and to charm the audience with a familiar face that was at once benign and tough.

Connolly reasoned that the choice of a popular street cop like himself had been part of City Hall's strategy to pressure state representatives into passing Mayor White's Tregor Bill, a bill which would make available funds to hire back the policemen and firemen who had been laid off as a result of Proposition 2½. The latter law, the result of a taxpayers' revolt, put a cap on the city tax. Though many people had hoped that Prop 2½ would force the mayor to cut back his staff of highly paid deputy mayors and public relations people, White instead began closing police and fire stations as well as schools.

When Burke asked Connolly about his position on the Tregor Bill, Connolly told her on-camera, "I hope that House of Representatives passes the Tregor Bill to rehire the laid-off police and firemen. I think money could have been found to keep them. There was no reason to lay them off."

Connolly's wife and daughter watched the Channel 7 telecast that night and said in the same breath, "He did it again!"

"I'll bet he'll be driving a wagon in a week," the younger Irene predicted.

Later on in the interview, Connolly took Burke to an area where narcotics were sold and then on to some "shooting galleries," vacant houses that addicts used as a place to shoot up and crash.

"Superintendent," the reporter finally asked, "What are we doing about drugs?"

"We're not doing enough," Connolly said flatly. "We don't have enough men in the Drug Unit to do anything. We have taken the men out of the Drug Unit and put them in uniform to fill in for the men who were laid off."

Eddie's wife threw up her hands. "That's it. He's gone this time, for sure."

Three weeks later Connolly found himself reassigned to the position of Chief of the Bureau of Administrative Services. For being so outspoken in the defense of his men, he found himself punished by being saddled with a desk job.

33

"Nobody Ever Leaves This Job Happy"

"Jordan must have some pretty evil reasons to do this to me!" fumed Eddie when he heard the news. Some people might have taken the transfer from the post of commanding officer of the city's South Zone to the top berth in the Bureau of Administrative Services as a step back up the ladder, but not Connolly.

"I'm not looking forward to my new assignment because it is not a police job," he stated flatly. He knew some reshuffling of the Department was inevitable in the wake of the retirements of both North Zone Commander Superintendent John F. Doyle and Bureau of Inspectional Services head Superintendent Earl A. Bolt. However, he didn't see why he should end up as Chief Clerk of the Boston Police Department, a position for which he was not suited either by training or temperament.

But on December 2, 1981, he reported on the 5th floor of Headquarters to start learning new skills as a paper shuffler. For the first few weeks, he paced in and out of his office and up and down the corridors like a caged lion.

Aside from a watercolor of Station 13 and some cards that his little grandson Anthony had made for him, the only decoration that Connolly brought to his new office was a framed blow-up of the front page of a *Boston Herald-American* story on the Sundstrom shooting with a headline that screamed "HE WAS NEVER A DESK COP" — a sardonic joke on himself and his new job.

He wasn't sure that he could learn all the intricacies of the accounting and number juggling that the position demanded. He would have much rather been cruising the side streets than reviewing purchase orders, but he would be damned if he would let this "promotion" get the better of him.

He soon discovered the scope of his varied responsibilities. He was the overall supervisor of the Hackney Carriage Bureau, Paid Details, various licenses issued by the commissioner, the police garage on Adams Street, the radio service shop in Southie, the video unit in Station A, the Police Academy, the revolver range on Moon Island, Mailing and Printing Department, the Warrants Unit, maintenance of all police buildings, motorcycle repairs, custody of money found or being held as evidence and the police Signal Service (an old name carried over from the days of the signal boxes for the Electrical Department).

Faced with the responsibility of reorganizing some of the units in the Bureau, Connolly found comparatively few people, either civilian or sworn, who were willing to help in the enterprise. There were a few notable exceptions. Captain Arthur Cadegan filled Eddie in on the workings of the Hackney Carriage Unit. Sergeant Maurice "Moe" Wall became Connolly's right arm.

Connolly helped Patrolman Fred Perkins and Detective Mike Riley with the colossal task of consolidating for the first time ever all the warrants from the various districts into one centralized office on the fifth floor of Headquarters. In the first weeks they pulled together 15,000 warrants; from then on they had to add 200 new ones each week.

Under the new procedure, warrants from the BPD as well as from police departments in outside cities and towns and from places like Transit Police, college police forces and the like were all put onto one computer network.

Every three weeks, the Warrants Unit produced a massive printout of all persons wanted on warrants and distributed it throughout the state. Policemen on the beat appreciated being able to access shorter "speedy" printouts with up-to-the-minute information on people likely to be in the officers' area.

As in the Bureau of Field Services, Connolly battled the political forces that interfered with police business. During his 34 years on the street, he had been able to ignore or sidestep this kind of involvement, but now he was forced to confront such matters as shady Department business contracts and appointments mandated by City Hall.

Connolly disliked having to work with political appointees, people who knew next to nothing about police life. Some people, like Administrative Services staffers Veronica Mahoney and Peg Leahy, had earned positions of respect by making their way up through the Civil Service, proving their loyalty to the Police Department by years of hard work. But most of the middle management — the supervisors, the head clerks, the administrative assistants — were political legacies of the mayor's.

They had been given these positions as a reward for their efforts on behalf of the mayor's reelection campaigns — answering phones, handing out cards or holding placards at the polls and, most importantly, contributing to the mayor's war chest. Civil Service personnel were likely to be overlooked when it came time for promotions unless they too had been very visibly involved in supporting the mayor.

It seemed that most of the top management and personnel jobs were being handed to favored outsiders and that the police were losing control of their own Department. All the high-salaried slots were going to people from outside the city, even outside the state, while the non-political folks who knew Boston and the workings of the BPD were often ignored.

City Councillor Albert "Dapper" O'Neil often vociferously deplored this invasion of the Department by "carpetbaggers and out-of-staters" at City Council meetings, but to little avail.

Not only did Connolly have to deal with co-workers whose allegiance was to the mayor and not to the Department, but City Hall often hamstrung him with all their red tape. Many of the jobs handled by Administrative Services were among the most touchy and thankless tasks in the Department. For example, Eddie's Bureau supposedly initiated the awarding of contracts to various towing companies. However, City Hall people always had the final say as to who got what contracts, no matter what the boards of police officers advised.

The city was a notoriously tardy payer of its debts. Some vendors might not be able to wait for months to drag by while bills remained unpaid. But with the millions of items needed to run the Police Department, the Fire Department, The Department of Public Works, etc., there were always vendors to be found who had the patience to wait for their money. Of course, they might add 10% to 25% to their bill as the price of their patience, but nobody ever said anything about such surcharges.

However, the vendors' willingness to wait had a limit. Connolly found himself locked into working with vendors who didn't want to cooperate until City Hall released some of the money due. The firms simply became as dilatory about deliveries as the city was about payments.

Urgently needed police cars would sit idle for a month "while parts were on order" until Eddie or the shop supervisor put some pressure on the Budget Management Bureau. As soon as the vendor received the check — presto! the parts arrived, and the vehicles were back in service.

Out of an order for 60 new cars, only five or ten might be delivered on time, but the dealer might hold onto the ownership papers until he got paid. Police lots might be cluttered with cruisers the officers couldn't touch because the final paperwork was all hanging on a payment to the dealer.

Because of the city's reputation, many contractors for services padded their bills, figuring that they were merely calculating in the interest ahead of time. Connolly was determined to serve the people of Boston by saving money wherever he could, but he was amazed at the reactions he got when he refused to pay outrageous sums for relatively simple jobs. More than one friend hinted that trying to save the city was not the name of the game. Elected officials who received big contributions from vendors and contractors frowned on Connolly's efforts to cut their supporters out of lucrative city contracts. But Connolly ignored the wishes of the politicians and did all he could to save the taxpayer a grand here and there.

With the advice and cooperation of Tom Terranova, a super-conscientious engineer in the Public Facilities Department, Connolly was able to save the city hundreds of thousands of dollars. Whether the projects were large or small, Terranova and Connolly tried to do any job that needed to be done for little or no money. If Connolly needed a door at Headquarters replaced, Tom hunted around vacant public buildings for one that was the right size.

Connolly was ordered to remove the cellblock at Station 6 in South Boston to make space for an Identification Unit in the remodeled substation. A contractor estimated the cost of removing the 40 sets of steel bars at $50,000. Connolly got his friend Bill Murphy, Deputy Commissioner of the Penal Department, to provide prison laborers to remove the bars from the reinforced concrete, using a front loader loaned by the Department of Public Works. The bars were then trucked over to Deer Island and used to build new cells there. Total cost to the city for the remodeling of District 6 — a mere $3,000.

Another contractor wanted $12,500 to erect and panel partitions for the Detective Unit at Headquarters. Connolly opted to pay four maintenance men overtime and got the job done in three days for $2,100.

Much of the work of maintaining the various police buildings involved repainting. When Connolly balked at having to pay $1,800 for one day's work painting the first floor of a police station, he decided to set up a regular program where most painting would be done by laborers from the Police Department, assisted by men ordered by the city courts to perform public service for such minor offenses as non-support or driving under the influence.

With a crew available to do painting basically at cost, Connolly decided to try something a little different. A friend had sent him an article describing research done in the mid-70's at the International Institute of Biosocial Research in Tacoma, Washington. Studies indicated that putting prisoners or mental patients in a room painted a certain shade of pink would reduce their tension, anxiety and hostility. A California clinical psychologist reported that over 300 jails, hospitals and institutions were using pink rooms to calm people down.

As a lark, Connolly decided to test the theory out on East Coast detainees. In June 1984, he ordered selected cells in Stations A and C, which needed repainting anyway, redone in pink. Floors, walls, ceilings and barred doors were covered with rose-colored paint.

The press had a field day, mocking the decision. In a phone interview with a *Globe* reporter, Eddie was asked to describe the shade.

"I don't know if it's a baby pink or a sunset pink or what. It's a very soft pink. It would be something you would have in a nursery."

"Why did you decide to paint the cells pink?"

"We've heard that it lowers blood pressure and heart rate. It does have a calming effect even as I look at it now. If it works, we'll paint every cell in the city."

"Any chance we'll see pink uniforms?"

"Of course not," Connolly sighed. "We're traditional. We're not going to go around in pink. The union would object."

There were plenty of jokes flying while the painting was being done, but very quickly the walls became so covered with graffiti and grime that it was hard to tell the difference between the pink cells and the regular ones.

Connolly was responsible for the other renovation plans that were far more important than the experiment with pink paint. One of the most significant projects that he ushered to completion was the establishment of a permanent Police Academy.

During the past decade, the Police Academy classes had been shunted from one end of the city to the other. When it had been displaced from its home on the fourth floor of the old Milk Street Station, where Connolly had learned the basics, the Academy had found temporary quarters in the North End, the South End, East Boston and later Roxbury. While a permanent site was being sought in the 80's, Academy classes reached an all-time low — literally: they were held in the basement of the gymnasium of Boston English High School.

City Councilor Joseph Tierney had proposed that the Fairmount Middle School, which had been closed down in the autumn of 1981, be refurbished as a permanent site for training police officers. Located on Williams Avenue in Hyde Park, the southernmost tip of the city, the school was far from the center of things, but it did have adequate parking space, and the local residents seemed to welcome the idea of having a lot of policemen coming and going all the time.

To finance the remodeling, Connolly had to transfer $250,000 out of the renovations fund for Headquarters. By watching every penny and only spending money on what was essential, he was able to give the Academy a home the force could be proud of. Lieutenant Robert Dunsford, the commanding officer of the Academy, got the cadets to do some of the painting and the moving of the furniture from Boston English to Hyde Park — further cutting costs.

Connolly rode herd on the contractors, whose progress was slowed by vandalism and exploding boilers. At first an officer from Area E had to be stationed on the premises sixteen hours a day to guard against break-ins. Finally, Dunsford and some sergeants rounded up the local youth and promised them access to the Academy's weight-room if they would behave themselves and stop wrecking and defacing the building.

Connolly was racing the clock to get the Academy completed. He had received Jordan's OK to name the new facility "The Deputy Superintendent William J. Hogan Law Enforcement Training Center" in honor of the man who had tutored thousands of officers in "Club 27," the school he set up in the basement of his own home. When he could no longer serve the force by patroling or doing detective work because of the injuries he had sustained in his fall down an elevator shaft, Hogan continued to make outstanding contributions as a teacher and a scholar.

Now, however, Hogan was lying terminally ill in the hospital, and unfortunately, the letter announcing that new Academy was being named in his honor arrived the day after he died.

Then too Connolly wanted to make sure that Joe Jordan was the one who dedicated the Academy. In late 1984 and early 1985, the papers were full of rumors about Mayor Ray Flynn's attempts to get the resignation of Commissioner Jordan, an unwanted legacy from the Kevin White administration. At long last, Jordan had consented to a buy-out. With Jordan's departure date fast approaching, Connolly had to see to it that the work on the building was pretty much completed before Jordan could officially declare it open.

On Friday, January 25, 1985, workmen were still busily slapping paint on the classroom walls while in the auditorium Jordan, as one of his last acts as Commissioner, declared the Academy open, though it would still be several weeks before the desks and students were moved in. Much of the ceremony was given over to eulogies of Hogan, whose 30 years of service to the Academy and expertise on criminal law were repeatedly acknowledged.

Connolly himself was working on borrowed time. Since he had reached the age of 65, he was officially forced to retire on November 30, 1984. Jordan, however, had granted Eddie an extension of 120 working days, which would carry Connolly into the regime of the new commissioner. The Department was abuzz with rumors of who Jordan's successor might be. Some said that the publicity-hound mayor would appoint a black woman just to get a mention in *Time* and *Newsweek*. Connolly laughed at other newspaper accounts that named him as a possible successor to Jordan.

Many of Eddie's long-time colleagues decided to retire around the same time that Jordan did. There was definitely change in the wind, and all the signs pointed to the fact that old-timers were no longer welcome. If Eddie wanted to avoid their fate, he would have to carry off a feat that had never before been accomplished by a Boston policeman. He would have to get a home rule petition passed through the city and state governments, allowing him to stay on for another five years. By that time, he would most likely be dead, and Eddie would get his wish to die on the job, as a working cop.

With the help of City Councilors Joe Tierney and "Dapper" O'Neil, the five-year extension petition passed the Boston City Council 13-0. The bill went to the desk of the mayor. Ray Flynn and Connolly did not see eye to eye on many issues, but the mayor did sign the bill. However, he amended the passage that guaranteed Connolly his rank as superintendent to a guarantee of his Civil Service status, that of lieutenant. (That was OK by Connolly; for the past three years he had submitted a request to Jordan to be returned to the rank of lieutenant and to be reassigned to a job on the street, but the Commissioner had denied him the demotion all three times.)

The next round was the state legislature. State Representatives Jim Craven of Jamaica Plain and Mike Flaherty of South Boston saw their efforts to get the bill through the Massachusetts House of Representatives stymied by a committee chairman, Nicholas Bagleoni of Methuen. The bill was held back until the final days of the 1984 session and failed to pass. Though Eddie had little hope that the bill would go through when it was submitted in 1985, Connolly's daughter Irene was determined to find a way to make it happen, and Eddie was not about to give up without trying everything.

While he was fighting to stay in the Department, he wanted to see that Jordan, who was often harshly criticized by the press and the Patrolmen's Association, was sent off with some semblance of dignity and a show of respect. Connolly scared up badges that represented every rank that Jordan had held and had them mounted in a circle on a large wooden shield-shaped plaque; in the center was an oversized commissioner's badge. He had the memento engraved simply "From a Grateful Command Staff." Then he went around seeing if the grateful command staff cared to contribute toward the price of the present, and Eddie found out just how little appreciation some of them had for the man who had given them their superintendent and deputy superintendent badges . . .

Jordan seemed pleased with the gift, and Boston seemed pleased with his successor. After Mayor Flynn had flown around the country seeking a replacement, he ended up selecting a man from his own backyard — Francis M. Roache, a jogging buddy of his.

In his sixteen years on the force, Mickey Roache had never been a frontline crime cop, but he knew how to take the heat. For the past couple of years he had headed the Community Disorders Unit, the outfit that investigated the sensitive race-related problems — checking out allegations that whites were breaking the windows of a black family that just moved into the neighborhood, harassments of Vietnamese and Cambodians, discrimination against Hispanics and the like.

Roache's popularity in the minority community seemed to make up for the fact that he, like the Mayor, came from South Boston, a section of the city that was still reputed in some circles to be a bastion of white supremacism. The new commissioner was known for bending over backwards to be fair and for being ultra-sensitive about racial niceties. This reputation was crucial to an ally of Flynn's who wanted to win over the supporters of Mel King, the black man Ray had bested to become mayor of Boston.

In February of 1985 Connolly had heard through the grapevine that at the end of the month he would be supplanted by a new Chief of Administrative Services. The papers reported that Peter Welsh, a 33-year-old city administrator and unpaid policy advisor to Flynn during the mayoral campaign, had been given the job. It would be the first time that the position had been awarded to a person outside the Department. Yet Connolly had received no official word that he was no longer Chief of Administrative Services. Though the sign in the fifth-floor hallway still accorded him that title, his staff was directed to send all mail upstairs unopened for Welsh's people to examine.

One morning in late February, Eddie returned from a few days off, recovering from a bout with the flu, to discover that a City Hall personnel director had taken over his office. Sergeant Wall and the rest of Connolly's crew were moved over to a cramped adjoining area with no direct exit in case of a fire.

Connolly was insulted for himself and his loyal staff. He was not reticent about letting his ire be known. Soon afterwards, Connolly was summoned for his first private interview with the new head man.

What had been Jordan's inner sanctum was now abloom with bouquets and potted plants, swathed with pastel ribbons wishing Roache "Good Luck." Seeing these messages, Connolly couldn't help thinking, "You're gonna need it. You're a nice guy, and I hope you don't get burned here."

In his new pinstripe suit, Mickey struck Connolly like a skinny kid in his confirmation outfit. Actually, Roache was in good condition and had a straight-arrow masculinity about him that made him the kind of guy you'd want your daughter to marry.

But his shoulders were distinctly hunched over, as if he were struggling under a heavy burden. He seemed uneasy in the high position to which he suddenly had been catapulted. He appeared to be excruciating over demotions and transfers; Mickey never wanted to hurt anyone, and now the changes he was implementing were making lots of people unhappy.

"Eddie, sit down," he said a little over-solicitously. "Look, I'm sorry about what happened to you. I didn't know about it. If you want your office back, you can have it."

"Thank you, but don't worry about it," Connolly replied. "I knew a change was coming, but I didn't expect it so soon. I just got back from sick leave . . . and now no office."

Eddie went on to explain that he was much more interested in an assignment that he could sink his teeth into than in a bunch of file cabinets and a view of the skyline.

"Listen, we're glad to have you aboard. I'm gonna find a job for you as soon as I get things straightened out here. Would you like to go back to Drugs? It's a big problem both inside and outside the Department . . ."

After a two-hour conversation with the commissioner about all phases of the Department, but particularly narcotics, Eddie left feeling that he would get an assignment that would let him use his street experience once again.

But week after week went by, and no orders came down. When Eddie and the commissioner saw each other in the elevator, Roache would engage anyone in animated coversation so that he wouldn't have to deal with the reproach that was written on Connolly's face. Every day, friends kept asking Eddie if he had any word yet what his new job would be. He was no longer notified of or welcome at command staff meetings; on the other hand, he received no official word that he had been demoted or transferred. Roache kept him lingering in limbo.

"Super, do you still have the patrol car that says Administrative Services, or did they take that away from you too?" someone inquired.

"I'll bury the fucking thing before I turn my car over to a civilian," he growled, half-wishing someone would try to make him surrender the vehicle.

Every day Connolly would come in and try to find a seat that was not occupied by one of his staff. He'd wait all day with nothing to do. He realized how quickly the days left on his extension were dribbling away; the new regime hoped he would just fritter away his reprieve sedately and then allow himself to be eased out to pasture.

Despite what they had said about being "glad to have you aboard," Connolly now felt that they couldn't wait to be rid of him. Massive wholesale changes were made in many of the units, changes that Eddie and other Department veterans thought were extremely ill-advised. Seasoned officers were being thrust aside for youngsters with ties to City Hall.

Connolly imagined that the brass would shake their heads when his name came up. "You'd think that old fart would take a hint and

retire before we have to kick him out of here . . ." Actually, Eddie
wondered why they didn't just break him. Was it because they really
respected him for his years of service to the Department? Or was it
because they were afraid of the all-important media repercussions if
they demoted him and then saw him championed by his friends in
the press and by community leaders? Maybe they couldn't afford to
antagonize a diehard like Connolly because he knew too much about
too many things. Were they counting on Eddie's loyalty to the good
image of the Department to outweigh any resentment at the kind of
treatment he received at their hands?

Perhaps they thought that by chasing him into this no man's land,
he would finally get so disgusted that he would resign and get off
their backs. These new guys obviously didn't know Eddie Connolly.
He was planning to hang in until the last minute of the last day . . .
and he was still calling his friends at the State House to see if they
couldn't get the bill passed which would put off that "last day" five
years into the future.

Without her father's knowledge, Eddie's daughter Irene determined to do what she could to get the bill passed despite the fact that she
had no political connections. Though the bill had been defeated in
the closing days of 1984, she thought she'd try writing to Ronald
Reagan to exert pressure from the top down.

She planned to ask Brian Donnelly, the Congressional Representative from her district, to hand-deliver her letter to the President.
When she contacted Donnelly's office, she ended up speaking with
young Joe Rowan, son of the man who had headed the Tactical
Patrol Force and worked with Eddie in so many riot situations. Joe
reminded Irene that her father's request for an extension was a state
matter and put her in touch with Tom Finneran, a State Representative, who ushered it through the Massachusetts legislature on April
24. Irene tracked down and introduced herself to all the State
Senators and Representatives she possibly could. She was overjoyed
to find that most of them knew her father and enthusiastically en-
dorsed her request.

One afternoon returning home from work, she spotted senatorial
license plates on a Volkswagen and recognized the distinguished-
looking black man at the wheel as Senator Royal Bolling. As Bolling
rushed to post his own mail before the Grove Hall post office closed,
Irene followed him to the stamp window explaining her problem.
Like most of the others, he promised to support the bill.

State Senate President William Bulger and Senator Royal Bolling,
Sr. whisked the bill through the senate the next day. On May 1,
Governor Michael Dukakis signed the bill into law guaranteeing Eddie employment with the Boston Police Department until he reached
age 70.

Representative Finneran phoned Irene that night to tell her the good news.

"Thank God!" she cried. "How can I ever thank you all?"

"You don't have to," Tom Finneran replied. "We just didn't want to lose a good cop — a cop's cop."

The Day the Governor Signed the Bill

Front Row: Sec. of Public Safety, Charles Barry; Clerk of Courts, Dan Pokaski; Irene Landry; Governor Michael Dukakis Superintendent Edward Connolly; State Rep. Jim Brett; State Rep. John McDonough.
Back Row: State Rep. Richard J. Rouse; State Rep. Tom Finneran; State Rep. Paul White.

Epilogue:
The Funeral

A Short Story by Edward F. Connolly

Again and again it will take place . . . maybe not in the same location, maybe with a new set of faces looking on. The center of attention will always be different, that's for sure, but he will always be in the same position: horizontal.

Real tears will be shed by the family and true friends, but the phonies will be out in force as well, ready to shake hands with the top brass, the commissioner or whoever could be a useful ally in their quest for power and promotion.

Some will fondly recall the deceased as a good and honest cop, but there will be plenty to malign him as a thief, a corrupter, a drunk or a general phony. But whatever the deceased may have been or was alleged to have been, he is not in a position to defend himself or his reputation as a cop. He remains forever silent, unable to graciously accept compliments about his heroic actions or to refute whispers of his misdeeds and wrongdoings.

Few present at the service will remember him from his days as a rookie, patroling lonely streets and deserted alleys on dark, windy nights. His private stands against the temptations of vice and corruption will now never be recorded . . . at least not on earth.

Only in the heavenly ledger will he get full credit for deeds that never made it into the police register: the family squabbles he settled, the old women whose fears he put to rest, the victims he comforted. Even the infants he brought into the world in some dimly lit tenement will not be there to remember the man who delivered them . . . .

Few officers, scrambling to make the early roll call, noticed that flags at the police station were flying at half-mast to honor one of their own dead. They had too many more important personal matters on their minds.

The teletype had rapped out an order for every station to send a pair of men to the town of Needham for a 9 am funeral service of a retired deputy superintendent.

At District 7, East Boston, Sergeant O'Hara, was working his way down the list.

"McLean . . ."

"Here, sir."

"Pilowski . . ."

"Present."

"You two take the 7-1 car, go off the air and get over to Needham. You're going to a funeral detail at . . ." O'Hara paused for a moment as he adjusted his bifocals to read the printout more clearly, ". . . at St. James Church on Washington Street."

Piloskwi just shook his head and rose, getting ready to leave, but McLean was not going to give up so easily.

"Hey, Sarge. I got to get down to the pier to pick up my fish at Louie's."

"Never mind the fish. Get out to Needham."

"But what about my fish? I'm having a big . . ."

The sergeant glared over his glasses. "You really want to know? Screw the fish! Now, get going right now."

At around the same time, roll call was proceeding in a similar manner in District 11 in Dorchester. Sergeant Parker was running down the roster.

"Patrolman Baker?"

"I'm here."

"Patrolman Wells? . . . Wells?"

"Right in front of you, Sarge."

"I want you two on a funeral honor guard this morning. Take the 11-9 car off the air and make sure you're at St. James Church in Needham by 9 am."

"I don't know where any St. James Church is, Sarge. Hell, I'm not even Catholic. Why do you keep sending me on these funeral details?" Wells whined.

"You and Baker have the least ugly mugs around here, but don't let that go to your swelled heads. Actually, I'm sending you characters because I can't trust you with more complicated work like filing warrants."

Now, it was Baker's turn. "I'm glad you appreciate my good looks," he grinned, eliciting some boos and wolf whistles from his brother officers, "but can't I get replaced on this detail? I was planning to take my car down to Rocky's Garage for a brake job."

"You heard me. Get out to Needham. Wells, for your information and that of any other non-believers in this sorry bunch, St. James is right on Washington Street. Baker, get your car fixed on your own time. In any case, stay the hell away from Rocky. He's a thief and he runs a chop shop. You and him will both end up in the shit, if you continue to do business with a bum like him . . ."

The two patrolmen huffed and grumbled a little longer.

"Wells, Baker . . . Needham, right now."

And so throughout the city assignments were issued in order to make up the 20-man honor guard for the funeral. The VFW drill team and the color guard had been notified earlier in the week to report for the ceremony.

Around 8:45, the cars from the different districts began to pull into the parking lot behind St. James. Still only half-resigned to their tedious task, the men reported to an old-timer, Sergeant Tim Murphy of District 4. Born in Galway, Tim came to Boston as a young man; he became a citizen while working as a longshoreman in South Boston. He studied at Matt Connolly's Civil Service School and passed the police examination. When he got back from a tour duty overseas in World War II, he was appointed to the Boston Police Department.

"Fall in. Come on, let's go," Murphy called, and the men reluctantly crushed cigarettes they had just started underfoot and began shuffling into position. "Let's make it look good today for this fellow officer."

"Who the hell is this guy anyways?" a voice piped up from the middle of the formation.

"Deputy Superintendent Robert J. Harrington," Sergeant Tim replied in his raspy brogue, "a fine officer and a fine man."

"That prick," Wells fumed. "I knew that guy. He was my sergeant in old 9. Gave me a trial board. I got 120 hours of punishment duty for nothing. Harrington was a real, first-class A-1 prick."

"Shut up, Wells," Sergeant Tim warned. "OK. Left face. Forward MARCH!"

The platoon moved along the side of the church and wheeled around at the front, coming to a halt opposite the steps.

"Platoon, halt . . . left face . . . OK, at ease. The funeral will be here in a few minutes."

"Hey, listen, Wells," whispered English of District 2. "I worked with Deputy Harrington in District 4 when he was a lieutenant. He was an alright, fair and honest guy as far as I'm concerned."

"Right, English," the sergeant asked.

"English, you always were an ass-kisser," hissed Lucas when Murphy seemed to have moved out of earshot. "Harrington was around a long time before you got on the job, and like Wells here says, he was a first-class prick . . . irregardless of what you or that mick sergeant says."

Apparently Lucas had underestimated Murphy's hearing because the old Irishman swung around and confronted him, "Mind your language in front of a church, and watch who you call a 'mick' or a 'prick' or it will be your ass."

"Now, let's be fair," interjected John Ralph of District 13. "I hear from a lot of people that knew Harrington that he was a good family man. He loved his wife and kids and gave them everything he could. My son lives here in Needham, right across from the Harringtons. He oughta know. So if a man is good to his family, what more can you say?"

"Ralph, you're full of shit," countered Rotondi. "That old bastard would fuck a snake if you hold it still for him. I even think he was playing with little boys."

"You fucking wops are always cutting down the superior officers," sneered Ralph, "unless, of course, he's a guinea, too."

The backbiting and trading of insults continued as the restless troops waited for the cortege to arrive. Ellison, a young rookie fresh out of the Police Academy and assigned to District 3, listened with wide eyes to the conversation. The way he had been brought up, no one would speak so crudely about the dead, especially on the very day the man was being put into the ground.

Ellison turned to Joe Haggarty, an Academy classmate who had been assigned to District 9, "Joe, I can't believe these guys are policemen. I hope we never end up feeling like them."

"I dunno," Haggarty replied, "My uncle told me most of the guys on the force with him were pretty damned cynical."

As soon as the cortege appeared at the next set of lights, Sergeant Murphy called the honor guard to attention. "Let's have a snappy salute to honor this fine man."

Some smart aleck in the ranks called out, "He gave you many a buck."

"Keep quiet. I know who said that," Murphy said. "Hand salute."

The first car laden with floral tributes slowly passed by the honor guard. The VFW drill team and the color guard were next. Then the hearse came to a stop at the door of the church, with the family limo and the other cars in the procession following.

The honor guard, who only moments earlier had been grousing and backstabbing, now sucked in their guts and tried to look as sharp as a platoon of West Point cadets. Miraculously, they did make a fine line of blue, standing there at attention.

The pallbearers eased the coffin out of the hearse and carried the deputy's body slowly into the church. The honor guard followed; the men uncovering as they passed through the portals, holding their uniform hats over their hearts. With a stately step, they marched down the center aisle to the front rows, leading the way for the family and other mourners.

The Mass was short by any standards, and the honor guard was the first group out of the church. Even the brief time they had spent indoors for the service was enough for the weather to change to a fine, misty rain.

The wait for the coffin and pallbearers to reappear seemed much longer than the Mass itself. None of the officers had raingear, so they simply stood in their assigned positions getting wet.

Young Ellison overheard Wells complaining to Baker, "If I get a cold, I'm going to sue this prick."

"Tell me about it," returned his partner from District 11. "This rain is going to ruin my uniform; I bought it new last week."

"You haven't bought any part of a uniform in years. You give all your uniform money to that girlie you keep on the side," Ralph laughed. "I hope you get pneumonia. Yours is one funeral detail I'd be glad to volunteer for!"

"Attention," called Sergeant Murphy. "Hand salute!"

The men once again assumed rigid, respectful stances as the pallbearers descended the steps and replaced the coffin in the hearse. The undertaker's aide popped open a black umbrella to shelter the bereaved family as he ushered them to the limo.

When the doors of the limousine were closed, the rain started to come down in torrents, and Sergeant Murphy decided to show a little compassion to the soaking troops.

"Dis-MISSED. Get out of the rain. The deputy would have wanted it that way."

The men broke rank and raced for the shelter of their cruisers. Ellison and Haggarty ducked under the canopy that overhung the church door, pausing to do a little reminiscing before heading for their vehicles.

Just then, the rear left window of the family's limo rolled down slowly. An elderly woman, her grey hair done up in a bun underneath the small black hat and veil, signaled for them to approach.

"Officers . . ."

The two rookies manfully braved the rain to see what the widow wanted.

"Yes, ma'am," Ellison said in his most respectful tone.

"I feel terrible holding you up in the rain. I know you're wet, but I'm Mrs. Harrington, the deputy's wife. I couldn't let you all go without expressing my thanks and that of the whole family to you and the other officers for being so kind in paying your respects to my husband. He loved his men as well as his family. I know he'll be missed by all of the officers. The patrolmen in particular . . . he had special admiration for them."

Suddenly a tiny towhead clambered up into Mrs. Harrington's arms. "This is our grandson," she sniffled, fondly running her black-gloved hand through his curly blond hair, "He was named after his grandfather."

"I'm going to be a policeman just like Grandpa," the little lad announced, rubbing his reddened eyes with his fist. "He was the best policeman in the whole world, wasn't he?"

"Yes, he was," Ellison answered hoarsely.

"Well," Mrs. Harrington sighed, twisting her handkerchief in her hands, "as I said, I'm sorry to keep you out in the rain, but I know that Robert would want me to thank you. Please tell the rest of the men."

"We will, ma'am," Ellison said. The window rolled up, and the long car pulled away, sending up a spray of water.

"If she only knew," Ellison said, following the car with his eyes until it vanished into the mist and traffic.

"Enough! Let's get out of this fuckin' rain," Haggarty replied.

"Before we go back, I've got to make a call to my wife," Ellison said, suddenly sounding very serious.

"You're soaking wet."

"There's usually a phone in the back of these school halls," Ellison continued, as if he hadn't heard.

Haggarty shivered and tried to pick his way through the puddles as they made their way into the hall and found the phone. "Why didn't I bring a raincoat or poncho or something?"

Ellison had dialed. After a few rings, his wife Mary answered, "John, why are you calling this early? You didn't have an accident!"

"Nothing happened. Everything's alright. I'm in Needham."

"Needham? What are you doing out there?"

"I was detailed to a funeral. Listen, Mary, when I die, I want . . ."

"Die? What are you talking about?"

"Just listen. Mary, just promise me that when my time comes, you make sure that there are no cops at my funeral."

"John, what do you mean no cops?"

"Just remember, Mary, no cops at my funeral. Bye, honey. See you tonight."